D1217708

THE
GOVERNMENT OF CORPORATIONS

THE GOVERNMENT OF CORPORATIONS

Richard Eells
Adjunct Professor of Business
Graduate School of Business
Columbia University

THE FREE PRESS OF GLENCOE

PRINTED IN THE UNITED STATES OF AMERICA

For information, address:
THE FREE PRESS OF GLENCOE
A Division of The Macmillan Company, The Crowell-Collier Publishing Company
60 FIFTH AVENUE, NEW YORK 11

DESIGNED BY ANDOR BRAUN

LIBRARY OF CONGRESS CATALOG CARD NUMBER: 62-15339

PREFACE

DURING THE PAST TEN YEARS, in various studies of the modern corporation and its role in our free society, I have repeatedly had to touch the subject of the present volume peripherally. But only within the past few years has it been possible to discuss the subject of corporate governance systematically, as I have tried to do here. Recently much attention has been given to it by many writers, and it has seemed timely to bring out my own analysis now, even though a definitive treatment of the subject must await far more extensive and cooperative work among many disciplines.

Almost twenty years ago Beardsley Ruml, in *Tomorrow's Business*, wrote of business not only as a producer but as a rule-maker standing "high in responsibility among human institutions, as a source of goods and services, to be sure, but also a source of order and freedom." In his view, business was "an instrument of authority and power" and "a source of direction and decision." But business, he went on to say, must not try to achieve order and certainty at the cost of the freedom of those whom business governs; and in a country deeply committed to the ideal of human freedom "the various subordinate governments—public and private—must conform in their rule-making" to this ideal.

This conception of business corporations as a species of

private government, though resisted at first, is now widely accepted. It is not universally accepted even now, and the reasons for this resistance are discussed at some length in the present book. They are not without interest to students of our mixed economy, and they throw considerable light on the problems of management in the corporation of the future. Ruml's own reasons for regarding a business as a private government are worth restating:

> A business is a *government* because within the law it is authorized and organized to make rules for the conduct of its affairs. It is a *private* government because the rules it makes within law are final and not reviewable by any public body. Some might say that the reason a business is a private government is because it is owned by private individuals, but it seems to me that the element of private authority is more significant than the question of ownership.

He thus raised a question, now pursued with profound interest by lawyers, political scientists, and business economists, concerning the nature and sources of authority in corporate governments.

The pluralistic implications of this question, and of a whole range of issues connected with corporate governance, have not been missed by contemporary observers of the governmental process in a free society such as ours. Thus, in the Rockefeller Panel Report on American Democracy, *The Power of the Democratic Idea* (1960), one finds this pertinent observation:

> It is a principle of democracy that the government will not be the only rule-making body in the community, and that associations that are independent of it will have the right and the power to make socially significant decisions. This implies, however, that these associations are themselves governments in the most meaningful sense of the term. They make rules and exercise genuine and effective authority over those who work for them or belong to them, and they establish arrangements that affect the general character of the community at large. The phenomenon of widespread private government, nourished and supported, indeed, by the deliberate action of the state, is an intrinsic feature of a free society.

Accordingly, the same sort of question that can be asked of other governments can also be asked of these private governments. The democratic ideals by which the state is properly judged may also be applied to the ways in which the lives of men are governed in the private sector. If the individual is smothered, if power is excessive, democratic principles are violated as surely as they are violated by similar conditions in the public sector.

It is now evident that the subject of governance of corporations must become a part of the curriculum of business schools if they are to face the realities of corporate action. The top business leaders of tomorrow will become managerial statesmen to the degree that they conceive of their task in larger terms than efficient administration for production alone and accept their responsibilities as officers of private governmental systems. Without denigrating the importance of the science of management and of operations research, one may suggest that the time is now ripe for adding a new dimension to the training of business executives—namely, the art and science of corporate governance.

We hear much today about the cybernation of the society of the future—the introduction of computers and automation into the work of public and private organizations. Such a development seems inevitable. Yet, regardless of the degree of centralized national planning and of centralization of controls in private or "alter" governments, the governed will not cease—if the tradition of constitutionalism survives—to demand of their public and private governors a polity rooted in what Hugo Krabbe called the "feeling for right and justice." Nor will this imperative be met adequately without due regard for the structure and processes of government in private as well as public sectors.

For this reason I have tried to emphasize, in this first general treatment of the subject of corporate governance, the importance of constitutionalism as applied to business polities. Only in Part V does the emphasis shift to corporate policy, strategic decisions, and the current problems of running a business. Later on, when the opportunity arises, I intend to press beyond this general framework to specific and comparative studies of corporate governmental systems. This further project, needless to say, demands the cooperative efforts not only of specialists in many disciplines but of the directors and executive managers of leading corporate enterprises.

While many of the insights contributing to the present work have been derived from my own experience in connection with certain large corporations, notably the General Electric Company and the International Business Machines Corporation, I owe much to others. So many persons and institutions have contributed, through advice, conversation, and criticism, to the development of the ideas here presented that I cannot hope to list them all, though the citations to references in the notes indicate a number of these. In addition I should mention, with gratitude, the conversations and communications I have had with corporate directors and executives; executives in investment banking houses; corporation lawyers, deans, and other faculty members of graduate schools of business; members of other university faculties in the fields of political science, economics, sociology, and psychology; and numerous advisers and consultants to large corporations and company foundations.

The present volume represents the first completed project sponsored by the Foundation for the Study of Human Organization, Inc. It is hoped that this study can be followed up with further exploration of the largely untilled field of corporate governance as well as other kinds of government in the private sector.

RICHARD EELLS

New York
March, 1962

CONTENTS

Part III. THE POWER TO GOVERN

Part IV. RESTRAINTS ON THE POWER TO GOVERN

Part I

PATTERNS AND TENSIONS

CHAPTER *1*

The Study of Corporate Governance

GOVERNANCE IN BUSINESS corporations is an old art but a new science. Long before the rise of the modern corporation to a dominant position among the various organizational forms of conducting business operations, corporate polities flourished here and in Europe; and those who governed the affairs of the older "bodies corporate and politic" were well aware that their business was the governing of men as well as the administering of property and the manipulation of things. But, while it was never doubtful that a corporation, like a church or a state, had a polity of its own—a governmental organization and a constitutional structure fitted to its special purpose—only in recent years has there been much scientific interest in corporate polity.

The study of corporate governments, as a special field of political science, is only now beginning to take on the contours of a new discipline. For some time there have been systematic treatises on "business administration," but there is still no comparable literature on corporate governance. Historical and comparative analyses of corporate polities, of sufficient scope and depth to be used, for example, as textbooks for students of corporate government in universities, have failed to appear for a number of reasons. Some of these reasons result from the natural lag between the development of an art and the appearance of a science which describes and explains it. Others grow out of a peculiarly persistent mode of thought about "business" and "government" as disparates.

A Tardy Science

AS TO THE LAG between art and science, one can observe it quite clearly in the delayed growth of the general science of politics. Politics as the art of government long antedated the first attempts in ancient Greece to study it scientifically by the Aristotelian method. Greeks of the Aristotelian school were interested in observing and noting down the diverse forms of government they saw around them in the city-states of their day. Politics, as a discipline, was not merely descriptive and taxonomic, however; it was knowledge of the political good, relative as well as absolute, and of governmental mechanics to be employed for chosen ends—whether good, bad, or indifferent from the point of view of the observer.

The result of disciplined observation of this kind appears in such ancient treatises as Aristotle's *Politics* and Polybius' *Histories,* which still impress us moderns as ground-breaking work in political thought. The polities they described and analyzed were not new, but the task of description and analysis was. There is a notable discontinuity in distinguished writing on the *science* of politics in the period between that golden age of learning and our time. The *art* of politics was continuously practiced, and undoubtedly with great skill, throughout the Middle Ages. But not until the recovery of the Aristotelian writings near the close of the Middle Ages were educated men again conversant with the "antique-modern" mode of thought about politics as a science. There was continuity in the discussion of political ethics, but not in the objective study of governmental institutions in the Aristotelian fashion and as it is pursued by modern political scientists. Political philosophy flourished without interruption in Western Europe, as the Carlyles have shown, from the beginning to the end of the medieval period, and normative theory was strongly influenced by Stoic and Christian doctrine, by the Roman law, and by feudal conceptions of personal obligation, contract, and property. But it was not until about the sixteenth century that men began again to undertake the task of political analysis, observing and writing about the political institutions they saw around them.

Even then there was a notorious lag of theory behind practice. The historian of the science of politics is struck, for example, by the fact that Machiavelli—sometimes called the first modern political scientist—was by no means a characteristic political commentator of his century, and that most of his contemporaries seem not to have observed the birth of a new age in the evolution of political institutions. Machiavelli himself may not have been aware of it any more than Aristotle was aware that the Hellenistic age was impending. Both, however, were deeply interested in the dominant political institutions of the centuries in which they lived.

The institutions which have especially engaged the attention of modern political scientists are mainly centered about nation-states, much as Aristotle's study of politics focused on the city-state. But it was long after the emergence of the modern states system that students of government began to see it for what it really was. Medieval assumptions prevailed as blinders inhibiting a candid assessment of political practices. The abhorrence of Machiavelli's blunt accounts of the political arts of his day is a case in point. Another is the failure of the conciliarists—in some respects "modern" in outlook—to observe the decline of the universal Church as the dominant political institution. Still another case is the hatred in the sixteenth century for Jean Bodin's theories of sovereignty and religious toleration.

During the past two centuries writers on the process of government have acknowledged the facts about the modern states system, and they have developed, especially in the past fifty years, a vast scientific literature on most aspects of modern political life. Yet there is still a lag in scientific analysis of government, and it results primarily from preoccupation with the state: that process of government within and among the nation-states which characterize modern politics. It may be premature to predict the passing of the modern states system and its replacement by other patterns of government, but there are many signs which indicate the emergence of a new era comparable to that which emerged at the end of the Middle Ages. The political scientist of tomorrow may find that the focus of his attention must shift to new governmental institutions.

World government is not just around the corner, and it may never come. But that does not mean the permanence of the nation-state system as we have known it. On the one hand, a United Nations of more than a hundred so-called sovereign nation-states may turn out to be less than a viable political institution for the art of governance in the twenty-first century. Many of the new "states" bear little resemblance to the nation-states which ushered in the modern period when medieval universalism vanished. On the other hand, new forms of governmental mechanism are rapidly moving onto the scene, and some of these bear slight resemblance to established nation-state political systems. Regional alliances for military defense, blocs of communist nations, "uncommitted" and "non-aligned" powers acting in common on certain policies, and functional entities with supranational governing bodies (Euratom, the European Coal and Steel Community, for example, and now the new European Economic Community or Common Market)—all of these developments portend epochal change in the world's political structure.

If it be true, as it may well be, that we are on the verge of a new epoch in the evolution of governmental mechanisms, it is inevitable that sooner or later the science of politics will shift attention to the emerging patterns of government. Nation-states will not soon disappear; the study of their governments will continue to be of major importance. But the newer institutions must also be put under the microscope, as it were, and analyzed with the same care and by the same methods that political scientists have used in studying the dominant political systems of our time.

Pressure Groups and Private Governments

THIS IS ALREADY being done, of course, by the Young Turks of the political science profession. In the United States, where political science is more highly specialized than elsewhere, the movement began two generations ago with respect to "pressure groups." Technically private associations, and not arms of public government, the pressure groups were in fact seen to be significant elements in the process of public government. Realism required the student of government to note that fact and to describe it in detail. The study of pressure groups has now become an established subdiscipline of American political science and has spread to other countries as well.

That particular field of the general discipline, however, is usually conceived of as a part of political science because of the nexus with public government—the government of the state in its many forms. Pressure groups, that is to say, exert private pressure on public government and are therefore properly within the scope of political analysis. Insofar as these groups influence legislation, administrative action, and the judicial process, in other words, they are quasi-political associations whose activities cannot be allowed to escape the observer of the political process—a process that by definition occurs in public governments.

The younger generation of Young Turks will not stop here, however. They insist, and rightly, that the student of governmental processes must not confine himself to public governments but must widen his horizons to take in private governments as well. They will not be bound by the etymological and traditional meaning of "politics" as the science of statecraft, whether in city-states or nation-states. They see the governing of men as a ubiquitous phenomenon not limited to public governments. The polity of any human association is grist for their mill. Groups which "pressure" public governmental agencies are, to be sure, appropriate subjects for study; but so are those which do no pressuring.

In every association, public or private, the art of governance can be observed, both as to the uses of power by the group in relation to outsiders and as to the uses of power by the governing elite within the group in relation to its members. In this sense every association has a polity worth studying, and not merely for purely scientific purposes. The concept of polity and private government in this broad sense is not only extremely useful for understanding the ubiquitous phenomenon of government; it becomes also a clue to a more mature philosophy of government in free societies.

Influence of Political Pluralism

AT THIS POINT one must note the influence of pluralistic theory in the growth of recent American political thought. The new emphasis on the significance of private government–including the private government of corporations, labor unions, universities, and other nonstate associations–is not motivated solely by scientific considerations. The desire to understand fully the pluralistic mechanism of modern society is buttressed by a widely held conviction that distribution of governing power among numerous decision-making centers, public and private, is indispensable to a free society. It is interesting to observe how frequently commentators on public policy now refer to our "pluralistic society," thereby putting the stamp of approval on the proliferation of private governments as a counterpoise to public authority.

To the historian of political theory this resurgence of pluralistic doctrine raises many questions. Political pluralism presumably had its heyday forty or more years ago. Its revival today is regarded by some people as a curious, and even a dangerous, anachronism. The emphasis on "group theory" as a basis for the justification of private government is thus attacked as ethically unsound. The reasoning is that, while the earlier pluralists (such as Gierke, Maitland, Figgis, and Laski) were worried about the dangers of excessive authority in an overpowering sovereign state, what we have to be concerned about today is that its competitor private governments will undermine the foundations of social order.[1]

Pluralistic theory, on the other hand, is invoked by writers such as Clark Kerr and Calvin B. Hoover to justify the preservation of balance in the economy as between public and private rule-making powers. Apologists of private government in corporations and labor unions do not fear the encroachment of these power centers on public government; on the contrary, they point to the opposite danger and the necessity for guarding against encroachment of Leviathan on private sectors. They also urge recognition of the need for sharing the burden of governance in our complex society, and of reserving to functionally defined groups the specialized kinds of decision-making that can best be executed by those closest to the functional operations which society wants to have carried out.

Pluralism today thus becomes a rationale, as well as a theoretic construct for political science, which seeks to justify an American type of political economy that is partly guided and planned at public governmental levels but left for the most part to private decision-making—which, in fact, becomes largely corporate decision-making. But this pluralistic rationale is increasingly the subject of critical reappraisal. On the one hand, there are critics who are alarmed at the encroachment of the state upon corporate autonomy. On the other hand, the whole corporate system, as we know it in the United States, is presented as an inchoate form of sub-public government destined at length to alter the foundations of modern political institutions.[2]

Corporations as Power Systems

THE NET EFFECT of all these strands of thought, whether pluralistic or monistic, is to bring to the fore explicit studies of corporate governments as a new field for political scientists. Whatever one may think of the positive or negative value of our "pluralistic society," and in particular that aspect of it revealed in the prominence of relatively autonomous business corporations as "systems of power," there can be no avoidance of serious study of the phenomenon. Nor in this study can the terminology of political science be avoided.

Businessmen frequently object to any discussion of the private government of the corporation on the ground that "business" and "government" are disparates, that governing is the exclusive business of the state and its agents, and that to concede the opposite is to open the door to unbearable public regulation. "Polity" is said to be a suspect word as applied to corporate governance because it connotes the police power—which managers presumably should neither have nor want to have. But the recognition of the existence of private government is not necessarily a threat to its continuance; the pluralists, indeed, insist upon its recognition precisely in order to preserve it. And in any case, quite aside from one's preferences, this terminology of political science has so long been used with reference to economic organizations that nothing can be done, short of a purge, to erase it from our vocabulary.

The advantages, from the businessman's point of view, of clearly recognizing the fact of private government in the corporation are many. Recognition of the fact will contribute toward a better public understanding of business polities: their special requirements for authority concentrations and distributions within the corporate structure, for example, and the reasons for great diversity in governmental systems within companies, depending upon the functions they perform. But, aside from public relations considerations, the directors of large corporate enterprises are in need of more substantial doctrine than legal and economic theory has provided as a rationale for the powers they must exercise. Faced as they are with demands for reform of their so-called despotic corporate governments, managers must look to new sources of knowledge about the great collectivities over which they preside. The modern corporation, as a relatively unsurveyed field of social forces, cannot be measured by the old instruments or accounted for alone by the old theories inherited from eighteenth- and nineteenth-century legal and economic theory.

Some writers have urged that the new age of collective action heralds the onset of new systems of "industrial government," and that a clue to these emerging systems may be found—as John R. Commons [3] thought—in the analysis of transactions of bargaining of the "managerial" type and of the "rationing" type. In transactions among legal equals, as in bargaining, there might be persuasion when the legal equals are also economic equals or coercion when they are not economically equal. In managerial and rationing transactions the relationship is between the legally superior and the legally inferior: the superior commands and the subordinate obeys; but in "rationing" transactions a negotiatory relationship prevails among those who are authorized to ration, to allocate, and to apportion benefits and burdens.[4]

This approach to the nature and purpose of the new collectivities and to an understanding of the dynamics of organization has been useful in directing attention away from the old clichés toward the essential authority relationships in any collectivity. If, for example, we avoid exclusive concern about the "business" and "economic" objectives of a corporation and its legal personality, we may discover, in the working rules of the going concern, certain principles that govern the transactions between real persons in the ongoing organization, and among its principals and outsiders.

Modern industrial enterprise requires large organizations in which, it is often charged, authority is centralized in a "self-perpetuating oligarchy." But is not this in itself a cliché that requires testing against the corporate realities? Like the stereotype of profit maximization as the sole objective of a business, this thesis can be tested by raising certain questions directed to facts. What authority does a business executive exercise? For whose benefit? With what sanctions (enforcement capabilities, rewards, inducements)? With what theory of legitimacy? With what effects upon "justice" in the organization and upon canons of right conduct in society?

Such issues arise in all ages and all places, in situations of collective action, whether transient or permanent, whether in political or nonpolitical associations. They arise whether there be a formal system of government in the political sense or simply informal arrangements that involve command-obedience relationships or relationships of other types which require persuasion, coercion, or negotiation by authorized agents. The nature and content of the working rules governing the situation are not always so clearly evident as in the constitutional law of a nation. But they are discoverable. And they need to be identified and subjected to scrutiny in any well-developed polity, or system of government.

The need for such scrutiny has always been evident in the polities of churches,[5] for example, and in public governments. The history of constitutional theory is drawn largely from the historic debates about church polity and about the framework of public government, from the Greek *polis* to the modern nation-state. Constitutionalism today is a historic precipitate of theory and practice resulting from the frequently violent interaction of powerful reagents in church and state over the past centuries. Men who fought in every time and clime for their rights, as they saw them, struggled not merely for temporary advantage but rather to establish certain enduring power relationships which became constitutional patterns, whether in church, state, or corporation.

Corporations and Constitutionalism

FOR IN EVERY constitutional system of government, public or private, there must be, first, adequate collective *power* to achieve common purposes and, second, workable *limitations* on this power. Those who make the decisions will thus have authority that is appropriately circumscribed. Constitutionalism today puts the major emphasis upon limitations, but a balanced view of any constitutional system will give due attention to both power-granting and power-limiting elements.

Constitutional government in this sense pervades the social structure of a free society, for it is not a totalitarian and monolithic pyramid in its structure. American society has grown as a dispersed and diffused power structure, with many decision-making centers, both public and private. Within this great design lies one key to freedom, as the pluralists correctly insist. This system provides for sufficient concentrations of authority, over many disparate matters and at many points, to get things done. We have always been interested—within the American constitutional tradition—in trying to achieve a proper balance between adequate powers in public and private sectors, and also upon effective restraints on those powers. Respect for the private rights of persons and their property has always been the reason for these restraints in our constitutional heritage. These private rights form the cornerstone not only of the polity of the state but also of the polity of churches, labor unions, professional associations, and universities. Thus, we find that the private rights of persons and property constitute a common denominator in the genesis of polity in all of these important institutions.

It is no different with the modern corporation, regarded as a basic pattern of authority relationships. Large powers are needed to achieve common purposes; it is equally important that these powers be circumscribed so that they will be used only for legitimate ends. The legitimate ends of corporate enterprise are certainly a debatable issue today. The scope and legitimacy of managerial authority are unresolved problems. That is why the demand for "due process" in the corporation is increasingly heard.

For these reasons alone it is timely to consider the nature of the constitutional crisis in the modern corporation and to clarify the basic issues involved. In much of the contemporary polemic against and apology for Big Business these issues are obscured. There are interesting historical parallels. The conciliar movement in the Church, before the Reformation, was to many contemporaries a personal struggle for power among contending prelates; yet in fact it was an epochal struggle over the constitution of the Church itself—a struggle that resulted in the victory of papal absolutism over a theory of representative government within the Church. Similarly, from the point of view of the American constitutional historian, the Age of Roosevelt is less significant as a struggle over New Deal policies than as beginning a new era in American government comparable to that ushered in over a century earlier by the sweeping constitutional doctrines of John Marshall's court.

Corporate government may well assume something of the same significance for the twentieth century that ecclesiastical polity had for the conciliar movement and the problem of church and state in the sixteenth and seventeenth centuries. We may be on the brink of similar, important new developments in political theory today. Just as the great councils introduced patterns of theory and practice that profoundly influenced the development of Western parliamentary institutions, so may the modern corporation elicit theory and practice that will shape many social patterns of the future. It could influence the pattern of law and order in the market place of the world community. It could influence our basic ways of adjusting conflicting interests within nations. And it could help to crystallize more meaningful and workable concepts of human freedom.

The development of a science of corporate government, like

the development of a science of politics, or like the study of any field of social interaction, calls for the penetration of an unexplored terrain of thought. Lord Russell once said, "Men fear thought as they fear nothing else on earth . . . more even than death." But we have come to realize today, perhaps more than in any time in our history, that the mind that works, whether in the natural or the human sciences, has to be open to concepts now unfamiliar.

Ultimately, an effort to understand business in such new terms will require the cooperative efforts of both academy and corporation. They must share the burden of theoretical analysis and practical observation of corporate government in action. Neither can afford to be merely grinding an ax as critic of, or apologist for, the corporation. The pursuit of truth must become and remain the objective. Legal and economic analyses, although different from the present approach, will continue to contribute to our understanding. The science and the art of management of business enterprise will continue to develop. Within this generation we may see the development of a theory of business government that will constitute a new and important chapter in the history of political theory itself.

Ethical critiques must be made from time to time. In the end, our pursuit, like most social inquiry, has an ethical goal. For just beyond the horizons of the research problems we have outlined looms the transcending question: how shall we design the patterns of our institutional systems so that we can preserve the values of our constitutional heritage of freedom?

CHAPTER *2*

Constitutional Crisis in the Corporation

MANY OBSERVERS DENY that the business corporation today has any "constitutional" structure. Others who concede the existence of a corporate constitution refuse to recognize that it differs today or will differ tomorrow from that of the traditional corporation. Yet closer students [1] of the modern corporation express profound interest in the problem, and it is not too much to say that in the decades ahead corporate constitutionalism will become one of the major issues confronting corporate executives and public policy-makers.

The idea of the modern corporation as merely the enlarged figure of the classical owner-enterpriser no longer suffices for the making of either corporate or public policy. The authority of executive managers of great collectivities is not in practice the translation of the property rights of stockholders into the "right to manage" large enterprise on behalf of absentee owners. So to regard managerial authority is to miss the significance of recent changes in the nature of property and changes in the concept of authority itself.

Even in the administration of a business enterprise below the board level, the question of corporate governance raises real problems of power and authority which one can usefully attack with techniques of analysis drawn from political science. But when one widens the scope of the inquiry and takes into account not only the board of directors but also the stockholders and the array of external groups with which a corporation carries on relations of many kinds, then one gets far beyond the mere administering of the enterprise through the organization of executives, managers, and individual contributors.

When one begins to ask about the influence of boards, stockholders, customers, the public, and—not least—the unions in the shaping of a company's objectives and even in the day-by-day running of the business, one gets into problems of authority and responsibility. When they occur *within* the organization structure below the board level, these problems are usually discussed in terms of "scientific management," business administration, and so on. But beyond these considerations there exists also the question of adapting and assimilating the corporation as a private government into the general social picture.

Let us consider for a moment some issues which are of universal concern to both businessmen and the public generally: Who really controls a company? What power does it exercise? To whom should the power-wielders be accountable, and how? Is the company a "self-perpetuating oligarchy," as some have charged, or is it a type of republic? And if one or the other, what difference does it make, so far as the public is concerned? What is the role of the large corporation in the total power structure of the nation? Is it an important element in the balance of social powers? Does a "free society" depend heavily upon the kind of pluralism we have in our economic and other sectors, with the private business corporation playing a significant part in sustaining a healthy distribution of power throughout society as a whole; or would we do better without it?

These are all questions that pertain to the government of society and of its integral parts. They are questions that inevitably draw the inquirer into the deeper issues of political science and political ethics—with respect not only to *public* government but also to *private* governments. The failure to acknowledge this omnipresent problem of government, especially as it arises in economic organizations like the corporation, is a dangerous oversight. The problem is there and cannot be escaped. So far, few answers have been given and those which have been suggested have originated outside, rather than inside, the corporate community.

The man in business is, quite naturally, so engaged in minding his business that he has little time to speculate about its nature. To get the enterprise going and to keep it going take all his ingenuity and energy. Like the medieval mystic who remarked that it is better to feel compunction than to know how to define it, the businessman is usually better at doing his job than at thinking about the governmental processes inherent in it.

Yet, with the growth of giant economic organization it becomes plain that underlying the superstructure of administration there is the substance of visible and not so visible private government. Students of the subject discern an evolutionary process imperceptible to those who see in the business corporation a clear and fixed pattern of authority relationships among stockholders, directors, executive managers, and employees at lower operating levels. Stereotypes of the corporation, provided by received legal doctrine and economic theory, have succeeded in obscuring its nature further. We are inclined to see the social institutions around us not as they really are, but in accordance with preconceived notions handed down to us by our predecessors.

The business corporation, like all social institutions, has such an image in our minds, but it has also an objective reality which may or may not correspond to the image. In static periods the lack of harmony between image and reality can to some extent be safely ignored. In a dynamic age the distortion creates dangers. A common-sense view of the corporation, based on the wisdom of the past and respectable dogma, would suffice were it not for the fact that political, economic, and social change has moved it so rapidly away from this base.

Evidence of Tension

THE GROWING DIVERGENCE of the corporate image from corporate realities has led to an accumulation of unresolved tensions. One example is the debate about the respective positions of share-owners and managers in the control of large enterprises where stockholding is widely dispersed: the so-called separation of ownership and control. Another example is the touchy question of social responsibility—the problem of the general public's share in the authority structure of large enterprises, since obviously responsibility and authority must somehow be linked together. A further example is the unresolved problem of union power vis-à-vis corporate managers: the encroachment of organized workers on managerial authority and the drive by labor unions to enjoy a "fair share" of the fruits of enterprise. Then there are the growing concerns about human relations in industry, the sensitivity of managers to the personality requirements of people in the workforce, the nature of authority at the workplace, and the right to discipline. At the outer reaches of the constellation of interests that make up a large corporate enterprise we find the pension and investment trusts of a "paraproprietal society." These trust funds are institutionalized share-owners who are far removed from the going concern; but by the traditional canons of corporate theory they are the ultimate sovereigns as they accumulate large blocs of stock in a concern.

All of these examples provide evidence that the traditional view of basic authority relationships in large enterprises is an unstable compound of hypotheses about relationships among the primary interests and the direct contributor-claimants [2] of the going concern. The instability of this outmoded compound of received doctrines becomes evident in relatively minor explosions here and there: the recurrent struggles over collective bargaining, the intervention of legislators to protect first the creditors and then the share-owners against abuses of managerial authority, the revisions by general incorporation laws accompanied by acute conflicts of opinion about the theory [3] that should underlie them, and the struggles for "control" in certain large companies.

Taken separately, these are but dramatic episodes in the long evolution of new constitutional theory for corporate enterprise. These episodes must be seen comparatively and historically in order to get the proper perspective for the evolutionary lines of development. The changes that are occurring in basic corporation theory are most clearly observable only over a considerable time span and after comparative analysis of many situations.

The Constitutional Pattern

As a point of departure one can begin with the traditional pattern of corporate constitutions, as expounded in the standard treatises and as they are generally understood by businessmen and lawyers. This constitutional pattern, it must be emphasized at the start, does not emerge clearly unless a distinction is made between the corporation as an economic unit and the corporation as a *decisional center* in a pluralistic society. We need to see it as a decision-making center with an impact on the larger society where many authority centers exist, and as a complex of forces seeking places at the table of power within the corporation itself.

As an economic unit, the corporation is a producer and distributor, a buyer and a seller, of economic goods. From the point of view of the economist it is an entrepreneurial unit; but our focus here is upon the corporation as an instrument of power and authority, an institution with its own constitutional structure, maintaining a system of organization, discipline, and morale within its own ranks as well as influential external relations with other authority centers public and private.

Thus, a corporation, like any other organization, exhibits certain more or less well-defined patterns of leadership,[4] subordination, superordination, and coordination within the boundaries of the firm, and patterns of authority relationships with other organizations and persons beyond its corporate frontiers. All organizations require some basic constitutional pattern of authority relationships, internal and external, to achieve unity of effort with a diversity of human resources. They all have common purposes defined by written or unwritten rules, expressed or implied by their basic charters. Though their objectives differ, all make more or less successful attempts to pattern the organizational structure in a functional way; the authority structure is presumably a reflection of the organizational goals.

One of the most important problems confronting the managers of the modern corporation is whether the basic pattern of authority relationships—internal and external to the organization—is functionally appropriate in view of contemporary corporate objectives and the organizational requirements for achieving these objectives.[5] The issue has become highly debatable today. Conflict of opinion on the point is one cause of the contemporary crisis in corporate constitutionalism. This is in fact a crisis of larger dimensions. Similar issues arise with respect to all large organizations and not least those public organizations which we designate as nation-states. The structure of authority is changing the world over, and we do not know what the future holds. The nation-state system, which reached maturity in the early modern period, is under heavy stress and may not survive such polarizing influences as international communism and Western constitutionalism, the "revolution of rising expectations" in the less developed regions of the world, and the phenomenal technological developments of the nuclear and space age. In the evolution of new patterns of authority, however, it is not improbable that the business corporation will play a telling part, perhaps as a catalyst, or perhaps as the forerunner of some new and still inchoate type of governmental pattern.

The tensions that are building up in economic organization are thus traceable to external as well as internal forces. Inside the company the stockholder-manager-employee complex reveals the tug and pull of certain easily definable forces. But outside, in the immediate neighborhood, there are the forces of labor unionism and plant-community interests; and in the farther reaches of the environment, the rising fiscal and other demands of public governmental agencies, the still quiescent but looming power of pension and investment trusts, the ever changing market picture at home and abroad, and epoch-making changes in the global patterns of political authority.

Control of Corporate Power

THE RESULTING constitutional crisis in the corporation derives from the extension of the authority relationships both within and beyond the firm. The major issues in corporate constitutionalism—as in traditional constitutionalism—center on the scope and legitimacy of power and the means of controlling it. Of these two major problems, the emphasis in contemporary writing on the corporation is given to the problem of control. A relatively undeveloped theoretical field is the question of adequate power in corporate governments to perform their legitimate tasks.

There are two major possibilities for the control of corporate power: controls of managerial power by external agencies; and internal controls through institutionalized devices within the firm, designed to secure responsible corporate government. Mixtures of these remedies for abuse of corporate power are likely, but here we are concerned mainly with the question of internal controls. What likelihood is there that such institutionalization will resolve the problem of corporate constitutionalism?

According to Carl Kaysen, "the development of mechanisms which will change the internal organization of the corporation, and define more closely and represent more presently the interests to which corporate management should respond and the goals toward which they should strive is yet to begin, if it is to come at all." [6] Yet the fact is that the trend in this direction is already well started, though the evidence is not to be found in too narrowly defined organizational terms within the formal structure of the firm. The evidence is to be gathered rather in such peripheral developments as collective bargaining and the attendant growth of the idea of the workforce as a corporate constituency, the newer relations between franchised dealers and manufacturing companies, the rise of pension trusts with their yet unrealized potential as corporate policy-determiners, and the gradual internalizing of cultural mores in the form of "social responsibility of the businessman" and what Berle calls the "corporate conscience."

In comparison with these developments, the attempts on the part of the "corporate democrats" to activate shareholder control of management have had insignificant results. Nor has the legislation, stemming from the 1930's, which seeks to protect stockholders from managerial abuse of power, effected any revolutionary changes in the corporate constitutional system. The legislation of the thirties on securities marketing, on the contrary, seems to have been based on a theory of corporate governance in which the stockholders were the sole relevant constituency. But this theory is hardly reflected in corporate practice. It is significant that in recent decades most critics of corporate governance have concentrated their fire on the separation of management authority from stockholder control. Only within the past few years has any systematic attention been given to the impact of other developments on corporate constitutionalism. And a great void is left—even by the latter-day critics—in the relatively untouched area of the nature and scope of corporate authority.

Adequacy of Corporate Power

AS WE HAVE SUGGESTED EARLIER, the issue of control of power is logically subordinate to (though not necessarily of less practical importance than) this question of legitimate power. The standards of justice to be applied in corporate constitutionalism will depend upon what we expect corporate power to accomplish. Because their aims are different, one has to be cautious in making simple analogies between the state and the corporation. Even in states, different systems of value are discernible, as was evident in the varying sorts of meritorious conduct esteemed in the classical Aristotelian classification of states. Democracy esteemed freedom; the quality of being a free man was the measure of control of power in a democratic state. Oligarchies esteemed wealth or noble birth, while aristocracies esteemed virtue or honor. The nature and scope of governmental power in these cases stemmed from different standards of value.

What standards of performance do we expect of a business corporation, and will these standards supply the key to the scope of its powers? At first blush the Aristotelian oligarchy, with emphasis on wealth, would seem to provide the key. If one assumes that the business corporation is some kind of self-contained society with its own full-blown concepts of internal corporate citizenship—a *koinonia* or fellowship standing alone, with consonant principles of the good life to guide its members—one might conclude that creation of wealth is the source of its standard of performance. But, while the production of goods for profit is undoubtedly the major business of the corporation, this is hardly the *sole* concern of its members, who are, after all, bound by ties to societies other than the corporate institution.

This multiplicity of ties is certain to modify the otherwise clear-cut purpose of a business corporation, and the modification is in the direction not of a narrowing but rather a widening of the scope of corporate authority. This is so in part because the pursuit of profit (wealth, by analogy, in the Aristotelian oligarchy) has to be conducted in terms of the dominant standards of justice in the greater society. But the enlargement of corporate objectives also arises from the fact that its people must commit much of their time and energy to its affairs. Nor is this involvement necessarily a function of organizational size; it happens in small as well as large businesses.

Given the fact that people "in trade" must invest so much of their time and energy in the particular business in which they are engaged, the organization inevitably assumes kinds and degrees of control over their lives that are not describable in purely economic terms. *Any* organization—whether it be political, economic, religious, educational, or scientific—involves some degree of teamwork in which controls only peripherally related to the primary function of the organization have to be set up and exercised by governing authorities.

Quite aside from the powers of officials in any organization, arising logically from its specialized purpose, there are always other powers growing out of organizational necessities of a more general kind. There are at least minimal disciplines to be enforced to build up and maintain an *esprit de corps* and to preserve unity of effort in the face of internal disintegrating forces as well as external threats to the common enterprise.

Emphasis is necessary on this point, particularly with respect to the business corporation as a going concern, because of the renewed emphasis on the value of human freedom, a value of high priority in our society. We do face, however, in today's struggle for power in the international arena, extraordinary pressures that enhance the countervalue of solidarity—a solidarity not only in the direct instrumentalities of national defense but also in the less direct. The large business enterprise is such an indirect instrument; and when we speak of the global struggle we need not confine our attention solely to its military aspects. Certainly in the economic and social phases of our global efforts the role of business and other nonmilitary organizations is vital.

To put the matter in another way: the *powers* required to sustain a viable corporate constitutional structure, especially in the larger business organizations, must be adequate at least to control the entropic tendencies in any organizational effort. So viewed, the mustering of corporate authority may in some cases leave something to be desired. A putative enemy could wish for no greater boon than the disintegration of civil organizations in the logistic lines of his adversary, and of course it is reasonable to assume that this method of undermining the foundations of national power is systematically pursued.

The problem of corporate power in these terms has hardly been faced squarely, nor is it an agreeable field of controversy. One too readily encourages the exorbitant claims of the authoritarians who would—in the name of national emergency—invoke the harshest forms of industrial discipline without sufficient proof of their necessity. Yet the potentialities of crippling blows to our social fabric by "the enemy within" have been dangerously evident in more than one area of industry and commerce. A serious crisis could very quickly impel national leaders to invoke legislation already on the books, and to enact even more stringent controls, all of which might make the older insistence on "managerial prerogative" look like the golden age of freedom by comparison.

Pluralistic Implications of Corporate Power

WE TEND TO ASSUME—perhaps too optimistically—that the pluralism of our relatively competitive economy is in itself an immeasurable source of strength for the nation as a whole. Undoubtedly there is much truth in this claim; yet the other side of the coin bears scrutiny—namely, the *adequacy of decisional authority in the dispersed centers of privately organized power*. If the authority is to be widely dispersed in the interests of liberty and freer choice, it must not be forgotten that choice in itself means decision-making, and decision is the most important component of power. The decision centers, in other words, are *power* centers; and in an increasingly *organizational* economy these *power* centers are found not entirely or even mainly in the individual human units of a completely atomized society but increasingly in the artificial units of capital aggregrates.

This means that, under the impact of the organizational revolution, a pluralistic society is not a society of individual free men who release bits of their primitive freedom of choice to public government alone, retaining all other decision-making power to themselves as private persons. Rather it is a society in which decision-making is transferred to a variety of public and private governments—that is, to various public and private officials who hold more or less extensive authority to act for otherwise free men on numerous issues that affect the lives and property of these individuals.

This transfer of decisional authority goes far beyond anything contemplated in the received doctrines of democracy and constitutionalism. It has long been a popular pastime to bridle at the extent of this transfer of authority to public government's decision-makers, but only in recent years has systematic attention been given to the extent of the transfer to the officials of private governments. In both cases there is a re-transfer: in the case of public government, for example, the delegation of powers by legislative assemblies to administrative agencies with "quasi-judicial" and "quasi-legislative" authority; and in the case of private corporate governments the delegation of decisional authority by boards to operating managers, on the one hand, and by shareholders, incipiently, to trust and pension funds, on the other.

In this process of transfer of decisional authority from the primitive units of a democracy of free men to the public and private governments of a pluralistic society the accretions of power by these governments are responses to the need (or at least the felt need) for collective action. The debate about shrinkage of individual freedom of choice, as this transfer proceeds apace, is not mainly a debate about the individual *versus* the state; it is a debate about the *kinds* of organization that ought to have the power to govern men, and about the distribution of powers among these public and private organizations.

It is from this point of view that one has to approach the normative question of power-mustering (that is, decisional authority) in the business corporation. What power has to be transferred to the private government of the corporation if it is to perform the tasks assigned to it? And how can one define those tasks in such a way as to make a rational distribution of decisional authority as between this particular kind of private government and other kinds of public and private government?

As a purely scientific problem—quite aside from one's preferences in the matter—one must also ask how in practice the muster of power in corporate governments has been effected. What, in other words, are the written and unwritten basic principles that spell out the nature and scope of corporate powers? For it must be conceded that in private as well as in public polities based on the traditions of constitutionalism, a constitution is an instrument of government as well as a symbol of liberty. The rule of law, as against the dominance of arbitrary will, implies rule as well as limitations on the rulers.

In very large corporations, moreover, the authority of corporate governments at the top must be adequate to meet the demands made upon them by outsiders. While a considerable delegation of authority is indispensable for extensive and diversified operations, the reservations of authority at the center must necessarily be substantial. This necessity was pointed up in the recent antitrust cases against the electrical companies. Decentralization obviously has certain limits; it can go very far with respect to some matters, but will be quite impractical in others. The distribution or allocation of powers within a firm to various divisions, committees, departments, branches, and individuals is not simply a question of power distribution for the purpose of checking the exercise of power. It is also a question of preventing the dispersal of power to that point beyond which the governing board and executive managers lose control over matters for which they will be held accountable.

In sum, then, we can observe a constitutional crisis in the modern corporation which raises two equally important questions: the adequacy of power in corporate governments, and the control of that power. Before considering these questions separately and in detail it is first necessary to examine the constitutional foundations of corporate governance.

Part II

THE CORPORATE CONSTITUTION

CHAPTER 3

Constitutional Foundations of Corporate Governments

THERE IS ALWAYS a tendency to draw analogies too narrowly between private government and American public government. But there is no obvious reason to suppose that our own patterns of public government necessarily have or always will provide the solutions for the problem of government in our private sectors. With respect to the nature of constitutions, in particular, the comparative study of constitutional systems can be enlightening.

Lord Bryce once distinguished between those nations which have created and maintained permanent political institutions—allotting special functions to each organ of government, and assigning to the citizens some measure of participation in the business of government—from those in which such institutions existed only in theory, if at all. Constitutions, in the "proper" sense of the term, were discoverable only in the former category. Other nations were "in a state of chronic political disturbance and were mostly ruled, with little regard to law, by military adventurers" [1]; or remained under autocratic monarchies with a small educated upper class and a predominantly backward population; or had a low level of intellectual life and were little influenced by ideas which permanent political institutions of the constitutional type presuppose. For Bryce, "a Constitution is a Frame of Government designed to prescribe the form which the administration of a State takes, to define its powers over the citizen, and the rights of the citizen against it." [2]

Since Bryce wrote these words, however, we have seen the rise of many regimes which he would have dismissed as having no "proper" constitution but which nonetheless have "basic" charters of government that are clearly oligarchical and dictatorial. In the broadest sense, constitutions are the fundamental laws and practices in accordance with which governments commonly operate, regardless of the degree of participation by citizens in their government and not excluding regimes in which citizens' rights are protected against their government hardly at all.

If a business organization were like a republic, it can be argued, then one could trace the democratic sources of corporate authority to the will of the majority and speak of a corporate "constitution" as though it had its roots in a popular constituency. But, while the charter of a corporation is indeed the result of a sovereign act by a public government with democratic roots, the managerial authority in a business is traditionally traceable not to any democratic majority but rather to the property-holders who merge their capital to create and maintain the enterprise. Managers must of course reckon with the will of the public majority as expressed in the corporate charter and in corporation laws, but they must reckon first of all with the will of the ultimate owners of their corporation.

This, at least, is the theory of the traditional corporation, which assumes a kind of responsibility on the part of share-owning corporate constituencies that is more mythical than real. Today's shareholder is often merely a tacit and irresponsible owner who plays the market more like a crap shooter rather than a knowledgeable investor of risk capital in companies whose affairs he helps to govern. Like the pension fund trustee, according to the critics, he shoulders about as much responsibility for influencing corporate governments as an irresponsible parent in governing a wayward child.

It is not usual—at least nowadays—to argue that the authority of the state rests on the rights of property or, in good Lockeian fashion, to insist that the purpose of public government is the preservation of rights in property. Nevertheless, it is argued that in corporations, as in churches, majority rule is not in itself regarded as a sacrosanct principle, in view of the special purposes of the respective polities of these institutions.

Further, one can object to the analogy between public and private polities from a historical point of view. It is not true, for example, that church and business polities have drawn primarily from the experience of public governments in drafting the basic patterns of their private governments. In many respects it has been the other way around. Presbyterian and congregational theories of church government had a profound influence on the earlier patterns of public government in the New England colonies, while—looking farther back—as we have observed, one sees the impact of conciliar theory on political doctrine in the fifteenth and sixteenth centuries.

Nor is it clear that earlier forms of corporate polity in England and the United States were inspired mainly by the examples of the constitutions of public governments; while in more recent times one can observe the pressures generated "to make government more businesslike." Finally, it is not unlikely that business polity in the future may develop theories of polity from sources quite independent of politics in the sense of public government. It is even possible that public polities may, in future, be profoundly influenced by the experience of private polities.

When all this has been said, however, the analogy between public government and corporate polity remains a useful method of inquiry because of the far more extensive and disciplined body of thought available to us under the headings of public law and constitutional theory. Except for the polity of churches and some discussions of the government of unions and guilds, there is virtually no systematic literature on other than public governments. To cast aside the concepts and terminology developed in that area as completely irrelevant to the problem of corporate constitutionalism would be a hasty and uneconomical procedure, to say the least. One does not need to work out an entirely new and different set of symbols and hypotheses.

Hence, in this discussion we shall refer, in using the term "constitution," to the more basic principles concerning (1) the mustering of power and authority in any organized group, and (2) the limitation of the power and authority of office-holders in the organization. These principles are "basic" in the sense that they are generally accepted as being less easily alterable than rules and policies subject to fairly frequent review. Some of them may be written down; others exist in the form of tacit agreement. Some may be in the form of laws and charters; others, in the form of mere regulations that are nevertheless seldom challenged.

What is important for purposes of definition is not the form of these principles but rather their credited priority as rules concerning the mustering and control of power in the organization as a whole. In every organization one can find such rules in more or less concrete expressions of command, superior to other commands in that they set the framework for a "constitutional" system of government under law.

The Tradition of Constitutionalism

THE TERM "CONSTITUTION" is historically grounded in a tradition of constitutionalism which has a very long history.[3] The tradition did not originate with American and French drafters of written basic charters, who were sometimes accused of believing that a constitution was "a pudding to be made by a receipt." Rather, it goes back at least as far as Plato and appears almost continuously in the political thought of the West in the idea that all legitimate governments must be limited in their power over men. Constitutionalism in all its successive phases, writes McIlwain, "has one essential quality: it is a legal limitation on government; it is the antithesis of arbitrary rule; its opposite is despotic government, the government of will instead of law." [4]

A constitution has been defined by T. M. Cooley as "that body of rules and maxims in accordance with which the powers of sovereignty are habitually exercised." It is "the fundamental law of a state, containing the principles upon which the government is founded, regulating the division of the sovereign powers, and directing to what persons each of these powers is to be confided, and the manner in which it is to be executed." [5]

In this sense of the word, all politically organized communities have constitutions. In some political communities the "powers of sovereignty" are not "habitually exercised," in accordance with constitutionalist principles. But constitutionalism means something more than having a constitution in the sense that Cooley defines the term. It means "government by constitution," [6] in which the constitution is not only an instrument that grants power but also one that effectively limits the use of power to legitimate ends and for the protection of private rights. There are governmental systems, as we all know, in which the "constitution" is solely an instrument of power, or even an irrelevant scrap of paper.

But in a still broader sense "constitution" means simply "the arrangement and distribution of the sovereign power of the community," as George Cornewall Lewis phrased it.[7] On the basis of his comparative study of the constitutions of Greek city-states, Aristotle concluded that the nature of the ruling class (*politeuma*) would determine the nature of the constitution (*politeia*) of a city. The constitution amounted to no less than a certain ordering of the inhabitants and thus became "as it were the life of the city" [8] and made the city what it was, with dominant values that would vary from city-state to city-state, and would even change abruptly in the same city.

Our modern idea of "constitution" is different in that we think in terms of a legal order, whereas for the ancient Greek the word denoted a whole way of life. Yet in contemporary usage among communists in the "people's republics" there is something of the ancient connotation: the ruling class imposes its way of life on the whole community through no less systematic an ordering of its inhabitants than in our Western constitutionalist regimes—though for quite different purposes, and for the preservation of "rights" not defined in accordance with the views of the liberal tradition of the West.

The idea of a constitution as a written document embodying the fundamental and paramount rule of law received its greatest impetus, no doubt, from the American examples, first, of the state constitutions and, then, the Constitution of 1789 for the federal system. There the attempt was made to bring together in one authoritative document, issued at a certain date, all those publicly acknowledged principles that were deemed fundamental to the governance of state and nation. In England, which offers the classic example of the "unwritten" constitution, these fundamental principles had been and still are scattered—in acknowledged usages and precedents, in various ancient charters and acts of Parliament, in leading decisions, and in the "customs and conventions" of the English constitution.

There the term "constitution" originally designated certain fundamental customs or ancient usages declared in solemn form by the English king with the assent of his Great Council. Henry II, for example, issued in 1164 a set of rules governing the relations between the secular and ecclesiastical courts—the Constitutions of Clarendon. Like Magna Carta in 1215, which the great barons wrung from King John, these were not new rules at all but rather the old usages put into written form and formally declared. Such charters were documents of definition, not of legislation, and bore little resemblance to our modern constitutions. In Cromwell's Instrument of Government (1653) there is a closer approach to the latter, for the Instrument was based on the Agreement of the People drawn up by Cromwell's soldiers in 1647, and was a formal *legislated* document setting forth the detailed powers of executive and legislative departments in the new republic. When the monarchy was restored, of course, Parliament—which had never accepted the Instrument—simply decreed that the government of England should revert to "the ancient and fundamental laws of the kingdom," and never since that day has England had a written constitution. The ancient and established ways of governing are not prescribed in a single assemblage of documents; and although new ways have been introduced, both by enactment and through more recently evolved "conventions," it was still true at the end of the eighteenth century that—as Tocqueville remarked—"the English Constitution does not exist" in the French or American sense.

The American experiment with written constitutions, while it was not completely successful as an attempt to write into a single document *all* of the fundamental institutions of government, was successful as an attempt to cover the more basic authority relationships. Any such attempt at comprehensiveness and exhaustiveness in the fundamental charter of a governmental system is destined to be only partially successful. Even if the basic charter, when framed, covers all the main principles on which the government is based, these principles almost always become modified in practice while others arise, so that the original instrument no longer fully corresponds to the actual government of a country, a church, a university, a trade union, a corporation.

The Unwritten Constitution

REALISM THUS REQUIRES the student of comparative constitutional systems to look beyond the formal instruments (and not merely to their clauses, important though they undoubtedly are), for these formal instruments can mislead as well as instruct. The actual "frame of government" must be sought in constitutional *interpretation* by courts, legislatures, and executives. The governmental framework is not derived from a mere private excogitation of the meanings of words and phrases in a written instrument. Not only is "the Constitution what the judges say it is" [9]; it is also what other authorized officers of government believe it means in crucial decisions that do not—and cannot under the doctrine of "political questions" [10]—come before the courts.

All of this is perhaps elementary, but needs to be emphasized here because it is true not only of the United States Constitution but of all written fundamental instruments of government in the several states of the Union, and indeed in all established organizations where a system of public or private governance prevails over an extended period. It is true whether we are speaking of an authoritarian regime or a democratic one, and regardless of the extent to which the basic instrument of government is regarded as "fundamental and paramount law." For a "government of laws and not of men" is impossible; only men can interpret and enforce the law, and it is their understanding of its meaning that is translated into those institutions of government that prevail.

A constitution of public government is "a system of fundamental political institutions," as Herman Finer [11] has phrased it, or "the autobiography of a power relationship" and, more specifically, the "power relationship between the individual and associated constituents" that prevails in that human grouping we call the state. The constitution is a "system" in the vital connections among fundamental political institutions and in the vitality of their relationship to the nature of the society in which they exist. A constitution's "fundamentality" refers to the exclusion of ordinary law: statutory law as opposed to the written constitution in the United States, *Gesetz* as opposed to *Verfassung* in Germany, *loi* as opposed to *constitution* in France, *legge* as opposed to *statuto* in Italy, *lag* as opposed to *grundlag* in Sweden.

Through its constitution, writes Finer, a people "seeks to establish certain institutions as fundamental . . . especially in the arena where uncertainties may cause conflicts of a radical and painful kind, that is, in political life."[12] We thus seek to avoid putting into daily jeopardy our liberty, our property, our family, our religion, our province, our country.

Constitutionalism, then, seen in historical perspective, indicates a persistent search, through centuries of human experience in the art of government, for basic principles both for the creation and the control of power to govern men. The most dramatic episodes in this long story have occurred, no doubt, in the public sector: in the struggles over power in city-states, empires, the medieval Church, and in modern nation-states. Yet we know that the struggle has gone on in the private sectors as well, though with less public fanfare and with little theoretic analysis by scholars.

Constitutionalism, as the traditional search for the justification of power and the means to control it, is currently changing its course in important respects. The search for workable and warrantable power aggregates at transnational levels is one example of this. In our own country the search for workable and warrantable power aggregates in industry and labor is another.

Some Proponents of Corporate Constitutionalism

THE ISSUE OF CORPORATE constitutionalization has thus to be seen in its historical and comparative context as one aspect of the wider problem of constitutionalism. In a recent essay by Scott Buchanan (writing for the Fund for the Republic, which is encouraging public discussion of "basic issues underlying a free society, especially as to constitutional questions raised by the emergence of twentieth century institutions") it is charged that

> the corporation, taken in its generic sense . . . has for a long time been generating and nurturing a set of habits of feeling,

> action, and thought that are only now becoming recognizable and articulate, and, as they are at present expressed, they appear to be incompatible with our understandings of the principles of the Bill of Rights by which we think we have been living our common life.[13]

And while it had often been said metaphorically, he continued, that the business corporation "is a government, private and invisible perhaps, but also touched with public interest," the statement could in fact be taken almost literally. For "the corporation is a government by and with the consent of the workers as well as the stockholders,"[14] and "more than we realize, our liberties are implicit in the separation and quasi-autonomy of self-governing corporations."[15]

But with "corporate linkages and affiliations" and "the web of filiations between business and government" the groundwork is being laid, as Buchanan describes it, for "the possibility of one master autocrat":

> the political, economic, and social phenomena of the twentieth century are marked by the mixing and confusion of corporate forms and functions. This may be partly due to the closing of the world, each part of which is in effective contact with every other part, all parts of which are penetrated and heavily influenced by our Western civilization, whose structure and style of operation are corporate; the result may be the congestion of corporations. This is no longer an unincorporated frontier; corporations everywhere meet and either conflict or coalesce, and consequently lose their identity and independence. Such a mixing and confusion of corporate forms may be comparable to the breakdown of the villages and the drift to the great cities which have marked the nineteenth and twentieth centuries in Europe and America.[16]

Buchanan then asks whether new doctrines of the separation of powers are not in order. According to the eighteenth-century rationalists, our liberties were ensured by separating governmental powers and trusting them to rational debate in their several compartments. Now "the addition of economic powers, money, industry, and welfare, to the fragile political forms of the republic is letting the bull loose in the china shop."[17]

Perhaps what is needed is some reasonable distribution of these powers to various corporate forms—not, as in the totalitarian pattern of communism, through a few giant collectivities, but through more imaginative structures better suited to our pluralistic society.

How, asks Buchanan, can we be assured that our corporations will have a republican form of government, in the same way that the Constitution assures such a polity to each constituent state? What principle of federalism as to reserved powers is to be made applicable to the corporate system? Corporation law could be regarded as a mere veil obscuring what is potentially another branch of public government. The charters of private corporations are remarkably reticent concerning the rules their internal governments are required to follow.

From a few charter specifications of offices to be filled—a president, a vice-president, a treasurer, a secretary—and a few lines as to broadly defined powers, the internal government expands into a self-generated system of bylaws and a huge, charted organization. Unlike charitable organizations—which, as they grow in size and function, differentiate their organs and functions somewhat along the lines of their predecessor and mother, the Church—the business corporation "shows the pattern of an amoeba increasing to the size of a whale."[18] There is no sharp differentiation of internal organs of governance but rather

> a series of fissions and fusions into colonies, such as the parts of General Motors, each with strong oligarchic controls within and weak federal connections with each other. It may be that there is still the implication of oligarchy in a plutocracy, and an incompatibility with democracy, but it would be interesting to see if replacing the Sherman antitrust law by the assurance of a republican form of government to all private corporations would not take the strain off the heavily pressed executive and hasten the present tendency of the business corporation to accept more community responsibilities.[19]

In our federal system the device employed to ensure justice and freedom both within the individual states and for the whole community was not a direct police power at the center (the national government), but a territorial distribution of powers that would guarantee the legitimacy and health of the separate corporate bodies (the states) under republican governments. By analogy, one might "redraft the categories of corporations according to their distinctive functions, assure them separation of powers and independence of one another, and restrict, or strictly define, the contracts or treaties (cartels) they are empowered to make." [20]

Buchanan also thinks that it might be necessary to redefine the terms of the Bill of Rights in the federal Constitution so as to cover the corporation as a body politic. In the confusion of our loyalties and duties to our many interrelated public and private governments, "membership" is badly defined. As a result, the meaning of basic rights has been eroded; and while we go on reiterating the ancient doctrines of justice with elaborate researches into the historic origins of constitutional rights, these scholarly enterprises "are not reaching the nerve of present political thought, either on the professional level or in the citizen's conviction." [21] The concept missing from this definition is the corporation as a body politic and the vital part it plays in promoting or inhibiting the great freedoms of speech, of religion, of association, and of the press. "The elegant eighteenth century words and propositions do not mean what they have always seemed to mean, and the bottom has fallen out of our political courage." [22]

Thus Buchanan raises basic issues of corporate constitutionalism. Has the political nature of the corporation been recognized for what it is? Would it not be better for our whole political life if the recognition were formalized in a body of corporation law? Should we not draw into the open such questions now "hidden in the phrase, private or invisible government?" How do the political habits formed by members of corporations fit with the habits that republican forms of government have developed in their citizens heretofore?

Mark Twain once observed that "it is by the goodness of God that in our country we have these unspeakably precious things: freedom of speech, freedom of conscience, and the prudence never to practice either." Would the corporation, asks Buchanan, become the school of political prudence in which men would learn not to practice what the political republic had always preached?

Similar questions were raised in a discussion [23] sponsored by the Center for the Study of Democratic Institutions in April, 1959. There Reinhold Niebuhr referred to corporations as "quasi-sovereignties," and Buchanan again raised the problem of their constitutionalization. He saw two possibilities: one was to "give the corporation a constitution and a rule of law within its own body"; the other, "to change the federal Constitution or state constitutions in such a way that they regulate and take their full responsibility with relation to corporations." [24]

Niebuhr asks what this "rule of law" would say to a corporation that the law does not say now. The law does say many things, as A. A. Berle, Jr., observed: "the corporation must not steal from its stockholders, it must not exploit its customers, it is not to exploit its labor." Moreover, "it is supposed not to discriminate in buying and selling. It must not monopolize. It must not grow too big, although the anti-trust cases are shifting. It must not contribute too much to political campaigns," [25] and so on. But as to its form of government, said Berle, "the traditional democratic process that we know about in politics does not work very well within a corporation for practical purposes, so there are oligarchies." How are the oligarchs kept in control? By "a public consensus which at any given moment may discipline the corporation with varying degrees of severity." Any "democratic" concept, as applied to corporations, is to be found in the working of this consensus, as, for example, through the regulatory commissions. In addition the consensus is now "beginning to demand some kind of planning." [26]

So far as internal constitutional restraints are concerned—

those which might arise from a corporate constitution's bill of rights or other restrictions on corporate power—Berle knew of no corporate charter that said anywhere "thou shalt not overcharge, or thou shalt not exploit labor." [27] These prohibitions came from the outside. As to its own institutionalized restraints, the methods by which directors are chosen present the almost unvarying picture of "an automatic self-perpetuating oligarchy." [28] But can and should a corporation be run democratically? For practical purposes, in Berle's view "the control or power element in most large corporations rests in its group of directors and it is autonomous—or autonomous if taken together with a central control bloc." [29] Because of inheritance-tax distribution of stock, moreover, management autonomy has developed.

But, in Berle's analysis, this is not the end of it. The management pyramid of power is "beginning to be balanced by a pyramid of men who have no possible property in the actual corpus [of the corporate assets] but do have the power of choice—the pension trustees." [30] He called these "naked power vehicles" because the pension trusts hold power without property. But it is a power that they do not in fact exercise. In fact, they refuse to exercise it. The situation has thus become fluid. For such power will eventually be used by someone. It demands legitimation, and will sooner or later have to find "a field of responsibility and a field of accountability." [31]

Berle perceived the probable development of a new federal constitutional doctrine to curb this "sheer power of invading personality"—a new doctrine that would "play a joke on our constitutional system." The joke is that, while our federal Constitution is based on the theory that corporations should be kept apart from public government, in fact they have not been. The forthcoming doctrine is that "where a corporation has power to affect a great many lives (differing from the little enterprise which can be balanced out by the market) it should be subject to the same restraints under the [federal] Constitution that apply to an agency of the Federal or state government." [32]

Thus the Bill of Rights and the Fourteenth and Fifteenth Amendments would become direct restraints on corporate as well as on national and state power. Berle conceded that this was a jump ahead of current law. But he thought it would be the next phase "just as we already have the constitutional doctrine that under the First Amendment you may not by private contract prohibit a Negro from buying land." [33]

The proponents of corporate constitutionalism, however, do not confine themselves to the device of public judicial review of corporate action that becomes in effect "state action." There are other public resources for "making just corporate government out of crude corporate power, commonwealths out of satrapies" [34]—to cite Professor Earl Latham's phrase. The problem, he insists, is "one of imposing on the corporation the same limitations that experience has shown must be laid upon the exercise of power in public government," [35] and by that he means not just the requirement of due process of law in corporate procedure but much more besides.

Latham calls for the "recovery of the constituent power" over corporations which, he says, has in practice devolved on the corporation itself to such an extent that its charter is really written by its managers and not by public agencies. He would revise incorporation laws so as to define corporate purposes more strictly and not leave corporate managers free to roam in an undefined field. He would institute active visitatorial functions in state agencies to supervise corporate affairs, and explore the possibilities of using federal commerce and taxing powers to keep corporate governments in line. The reforms he contemplates might even extend to the compulsory federal incorporation of business in interstate commerce.

Latham proposes, further, the revision of the electoral process within the corporation so that the present "make-believe democracy" would be replaced by one in which the "owner constituency" would be an effective force for self-government. Possibly the state would intervene to police the intracorporate electoral process in much the same way that the National Labor Relations Act authorizes federal supervision of workers' voting in the collective-bargaining process. He also suggests the possibility of assigning a certain amount of voting power in corporate affairs to the state.

In addition, Latham holds that the state might also lay down certain standards of due process—presumably by statutory or administrative rule—to govern the exercise of corporate executive power in the administration of a company's internal affairs.[36] But perhaps the most interesting of his proposals is the requirement that "corporate states," like the states of the Union, be guaranteed a republican form of government and be required to meet certain minimal criteria under this heading as a prerequisite to doing business in corporate form. Like the states of the Union, the "corporate states" could, he suggests, be required to purify their electoral machinery, to meet the demands of the due-process, equal-protection, and privileges-and-immunity clauses, and to use their taxing power and their quasi-police power only in the interests of safety, health, morals, and the welfare of those under the jurisdiction and authority of these "corporate states."

In this way, argues Latham, it might be possible to transform the corporate state into a true commonwealth—though not very quickly or without careful preparatory studies. Since it took centuries to develop constitutionalism in public governments, the constitutionalization of corporate governments could hardly be achieved overnight. As a first step, he calls for extensive congressional investigation of "the politics of the modern corporation" patterned somewhat along the lines of the TNEC. This is an inquiry that he considers long overdue.

Now, these views, which Latham has expounded at various times and places,[37] may or may not be widely shared by students of corporate governance, and it is not always certain that Latham himself takes all of them quite seriously. But it can hardly be doubted that he does take seriously the basic problem which he regards as a problem of political science *par excellence* and not just an "analogue" to the problem of public government. Nor can there be any doubt that many of his colleagues will agree with him on this point. But among the lawyers there seem to be doubts, even though they may agree that the issue of freedom somehow applies to corporate affairs.

As a lawyer, Professor Bayless Manning, for example, is highly dubious about the way the political scientist states the basic problem. He has called for a restatement of it that abandons the "poetic level of discourse" about corporate power and individual freedom in the abstract and gets down to more concrete and particularized analysis.[38] Manning is against the use of terms like "constituents" and "freedom," drawn from the special historical context of American public government and applied to the very real problems of the modern corporation. He regards these "political analogues" as highly misleading because they do not, in his opinion, get to the heart of the matter. What we want to find out, he insists, is *who* is hurting *whom* and *how*, in specific situations, and then to get on to some workable remedial measures.

All of the major terms in the contemporary political sociology of the corporation are swept aside by Manning as almost useless in getting at the "particular acting institutions, particular acts, particular victims, and particular injuries" [39] that need to be isolated for analysis in order to wind up with usable policy solutions in corporate affairs. He challenges the idea that the "corporation" *per se* is at issue, indicating instead the relevance of economic concentration in whatever organizational form. He dismisses "power" as a term without any clear referent in the current discussion, and urges instead that we talk about definable policy issues. He asserts that "freedom" is a useful enough shorthand term when we talk about the public constitutional system, since it calls up a definite body of law and practice with which the knowledgeable are familiar; there is an "area of normative consensus" [40] and there are precise referents for the elements in communicable statements about encroachments on freedom by public governments.[41] He denies that it is now possible to make any such precise statements about encroachments on "individual freedom" by "corporate power."

"Corporate power," he correctly points out, has no unambiguous referent. If we say that the "corporation" is depriving someone of freedom, who is the offending actor? Do we mean the legal form, the fictitious person, or "large business enterprise" in general, or some particular company, or some particular group or person within it? In public law the identifiable actor in an encroachment on liberties protected by bills of rights is always some specific state or federal official (or body). The things they are forbidden to do have been spelled out with particularity in constitutional interpretation over the years,[42] and the aggrieved parties are identifiable, case by case. The First Amendment, for example, has a subject, a verb, and an object: "Congress shall make no law . . . abridging the freedom of speech or of the press," and the Fourteenth Amendment specifies that "no State shall . . . deny to any person within its jurisdiction the equal protection of the laws." But who, asks Manning, is supposed to be protected against this abstract "corporate power"? Are we worried about "customers, employees, executives, junior executives, shareholders, some classes of shareholders, suppliers, creditors, some class of creditors, other institutional bodies such as the legislatures, the churches, the schools, the press," or only some of these—or perhaps some not even included in this list?

The questions of whose ox is gored, who does the goring, and whether, in fact, it is a goring at all or something else that worries people who talk about "corporate power and individual freedom" are salutary ones to raise at this point in corporate constitutional development. For, while one may not agree with Manning that the "analogues" of political science are irrelevant and obfuscative—the position taken in this book is that we are talking not about analogues but about identities—one may certainly agree that the questions he raises demand clear answers. And so do the other questions about the subject and the verb in the formula: *who* is supposed to do *what* in a truly constitutional corporate system of government, and would any reform of the present system produce the results that the would-be reformers contemplate?

It is by no means clear that the reformers are in agreement about any of these matters. Take, for example, Manning's interesting list of the "gored." Here there is a formidable array of interests, and the current discontents spring from many diverse sources. Manning himself is inclined to dismiss the grievances of those whose interests lie near the center of the enterprise,[43] and to show far more interest in the impact of corporate policies on "society"–whatever that may mean. But every group of interests he lists is somehow involved in the whole question of corporate constitutionalism–and certainly none to the complete exclusion of others. We get back to the problem of the real scope of the corporate community, a question that has to be settled before any substantial progress will be made toward corporate constitutional reform. This question does raise–Manning to the contrary notwithstanding –the problem of identifying the corporate constituency and the appropriate constituent power.

The so-called "owner constituency"–the shareholders–gets short shrift from Manning as the basis for the legitimacy of corporate government, a term which he avoids using. But, without so designating it, he does tackle the problem as a problem of political science. He attacks the thesis that in the loss of linkage between power and property in the large public-issue corporations there is no "legitimacy" in the acts of an unpropertied corporate management. He calls this an "involuted-Marx-upside-down argument" that

> assumes what must be challenged–that the rest of society need not worry about corporations so long as the "owners" are running them. Then it challenges what must be assumed–that corporate policies socially satisfactory when set by shareholders are no less so when set by others. The argument is based on *a priori* conceptions of right and legitimacy in a particular distribution of decision-making power within the corporate legal structure. Our concern about the large business enterprise is made to hinge on the degree of dislocation from this ordained internal legal order, rather than upon the functional social consequences of corporate policies. Again we forsake substance for form.[44]

But the basic concern of Manning is for the particular *policies* of particular corporations as determined by specific persons and as affecting other persons in identifiable ways that we ought to be interested in as defenders of "freedom" in the abstract. How should we allocate the decision-making power, *on specific types of issue*, to those persons and institutions most likely to exercise that power to produce the policy results we want? This kind of question, he thinks, is going to be more fruitful of solutions to the grandly posed problem of corporate power and individual freedom than theorizing about corporate governance in the large.[45] The kind of result wanted will be differently defined, certainly, by the various groups of interested persons who participate in corporate affairs, either as members of the organization or as more remotely located persons affected by policy.

But Manning is not interested in corporate constitutional structure or in blueprints of a corporate commonwealth. He would approach the problem pragmatically, case by case, situation by situation, hoping that eventually it might be possible "to put together a new general theory of the relationship of men to groups of men" and to break away from the old stereotypes. Thus we could arrive gradually at "a new set of institutional arrangements hand-built to accommodate the Demipublic Alpha Institution" [46]—a symbol he suggests as one way of indicating the more specific referent of large industrial enterprise. Then, perhaps, we might discover how to cope with the more general Alpha Institution—a broader category—and even find that we have at the same time "helped ourselves to a better theory of Individual Freedom and Government." [47]

Perhaps—but not necessarily. Radical empiricism alone does not produce the stimulating hypotheses from which general theory develops. From the lawyers' point of view it may seem more realistic, and sounder, to proceed case by case, taking one policy problem at a time, thus building up in a quasi-judicial process a series of precedents that will become the building blocks of a new corporate constitutional order.

But the proper allocation of decision power in the corporate structure is a question not likely to be answered with any reasonable degree of symmetry by the case method. This is pre-eminently an area in which hard cases make bad law—and, indeed, where the revered method of verbal combat through adversary proceedings before judicial tribunals will not be available for settling all the important issues.

Congress and the state legislatures are undoubtedly going to be forums for future discussion of corporate constitutionalism. But will they be the best forums for this purpose? Does the system of representative government, as practiced at local, state, and federal levels today, assure the primacy of the *public interest* in resolving such issues as that of the corporate constitutional structure? Or is the legislative forum more nearly described as a public arena for the battle of *private interests?* What assurance do we have that the problem of allocating decision power within business enterprises can be solved in such an arena? And if legislatures do, in fact, speak the public interest, how can one be sure that the legitimate *nonpublic* interests of many participant persons and groups in a large industrial enterprise will be adequately represented when the question of corporate constitutionalism is debated?

An alternative path toward constitutionalized corporations, of course, is the introduction of bills of rights and other methods of regularized restraint on corporate decision-makers by the corporate community itself, without any intervention whatever by public governments.

The general patterns of constitutional restraint on corporations discussed in this chapter are drawn from the experience of public governments. It is arguable whether these patterns should be imposed upon corporate governments by legislative, administrative, and judicial action in public agencies, federal and state. Thus one would have a system of extrinsically initiated constitutionalization of corporate governments. It might not be possible, or wise, to impose on corporate governments all of these patterns of restraint. But, as we have seen, there is now a growing body of opinion that at least some of them should be imposed, especially those involving the protection of private rights through public judicial review of corporate governmental actions.

But would it not be possible, alternatively, to stimulate in the corporate community itself a fundamental re-examination of the whole corporate constitutional system with the purpose of self-constitutionalization? Let us consider next whether there is any built-in potential for gradual internal development of restraints tailored to the specific nature of the corporation as a private government.

CHAPTER 4

Roots of Authority

IN THE STRICTLY LEGAL SENSE, corporate powers rest entirely upon grants of authority by public governments—as by charter or certificate of incorporation—and the concession of these powers is held to imply the withholding of authority not granted by sovereign act. The corporate constitution, in this strict sense, is a written constitution. The basic written constitutional documents that make up the corporate constitution include statutory, judicial, and administrative rules governing the exercise of corporate powers.

One must also look farther than the written constitution to discover the basic principles of a corporate polity. The written rules are both too narrow and too inclusive to give a true picture. For an understanding of the real decisional authority of corporate governors, and the actual limitations on that authority, one has to go beyond written documents, if only because charters, statutes, administrative regulations, and court decisions often go into matters that bear little direct relation to the major issues of corporate constitutionalism.

For the delineation of basic principles concerning the "authoritative allocation of principal functions . . . [the] system for the ratification of collective decisions, [the] operative system of command, [the] system of rewards and punishments, and [the] institutions for the enforcement of the common rules,"[1] as well as for those principles that describe the enforceable restraints on the powers of corporate governors in each of these areas, one must enter the unexplored terrain of corporate constitutional history.

The great company precedents that guide corporate decision-makers may never be written down. The basic "rules of the game" in business are largely uncodified. The more reliable sanctions—both for exercising corporate power and for resisting the arbitrary rule of corporate governors—are not likely to be found in the jurists' briefs and opinions. But they will not be unknown to those who manage a company's affairs or to those on the outside who know when and how to influence managerial decisions.

Here it is useful to point to a parallel in the study of public constitutional systems where reliance upon strictly juristic sources has long since ceased to be an adequate guide to the political scientist. The constitutional principles of American government are to be sought not alone in the basic document of 1789 and its successive amendments or even, by extension, in the judicial, legislative, and executive interpretations of the clauses of this charter of public government. One has to look into the deeper historical roots of our constitutional theory—in England, in medieval Europe, in Rome—and into the wider patterns of our own American political experience in peace and war since 1789, in order to appreciate the basic operational principles that govern the mustering and the limitations of public authority at the federal level.

The vital role of the party system is a case in point. The Constitution of 1787 said nothing about it, and, for reasons that history discloses, the omission is understandable. There are few Supreme Court decisions on the subject; and legislation, even if it were brought together from widely scattered statutes, would not adequately explain to a foreign observer the essential part played by political parties in the muster and control of public governmental power. Similarly, no mere exegesis of the texts of corporate charters would illuminate the governmental system of the Hartford Empire Company through license agreements and its "committee on character," or of N. V. Phillips Company in Holland, which, under the Corvo Law, was said to be able in time of war to follow the example of the amoeba and divide itself into two parts, with its western operations controlled by deeds of trust in British and American banks. For an attack on the *zaibatsu* system in Japan, the Occupation authorities under General MacArthur had to make exhaustive political as well as economic analysis of these intricately related industrial enterprises. The policy of the New York Central Railroad would be understandable only after careful study of the struggle for power in which Young was a dominant personal influence. For an understanding of the polity of General Motors, one turns to Drucker's studies, among others, and not to its charter and bylaws.

There are, in corporations as well as in public governments, established and difficult-to-change ways of doing things which one discovers only through close observation of practice over an extended period. Yet the charter is of such major importance from several points of view that we must single it out at the start for special attention.

The Formal Charter of Corporate Governance

THE CORPORATION CHARTER ("certificate of incorporation," "articles of incorporation") is the central document in corporate governance. Originally granted only by special act of a legislature, state or federal (after more or less careful consideration of the public and private interests to be served by granting a license to do business in corporate form), the corporation charter today is usually obtained with minimal formalities such as filing the articles with the secretary of state or other state agency. What was once regarded as an unusual privilege is now widely regarded as a "right" not to be denied to any lawful association.

Since, however, the grant of corporateness does create a new entity endowed with special powers, it is important to inquire into the source and nature of these powers. Who is the grantor? What is the "constituent" authority to which grantees must return for revision of the powers granted? For what purposes are the powers granted?

The *grantor* of corporate powers is, in legal theory, the state (or Congress, in the case of corporations in the District of Columbia and of other federally created corporate entities) through its legislature—or, by delegation under a general incorporation statue, through a state administrative agency—as representative of the people. Without this "sovereign act" of incorporation no person or group of persons could lawfully set up a corporate government. But here some important distinctions must be drawn.

Concession theory to the contrary notwithstanding, the principle of freedom of association prevails in American public law. If corporateness is a privilege that may, in principle, be withheld at the discretion of the sovereign, it is a principle which has been considerably vitiated in American practice because of the widespread adoption of general statutes of incorporation. Nor do these statutes raise, in general, any real difficulties against the grant of corporateness to outsiders from other states who intend to establish the corporation in the granting state only to maintain a small office there while operating the business elsewhere. Far from being jealous guardians of the corporate privilege, some states see it as a source of revenue. Delaware, New Jersey, West Virginia, Virginia, Maine, and Arizona are states which offer distinct advantages in this respect.

Freedom to associate in noncorporate form is of course unhampered except by the usual provisions against unlawful activities. Some privileges of corporateness without incorporation, it should be added, are obtainable even without any semblance of sovereign action. If this astonishes anybody, he might well compare the law and practice in certain industrial countries, such as Sweden, where the concession theory is quite unknown and in which the creation of a legal entity depends solely upon voluntary action of citizens in agreeing to a constitution and bylaws for their association. And in our own legal system the corporation *de facto* possessing all the responsibilities, privileges, and liabilities of the *de jure* corporation is far from rare; and although the *de facto* corporation may be regarded as a technically defective corporation, there have been many instances in which its official acts were held valid as corporate actions.

Certain attributes are nevertheless necessary conditions for the creation of a corporation *de jure:* (1) the common purpose or purposes of the associates must be set forth in a formal contract; (2) "the creating touch of a sovereign power" must be evidenced; and (3) the association must have a separate "entity" distinguishable from the identity of its human associates—a "life," that is to say, of its own not dependent upon the continued viability of the associates.

Noncharter Elements of the Corporate Constitution

CLEARLY, THE FIRST of these conditions is in no way dependent upon the sovereign will. Agreement on common purposes is the indispensable ingredient of unity in collective action of any kind; and agreement to pursue a common path can generate power in delegated leaders or officials without the "creating touch" which is indispensable to corporate effort *de jure*.

The power to sue and be sued as a unit is not uniquely a corporate power; it can be conferred by statute on unincorporated associations. Nor is limited liability obtainable only through the corporation. The "corporate veil," on the other hand, is of the greatest practical importance as a condition of organizational power in corporate polities. This entity, independent of the human beings who make its decisions, provides an instrument not easily available to men who are otherwise associated. This is not only because the entity's decision-makers are able to exercise implied as well as express powers conferred on the entity by charter, and these powers, however limited in number, are very great. The indefinite (not necessarily "immortal") life of the entity, and its very impersonal personality, encourage long-range planning for an enterprise whose potential for good or evil far exceeds that of any man or group of men as a sum of human units only.

These aspects of corporate power are probably of far greater practical significance than the specific issue of *ultra vires* action by the corporate entity, or whether its officers have acted outside the scope of the authority granted in the charter. Attacks upon corporate action as being *ultra vires*, for the purpose of limiting corporate authority, have been infrequent, at least in this century; often the issue has been raised upon suit to enforce contractual obligations of a corporation when its officers have pleaded invalidity of the contract because it was allegedly beyond the power of the corporate officials to obligate the entity. Thus, the *ultra vires* doctrine does not at all, in practice, have the same effect as judicial review in limiting legislative powers of public governments.

On the contrary, while judicial review was being developed as an effective means of curbing the authority of public governments, the trend in the private governments of corporations was toward the broadening of directors' powers (particularly as to the issue of shares), the imposition of restrictions on shareholders' suits, broader statutory provisions for the amendment of the charter by majority vote of the stockholders, and permission for mergers between corporations of widely differing powers and organized under the laws of different states. E. M. Dodd, Jr., a leading authority on corporations, in listing these trends in corporate powers for the first fifty years of the present century,[2] goes on to say, however, that the aggregate effect of these changes in corporation statutes was more than counterbalanced by regulatory federal and state statutes and judicial decisions with respect to public offerings of corporate securities, solicitation of proxies in the large corporation, accounting methods, security issues, consolidations of railroads and public utilities, and the reorganization of insolvent corporations.

To read the corporate charter alone, then, is not the way to discover the real ground rules for the scope and nature of corporate powers. The charter itself may be quite general in language. It may simply assign the corporate name, the place in the incorporating state where the corporation must have an agent on whom legal process may be served, the nature of its business in quite broad terms, the number of shares authorized, the initial minimal amount of capital, the names and places of residence of the incorporators, the limits on shareholder liability, and the duration of corporate life. Classes of shares and their respective rights may be specified, though in some cases the directors are empowered to determine these matters as shares are issued. Usually there is granted undefined contractual authority for directors and shareholders. The Delaware statute gives only certain express powers to shareholders: the power to elect the directors; the power to enact bylaws (the certificate of incorporation, however, may confer that power on the directors); and the power to approve or disapprove directors' resolutions proposing charter amendments, reduction of capital, merger, consolidation, sale or lease of all the corporate property, and dissolution. The shareholders have "the implied power to ratify certain voidable acts of the board and probably have implied power to appoint an auditor and power to remove a director if, but only if, he has been guilty of misconduct." [3]

The business corporation thus functions, as Dodd has said, like a representative government rather than a pure democracy, since shareholders elect the board, but it is the board which governs with broad powers of business management. Nor is this all. When the board is large, delegation of broad powers to an executive committee is usual, and many statutes expressly authorize such delegation. Furthermore, there is in practice—though seldom provided by statute—a next-step delegation of broad powers to individual officers. The functions of these officers, such as president, chairman of the board, secretary, and treasurer, are almost never defined by statute or charter, so that their governing powers (like those of the president of the United States) are left to implication from their titles. Even bylaw specifications are usually so general as to add little or nothing to what may be inferred from the title of the office.

Authority by Acquiescence

AUTHORITY IN THE PRINCIPAL OFFICERS is, as a result, a power to govern that is largely created by acquiescence, a well-settled principle of law. As Professor Dodd has put the matter: "There is no doubt that broad powers may in all states be conferred on the president or any other officer, either expressly, by bylaws or directors' resolution, or implied, by tacit acquiescence by the board in the officer's exercise of such powers."[4] While the principle of authority by acquiescence technically applies here only to those elements of power not expressly granted in some way that reaches back, ultimately, to the people of the incorporating state, it is not incorrect to assume that in a broader sense the so-called "oligarchical" powers of corporate governors rest essentially on the norm of legitimacy prevalent in our society—namely, consent.

This somewhat legalistic tracing of corporate officials' powers to the people of a state is, however, not the only basis for such a conclusion. In business practice it is generally assumed that when one deals with the president of a corporation one is dealing with its chief executive, and that the chief executive has rather broad power to bind the corporation by contracts and other business transactions entered into on its behalf. Not all courts will so agree, of course, and, as Dodd points out, the creation of authority by acquiescence is hard to reconcile with another well-established principle, that directors cannot properly act except by formal resolution at a board meeting, while "the courts have become increasingly reluctant to permit business corporations to repudiate obligations incurred in their name because of informalities in the authorization or execution of the instrument in which the obligation is embodied." [5]

If state legislatures, as representatives of the electorate, so desired, they might have forestalled the development of undemocratic private polities. They might still undertake a radical transformation of these as governmental systems. One must ask why they have not done so and what the prospects are that they may do so in the future. A partial answer lies in the principle of acquiescence, noted above, together with the judicial trend toward enforcement of corporate obligations "undemocratically" incurred. The courts, in such matters, probably reflect a general opinion about the relative importance of contractual obligation—however undemocratically arrived at—on the one hand, and the imposition of democratic principles on private governments, on the other.

The latter trend is certainly to be noted in certain sectors, especially the labor unions. But is this a *general* trend? Probably not, in view of public acquiescence to undemocratic polities in many churches, educational institutions, the civil and military services, to say nothing of the family, the most basic unit of society. There is no evidence to support a prediction that democratic procedures will sooner or later be forced upon the business corporation.

Yet one must note certain significant recent trends in the philosophy of corporation statutes which do indicate more than superficial probing into the nature of the corporate polity. These statutory trends, moreover, are fortified to some extent by the statements from many quarters (Latham's comment is but one index) which question the legitimacy of managerial authority and the locus of the corporate "constituency."

Constituent Power and Constituent Authority

THERE IS A CONSTITUENT GROUP in the background of every polity: that group of people, large or small, obvious or covert, in whom lies the power to establish, maintain, or sweep away basic relationships between officialdom and the governed and among the various functionally and geographically defined units of officialdom. The constituent group, following C. J. Friedrich's definition, is "that part of the community which is capable of wielding the *de facto* residuary power of changing or replacing an established order by a new constitution." [6] Power, in this sense, is based on organization of some kind: there is a relationship in which the leaders and led are banded together for the accomplishment of some common objectives, partly by consent, partly by constraint, and sometimes even by force. The organization may be informal, and indeed in a constituent group the power exercised over constitutional form and procedure is by no means derived from a *constitutional* authorization.

One must distinguish between the constituent power and constituent authority to make or amend a constitution. The constituent authority may be constitutionally prescribed as power could not be, for the right to make or abolish a constitution calls on antecedent principles—anterior, that is, to the constitution itself. The constituent authority in free societies is in theory "the people." The doctrine is thoroughly established in American constitutional theory, as Corwin has shown with historical insight in his essay [7] on the "higher law" background of American constitutional law.

For centuries the idea of a "higher law" or a "law of nature" had prevailed in Western thought: the idea that the laws by which men live can and should be the embodiment of essential and unchanging justice. Yet, for the purpose of translating such a higher law into stable and workable systems of restraint of governmental power, the "law of nature" long suffered what Corwin calls a "fatal nebulosity." Through gradual development of English and colonial American political thought, the theory of natural law emerged at the end of the eighteenth century in the idea of written constitutions which were enforceable by courts *against* government: "in the American *written constitution*, higher law at last attained a form which made possible the attribution to it of an entirely new sort of validity, the validity of a statute emanating from a *sovereign people*." [8]

Popular sovereignty is the prevailing doctrine of constituent *authority*—but not necessarily a scientific statement of the locus of constituent *power*. The analyst of polities must be alert to both, however; and in the search for constitutional indices in the government of corporate entities both are as significant as they would be in the analysis of constitutions of public government. There may or may not be congruency in comparing the group holding constituent *power* with the group which claims constituent *authority* as legitimized power. The problem of legitimation always raises the question of right as distinguished from might.

Constituent Groups in Nonstate Polities

THE LEGITIMACY OF PUBLIC GOVERNMENT, in the dominant strain of American political theory, undoubtedly rests on the consent of the governed. But it would be incorrect to assume that Americans accept this principle of legitimation for all of their nonstate or private polities.[9]

A good example of this is the rejection in some churches of the principle of congregational polity, in which original authority belongs to the whole congregation and only by delegation of its members to ecclesiastical officers.[10] The Church may be regarded instead as a monarchy, indeed "an absolute monarchy wherein Jesus is King forever and His word the unalterable constitution." [11] The constituent authority in this latter case is in no sense mundane and the theory of church polity is as far removed as possible from the doctrine of popular sovereignty that prevails for secular governments.

But, clearly, there are many secular governments that are also far removed in the theories of their polities from the political theories of democracy. It is sometimes claimed, as has been indicated, that business corporations resemble representative rather than direct democratic government: their shareholders elect boards of directors who in turn run the business, mainly through delegation. Others would go further in qualifying the republican character of corporate polity in business enterprises. Corporations are said to be "self-perpetuating oligarchies" because directors in fact select their own successors. It is even alleged that business corporations have "fashioned massive clusters of undemocratic force and influence," and that from "the constituent power which they have preempted from the state" they have designed the basic functions and distributed the power within their own bailiwicks which "violates the prevailing values of American democracy." [12]

But where do the constituent power and the constituent authority of a church or a business corporation or a state reside? The nondemocratic form of corporate governance is not peculiar to business corporations. As has already been mentioned, nonprofit corporations such as colleges and universities seldom have democratic polities. They are governed by boards that are usually not held accountable in any way to faculties, students, and alumni; and visitatorial supervision of these academic corporations by attorneys-general, in the old style of the King's surveillance over his corporate creatures, would hardly be welcomed by academic critics of business corporations because of the latter's "preemption" of constituent power from the state. In both profit and nonprofit corporations the ultimate source of *legal authority* to govern is clearly the sovereign creator. But one cannot press that argument so far that the *de facto* powers of governing bodies in all corporations are thus traceable.

If one were to run through the whole gamut of incorporated institutions in American society, one would find comparatively few in whose constitutional structures "the prevailing values of American democracy" were not violated, and even fewer in which the *de facto* constituent group would change the structure over to a democratic form. The fictions of ultimacy in authority rarely conform to the realities of power structures; and even where the contrast is glaringly evident, movements for radical reform in private polities are neither numerous nor markedly successful as a rule.

The Corporate Constitution as a Compact

THE CONTRAST BETWEEN constituent *power* and constituent *authority* is especially striking in the case of the business corporation. What is the ultimate source of authority for corporate governance? Where, on the other hand, is that constituent group which can make, alter, or abolish the form of corporate polity?

In strict legal theory, the corporate constitution, like the federal Constitution, is a grant of limited powers by a fixed constituent group. In practice, the powers of corporate as of federal governments grow by usage and the imperatives of changing environments.

The compact theory of public and private governments is more than "government grounded in consent." In the classical form of contract theory underlying American political philosophy, government is not a natural institution, but rather a "conventional" arrangement made voluntarily by men who are antecedently—by hypothesis—in a "state of nature." Constitutions are agreements of the people freely associated for specified public purposes that do not preclude other kinds of association for other purposes. The more limited the public purposes, the greater the range of freedom of association for private purposes. Thus the compact theory means not only "government by consent," but a pluralism of associations voluntarily entered into, with a resultant complex of public and private governments for these associations.

"Government by consent" could be interpreted quite differently as public government by consent of the whole people, but *private* governments only as a special privilege granted by the whole people's public government. The basic issue concerning freedom of association in modern times hinges on the validity of this claim. Obviously, the concession theory is aligned with it, as it excludes all corporate private governments except as they hold sovereign concession.

It is remarkable that in our free society the concession theory of business corporations should have taken root at all. In practice, this theory is on the decline and on the defensive today, and has been for many decades. As early as the Dartmouth College case (1819), where Marshall paid lip service to the concession theory, he also took pains to establish the compact theory of corporate constitutions. The charter of Dartmouth College, he argued, was a contract between the incorporators and the then king of England as well as a contract among the incorporators themselves to establish the college. New Hampshire, as a sovereign state, succeeded to the obligations of the former contract, and was therefore bound under the United States Constitution not to interfere with the internal government of the college.

The principle thus established was soon extended to business corporations and has stood to this day, although the force of it as a limitation on state police powers over corporations has been considerably diminished for reasons that need not detain us here.[13] More important is that the corporate charter of a business is regularly regarded as a *compact*, sometimes a very complicated contract among (A) the state and the corporation, (B) the corporation and its stockholders, and (C) the stockholders themselves.

These contractual relationships are not only of technical interest to lawyers; they reflect some basic theories about the very nature of the corporate polity. A corporation arises, in the first instance, not from a sovereign concession, but rather from the initiative of its promoters. They agree to act in association to pursue common purposes, and they pool property in order to achieve these purposes. The purposes to be pursued are not unusual, nor are they granted by a sovereign as special privileges. Engaging in a profitable and legitimate business is regarded as an inherent right of any citizen. But the *method* by which this purpose is pursued in corporate form is regarded under our law as a privilege. It is this method, or particular form of association, that only the sovereign can grant.

There can be some doubt that the thing thus granted, or permitted, is essentially a form of private polity. This peculiar form of governance for a business can be approximated but not fully achieved by private contractual arrangements.[14] It is not, therefore, correct to speak of the corporate constitution as based upon compact alone. The governmental system of a corporation derives essentially from the *permissive* action of states, by legislation, through administrative rulings, and in judicial interpretation of charters and general corporation law.

The emphasis on "permissive" is important. With the growth of general incorporation statutes, corporate organizers were permitted increasingly to write their own clauses into charters, and these clauses frequently conferred upon managers very large discretionary powers, including the authority to change pre-existing rights of the shareholders. The theory that the corporate charter is in part a contract, moreover, has been interpreted to mean that when shareholders buy stock, they assent to all the provisions of the charter and the general corporation law governing the charter. The stockholders, in other words, commit themselves by this original compact to be governed by *prospective* changes in the governmental system of which they are nominally a constituent part.

The result has been, as Berle and Means predicted thirty years ago, an emerging doctrine of corporate governance that "all powers granted to the management to shift property interests in earnings or in assets must be considered as having been granted as powers in trust to be used only for the general benefit of all concerned," [15] and that the directors' duties in the supervision of *corporate* affairs are highly generalized. Their liabilities have to do only with corporate interests as a whole and not the interests of *individual* shareholders. The security-holder "becomes a petitioner for the wages of capital," and is "safeguarded rather by business ethics and policy than by easily enforceable right." [16]

The Larger Corporate Constituency

HOW IS THE SHAREHOLDER safeguarded by business ethics and policy? Not primarily through the clauses in charters and bylaws, nor in the general corporation laws, which theoretically assure him of a voice in corporate governance through ordinary stockholder's suits or voting at annual stockholders' meetings. To the extent that a shareholder has any safeguards aside from these, they lie in the constitution of that larger area of corporate community—the mechanisms of the economy, the securities markets, and the pressures of the political arena as they affect management policies.

What becomes of the stockholders in this situation? Are they not in reality the true corporate constituency? Obviously not, for several reasons. By definition, stockholders are not a constituent group, for their very powers to act in the corporate polity are legally derived from the charter, and are not, therefore, anterior to the corporate constitution-making process. More significant, perhaps, is the practical objection that the shareholders cannot be relied upon as a constituency "to keep power responsible by the exercise of franchise," as Professor Chayes puts it,[17] or to make, unmake, and remake the corporate constitution as institutionalized power harnessed in the service of society. "Shareholder democracy," he rightly observes, "is misconceived because the shareholders are not the governed of the corporation whose consent must be sought" for the exercise of corporate authority. Why, Chayes asks, should they have any voice, direct or representational, in corporate decisions on prices, wages, and investment? "They are no more affected than non-shareholding neighbors by these decisions," and "they deserve the voiceless position in which the modern development left them" with "perhaps an exception for those corporate actions which alter the security holder's position as such."[18]

Chayes wants "a more spacious conception of 'membership' [that] would include all those having a relation of sufficient intimacy with the corporation or subject to its power in a sufficiently specialized way." This would call for the properly institutionalized representation of "the interests of a constituency of members having a significant common relation to the corporation and it powers." [19]

In what Professor Eugene V. Rostow calls the "endocratic" corporation (where because of wide dispersal of stockholding "the directors normally control, or come close to controlling, the electoral process from which their powers normally derive" [20]) corporate democracy is "not addressed to the prevailing reality" at all. The stockholders, he insists, resolutely refuse to participate in corporate affairs; they obey the management; they are interested in their stock only as investments; and their participation in the corporate electoral process, so far as it goes, is an empty ritual. The weak and scattered individual investors will not take any effective part in this process. It becomes almost a total farce. All this is impressively true; but when Professor Rostow proposes the optional delegation by the stockholder of his voting rights to a trustee he does not take us very far toward a solution of the problem of the corporate constituency but suggests only one way in which a doubtful element in that constituency could better meet its responsibilities.

The case for stockholder constituency, however, is not easily disposed of; in fact, it is probably the foundation stone of the most widely received dogmas about corporate governance: not only that a board owes to the stockholders alone its single-minded duty and unswerving loyalty, but, far more importantly, that the stockholder's *property interests* make the corporation what it is. Dewing's emphasis on the common purposes of those who merge their property interests in an enterprise as the nuclear reality in corporate life, and his somewhat cavalier treatment of the lawyers' arguments about the legal conditions of corporateness,[21] are illustrative of what might be called the "hard-boiled" school of corporate political theory. The newer "apologetics of managerialism" and the New Capitalism with its concepts of broadened corporate responsibility have made very little dent on the received dogma.

Thus, we observe that the "constituent group" in corporate government is not easily discerned, whether through the concession theory or the compact theory. It appears to be widely diffused through the larger community, and operates with respect to the corporation with a degree of complexity that is not easily understood. On the one hand, we have a greatly expanded managerial authority and, on the other, a body of corporation law that presumably prescribes limitations on that authority without, however, providing a working nexus between constituent power and those who actually run the corporation's affairs. This complexity is a considerable factor in the constitutional crisis of the corporation as a private government.

What can be discerned is that the business corporation, like all organizations, public and private, has as a constitution a basic structure of authority relationships. A constitution in this sense is made up of unwritten as well as written parts. The authority relationships are determined by a constituent group or groups, the identification of which is frequently obscured because a distinction is not drawn between constituent power and constituent authority.

In the business corporation the orthodox theories place constituent authority in the state (concession theory) and the contracting parties as incorporators and the stockholders (compact theory). But in fact the constituency is more diverse and more diffused, so that the forces which shape a corporate polity—and continue to reshape it as time goes on—are discoverable in what we have called the corporate constellation of interests or the large corporate community.

Thus there seem to be two fields for constitutional codification, or at least for hypothetical structuring of the larger corporate constitutional system as a whole: the code of authority relationships at the center—the core area of administrative coordination; and the code of authority relationships in the peripheral reaches of the corporate constellation of interests.

CHAPTER 5

The Core and the Periphery of Corporate Constitutional Law

THERE ARE MANY FORCES that shape the form of corporate polity. If we want to know the real pattern of authority in a given company, how the powers of various persons arise and are in fact exercised, the nature of the real limitations on those powers, and the identity of the ultimate constituent groups that can alter this basic pattern, we must look far beyond the formal elements of the charter.

Statutory Principles of Corporate Constitutionalism

WHEN ONE TURNS to the recent trends in state corporation laws, one finds that the 1950's brought many new statutes, some of them in the wake of the Model Business Corporation Act drafted by the Committee on Corporate Laws of the American Bar Association in 1953 and revised in 1955. Careful studies of these acts lead to the conclusion that, in prevailing theory, the states should impose a minimum of special conditions and limitations on corporate governments, and that the privilege of incorporation should be made freely available.

There are various theories that underlie, and should underlie, these general corporation statutes. The "enabling act" theory is at one extreme in a scale with increasing emphasis on the public interest in corporate governments. At the other is the "social responsibility" theory, according to which the powers of corporate governments would be exercised not primarily for the benefit of investors and creditors, or even customers and employees, but rather for the general public. In between are theories which would be less insistent upon a corporate polity designed to serve the public interest but still insisting upon some restrictions of the exercise of corporate authority, with various degrees and kinds of state intervention to safeguard investors and creditors. Unlike the enabling-act theory, these intermediate theories require more or less systematic control of freedom of contract as a basic principle in corporate polity.

Legislators have not regarded themselves as corporate constitution-makers, however. Their main concern has been the definition of the area within which parties should be free to allocate risk, control, and profit in any business organization and the question of power within such organizations to allocate these elements in the absence of express agreements. These, as Professor Katz has indicated,[1] are the primary issues in the law of agency, partnerships, and corporations alike. In the endocratic corporation the separation of risk, control, and profit has raised the problem of managerial responsibility in a form that would hardly arise in simpler kinds of business organization.

What margin of safety, for example, should be provided by law for creditors of a corporation—in a capital fund, for example, protected against distributions in "partial liquidation"? Should the creditors be left to their own devices by bargaining to limit their risk? Or should the statute intervene on the "paternal responsibility" theory of the Public Utility Holding

Company Act and the Bankruptcy Act controlling debt-equity ratios? According to Katz,[2] none of the statutes does reflect that theory.

Or take the question of tightening fiduciary standards for corporate officers and directors. Katz reports [3] that, with few exceptions, state legislation makes "little effort to keep corporate fiduciaries away from temptation" in such transactions as profiting from "short-swing" stock trading, dealings with individual shareholders, authorizing stock options without stockholder approval, and idemnification of defendant directors for litigation expenses in "strike suits" by disgruntled stockholders. The recent legislation "illustrates the 'enabling act' theory, since its major concern has been lest application of common-law doctrines should be unduly restrictive of corporate management." [4]

Similarly, as to the election of directors there is little evidence of any trend toward a more representative type of corporate governance through allocation of voting rights to secure managerial responsibility to those who bear the ultimate risk. Most American statutes, Katz reports, do not regulate the allocation of voting rights, though removal of directors with or without cause has been increasingly provided for. Although the New York Stock Exchange refuses to list nonvoting common shares, the statutes permit them, and express authorization of voting trusts is now customary. The drive to make cumulative voting mandatory, though successful in a number of states, seems to be losing force. But in general there seems to be "statutory freedom to separate risk and voting control," and most of the recent statutes make no provision for "restricting the allocation of risk, control and profit among holders of various classes of shares."

The "social responsibility" philosophy seemed to Katz to have had hardly any influence upon recent corporation statutes. The exception was the trend toward authorization of corporate giving in many states. Otherwise he found a more or less unmodified "enabling act" philosophy to be dominant, despite the movement (which began with Veblen and has extended down to the present) urging more effective devices to ensure responsible government in the corporation. Responsibility to the shareholders was the more conservative of these proposals, but even this was not a conspicuous principle (and certainly not a well-articulated theory) in the recent statutes widely hailed as the "New Look" in corporation law.

The "enabling act" theory had indeed been to some extent "modified by the theory that corporation statutes, while assuring freedom of contract, should reinforce in various ways the responsibility of individual decisions; and the theory that freedom of the parties should be limited in order that the results of responsible freedom may more nearly be approximated." But even these latter points of view found little expression except in the North Carolina statute. The Model Act has been said to contain little that is modern.[5] It changes the method of electing directors, curtails the stockholders' traditional rights to initiate and to achieve fundamental changes in the charter and bylaws, abridges the shareholders' inspection rights, is outdated in its provisions for availability of the voting list, and is inadequate as to the furnishing of financial information. If these charges are true, the states which have adopted the Model Act have not moved away from the traditional principles of corporate polity. The corporate constitution, except in rare instances, has not become an instrument of government for reform that corporate democrats would regard as even modest, to say nothing of those who would greatly widen the corporate constituency.

Those who favor wide discretionary authority for corporate boards, with limited protective provisions in state statutes, see in the Model Act, on the other hand, an excellent point of departure for strengthening the power-mustering phase of corporate constitutionalism. They do not regard the reformers' emphasis on shareholder authority as realistic. To them the real problem is adequacy of power for management. They play down the necessity for constitutional revision in the corporate polity, either by statute or by shareholder amending authority. They acclaim such developments as the short-charter "all-purpose" corporation "in which the stockholder has no right to expect management to adhere to enumerated channels of economic activity, but, rather, may well expect management to pursue any line of activity that bids fair to earn an honest dollar." [6] They welcome what they believe to be "a decided trend away from that distrust of corporate enterprise which manifested itself in extremely strict views of *ultra vires* and in doctrines that always created doubt when a corporation contemplated the employment of new techniques in keeping with the advancing science . . . of management." [7] And the inclusion in recent statutes of express authorization of powers to pay pensions and to establish plans for profit sharing, stock bonuses, and other incentives for directors, officers, and employees, while regarded as perhaps superfluous, is thought to be wise even though verbose through "excess of caution."

All of these factors in one way or another shape the constitutional pattern of a business corporation. The interweaving of these forces yields that "autobiography of a power relationship" to which Herman Finer referred in speaking of the constitution of a nation. Realistically, one looks for the living and working constitutions of organizations in the power relationships among their participants [8]; and in the larger corporate constellation these participants are located both at the core and in the peripheral reaches.

To delineate the constitutional pattern of a corporation in its wider reaches one needs an organizational model different from that which is ordinarily found in the orthodox studies of corporate organization. The rational-legal model will suffice for the inner "bureaucratic" core but the "natural-system" model [9] may prove to be more useful for the larger area. Both types of model will be needed, since, as Gouldner has observed, a modern organization is subject to tensions that derive from "the relation between its bureaucratic rationality and its social-system imperatives." [10] The latter imperatives do not always show up clearly in the formal authority structure at the bureaucratic center.

Rational-Legal and Natural-System Organizational Models[11]

ORGANIZATIONAL ANALYSIS of the rational-legal model, developed first by Max Weber and later by many European and American writers, conceives of an organization as a rational instrument for clearly expressed group goals. Legally and formally prescribed authority structures are at the center of attention in this kind of analysis. The organization and its component parts are blueprinted and diagramed. It is a structure that can be manipulated in a somewhat mechanical way in order to achieve the group goals more efficiently. In this rational type of model it is possible to specify with a high degree of exactitude the fixed and official jurisdictional areas wherein official duties are prescribed by rule, to distribute functional kinds of work with some accuracy, and to make methodical provision for the regular and continuous fulfillment of duties assigned, together with the execution of corresponding rights.[12] Management procedures are based to a large extent upon written documents, and there are staffs of officials in charge of systematic files. The officials are experts in their respective fields who devote their full time—and perhaps long careers—to their specialized tasks, and theirs is thus a degree of professionalization. Knowledge of the rules is one basis for occupancy of office, and officials are paid regular salaries in accordance with rank and function.

The natural-system model, on the other hand, sees the organization as an organic evolving whole, and "the component structures [as] an emergent institution, which can be understood only in relation to the diverse needs of the total system."[13] Equilibrium and survival are imperatives of the system, quite aside from the efficiency of the formal nuclear organization as a means toward rationally predetermined goals.

"Once established, organizations tend to generate new ends which constrain subsequent decisions and limit the manner in which the nominal group goals can be pursued." [14] The structures of organization, from this point of view, are maintained by homeostatic and spontaneous processes; and changes in structure are less the result of mechanistic manipulation than "cumulative, unplanned, adaptive responses to threats to the equilibrium of the system as a whole." [15] Whereas organizational analysis in the rational-legal model looks for deviations in the structure from norms of rationality, in the natural-system model the focus is on disruptions or organizational equilibrium. An organization, from the latter point of view, "grows" and cannot be—perhaps ought not to be [16] —modified by plan.

These two contrasting models, as Gouldner points out, are ideal types, neither of which is adopted exclusively by any modern organization analyst, though some tend to stress one more than the other. Writers who emphasize the significance of "informal" organizations, "human relations" in industry, and institutional approaches to the study of industrial corporations may neglect the rational patterns. Those who focus exclusively upon the legal structure, the bureaucratic mechanism, and the canons of scientific management at the administrative core of the organization may neglect the "natural" elements in the total constitutional structure we seek here.

Two Fields of Constitutional Codification

BOTH OF THESE ORGANIZATIONAL MODELS will be useful, however, in an eclectic approach to the nature and scope of corporate constitutions. One may look at the corporate constitution from many different points of view, in fact, and none can be excluded in a comprehensive analysis.

The jurist sees in charters, bylaws, and general corporation law the essential understructure of corporate authority. The administrative analyst looks for organizational charts, well-reasoned policy documents, job-analysis sheets, and so on, as the major indices of the company's ground rules. The financial analyst looks for the ground rules in the accountant's language. The economist looks at the company as an input-output system. The public relations specialist sees the company basically as an external communication system in which certain ground rules prevail. Each of these specialists' approaches to what we here call the corporate constitution is fractional, but, added together, they more nearly form a rational than a natural-system model that takes into account the "social-system imperatives" for the environment.[17]

There are really two distinguishable fields in which the process of constitutional codification proceeds: *first*, the core area where the ground rules of authority structure are already to a large extent codified by law and managerial science; and, *second*, the outer area where participation is mainly by nonmembers of the formal core organization and the ground rules are far less formalized.

The distinction between these two fields of codification and rationalization can be clarified by an example. Let us assume that the hypothetical XY Corporation has for some years made considerable progress, through a major component in the company's organization devoted exclusively to the problem of the managerial function, toward rationalization of the administrative core. This component has produced a substantial body of authoritative documents, well codified and made widely available to all managers, which spell out clearly the authority structure *from the board level down* and within the *formal administrative organization.*

All major function types of work within the four walls of that organization are accounted for in this corpus of policies, directives, organization diagrams, and so on. The research-and-engineering, manufacturing, marketing, financial, legal, and employee relations functions are all clearly marked out substantively, with appropriate allocations among defined organizational components. The distinctive elements of managerial work, moreover, are clearly classified within every functional component. The four elements of managerial work—planning, organizing, integrating, and measuring—are spelled out in detail. No weak spots or holes in the fabric of industrial business management at the administrative core are discernible.

The XY Corporation is a large, decentralized company. The constitutional structure of this whole quasi-federal system is as clearly codified as are the internal authority relationships of the individual semiautonomous production and marketing units. These operating units are organized separately from the staff units at a company-wide level. Central staff services are available to all operating components in accordance with well-codified principles of nonintervention by staff officers in operating work. The respective fields of operating and staff responsibilities are well demarcated.

The constitutional structure of the administrative core of this corporation will be found in fairly explicit language in the corpus of documents fathered by the staff component to which management analysis, as a functional kind of work, has been assigned. It is true, of course, that there are unwritten ground rules as well. Many principles governing the allocation of authority and limitations on managerial autonomy at various levels exist in the form of precedents, declarations of the president in less than formal documents, disciplinary action in notable cases, and so on. But the written elements in the corporation's constitution, in this inner core of the bureaucracy, are dominant as compared with the unwritten elements in the corporate constitution for the larger area of the corporate constellation.

This wider organizational area includes (A) the relationship between this inner bureaucratic core and the board of directors; (B) the relationship between the board of directors and the shareholders; and (C) the relationships among all three of these elements—the administrative core, the board, and the shareholders—on the one hand, and external groups, on the other, such as the financial community; suppliers; labor unions; customers; governmental agencies at local, state, federal, and international levels and in foreign states; plant communities;

recipients of corporate giving; scientific and educational institutions; professional societies; and so on.

The XY Corporation, like most companies, can refer to a definitive corpus of documentary rules governing the first and second of these wider relationships. Relationships (A) and (B) are governed by the articles of incorporation, the rules of corporation law as found in statutes and judicial precedents, and the minutes of the board. These relationships are also governed by certain ground rules that do not appear in codified form, arising rather from custom and convention developments. The active participants in this somewhat extended organizational area are relatively few, however, and the mutual understandings with respect to such uncodified ground rules are seldom ambiguous. This is true even of stockholder relationships where the law leaves comparatively little room for doubt about allocations of authority and responsibility.

But with respect to relationships among the administrators, the board, and the stockholders, quite a different situation is presented. These relationships reach so far out into the environing society that it is difficult to say where the outer boundaries of the larger corporate "community" or constellation really lie. With some of the "external" groups in this larger constellation of related interests, the administrative core of the corporation maintains contractual relationships of a clearly codified character. This is true of suppliers (including some financial institutions, as suppliers of credit), customers (including dealers and distributors, and governmental agencies as product-purchasers), and labor unions. As to others, such as potential customers (the "consumer public"), potential suppliers (including the hoped-for labor supply at all levels of skill and competence), potential regulators and protectors of the business (legislators, public administrators, judges, voters), the more important professional, scientific, and educational groups, and the local plant communities, the relationships are rarely codified and are often ambiguous and differently understood on both sides.

Codification of "External" Relationships

THE RELATIONSHIPS to be established and maintained by the administrative core of the corporation with all of these relatively peripheral groups [18] are usually regarded as completely *external.* Any attempt to hypothesize a corporate constitutional structure so as to embrace such "external" relationships is likely to be regarded as unnecessarily abstract and comprehensive. Yet in every large company today increasing attention is given to the so-called public relations function of management. Except among the more primitive types of corporate structure, the "public relations" function is no mere extension of the marketing operation. Selling the public on the "corporate image" is, of course, a reasonably legitimate phase of this work; but a more sophisticated view of public relationships is rapidly developing. Every perceptive chief executive today sees the need for a "relations" counselor—or, rather, a whole component of relations specialists—to advise him on the *scope* as well as the substance of the relationships just described. These advisers are expected to develop a systematic and comprehensive synthesis of all relationships of the managerial corps with both the immediate and the more remotely located groups of interests that contribute to and have claims on the enterprise.

Properly developed, this synthesis of all contributor-claimant interests will exhibit the outlines for a corporation's true constitutional structure. The synthesis so presented will not be confined to the traditional factors of production or to the authority structure in the administrative core of the firm. Rather, it will reach out into areas that are ordinarily excluded from the managerial view of the *total* enterprise operation. Each functional specialist, to be sure, sees these peripheral reaches of the operation for his own purposes—for marketing, for example, or for finance or union-management relations. But a unified view of all these functional kinds of work can be achieved only by a chief executive officer who—with adequate staff assistance—can draw all of the threads together at one vantage point.[19]

At the top, the chief executive officer is inclined to see his job as arbitral: the weighing and balancing of the many competing claims on the enterprise in terms of the respective contributions made to it by various groups, and the pressures that these groups can bring to bear at points of strategic decision-making for the corporation as a whole. This conception of the executive function in business corporations has been much criticized for several reasons. In the first place, it is said that the executive's function is not to *balance* interests but to pursue single-mindedly the share-owners' interest in profitability. In the second place, it is said that the usual *formula* for interest-balancing—to balance the best interests of shareholders, customers, employees, suppliers, and the general public—is patently unworkable and inequitable since the balancer is a party at interest.

These criticisms, however, raise counterquestions. Is it not true, in fact, that the large industrial corporation today really does represent a diversity of interests that must somehow be brought into productive equilibrium? And if the formula for achieving this equilibrium be faulty, what formula shall replace it? That large enterprises can and will be run exclusively for maximization of shareholder profits is a proposition that few would maintain. And the danger of conflict of interest, while theoretically obvious, has always to be weighed against greater dangers that would arise from displacement of the present system of managerial arbiters by new and untested methods.

Need for a Mature Formula of Corporate Relations

THE MAJOR DIFFICULTY about the prevailing conception of the top executive's arbitral function is the formula. The usual formula includes an inadequately drawn list of participants in the corporate enterprise. It also fails to assign priorities on the basis of a mature constitutional theory of the corporation. Let us take these two points in turn.

The usual list of participants includes five major groups of interest: shareholders, customers, employees, suppliers, and the "general public." Each of these five groups can be subdivided into classes of interest which present very different claims on an enterprise and make quite different contributions to it. Shareholders include holders of preferred as well as common stock, and the subclasses of each are several. With the appearance of pension trusts and other forms of security holding, the characteristics of the "shareholding" constituency become even more complex. What status should be assigned to each subclass of "owners" in the constitutional structure of corporate authority?

Customers constitute not one homogeneous group of interests but a wide range of interests that may be in mutual conflict. Distributors and dealers are customers whose interests may be at odds with ultimate consumers. The customer relation with big buyers of capital equipment (railroads, airlines, public utility companies, for example) is hardly governed by the same norms as customer relationships with household units. The national government as a customer—under defense contracts, for example, that are negotiable and renegotiable under terms imposed by law, and involve penetration of various kinds into the citadel of private corporate management—is certainly in a special category, both as a contributor to and a claimant on the enterprise.

Employees include blue- and white-collar workers, some of the latter being highly placed in the managerial structure of the corporation. A more realistic formula for interest balancing would distinguish between managerial and nonmanagerial employees and, as to the latter category, between middle-management and top-management groups. The effectiveness of the claims of all these subclasses of "employees" on the enterprise depends upon their authority status in the entire constitutional structure. In some industries the nonmanagerial employees exert an influence on corporate decisions through a type of "external" relationship—such as labor unions—and not at all, or very little, through the authority structure in the administrative core of the corporation.

Suppliers, like customers, may be other large corporations or public governmental agencies. But all large industrial enterprises depend for supply on a host of small businesses and individual contractors. The relative positions of these varied suppliers in the wider constitutional pattern of a large enterprise are seldom accounted for in a systematic *schema* of "external" relations, although in recent years many companies have taken pains to publicize their vital interest in small business as suppliers. The point is that a systematic services-of-supply diagram for a corporation, drawn in terms of authority relationships as well as input-output systems, would contribute to a better understanding of the larger constitutional framework of the enterprise.

The "general public," finally, is obviously a catch-all for the more remote claimants on and contributors to a large corporate enterprise. Strictly speaking, the term "general public" does not refer to the public as customers (already listed in the usual formula) or as consumers (potential customers). In the public relations work of some companies an attempt to reach the "general public" through institutional advertising (properly, an aspect of marketing relations) is the extent of the corporate relationship with that so-called contributor-claimant group. In other companies the general public is linked with the public's representatives in local, state, and federal governments. So conceived, the general public is not so much a potential customer as a potential regulator and inhibitor of, or a defender of, or voter for, free enterprise. The corporate relationship with the public and its representatives is then a compound of diplomacy, a petitioning for redress of grievances, and the eliciting of protective services and subsidies in some form.

The conclusion, after this brief review of the inadequacies of the prevailing formula for interest balancing in the corporate constellation of interests, must be that, while the arbitral concept is not necessarily invalid, the authoritative roles of arbiters and the respective parties-at-interest are not sufficiently defined. If they were so defined, the result would be a pattern of relationships that would approach what we here have in mind as the broad constitutional pattern of a corporation.

Tentative Definition of the Corporate Constitution

THE CORPORATE CONSTITUTION may now be defined as that body of fundamental principles, whether codified or uncodified, written or unwritten, which in practice determines the authority and power relationships within the core area of administrative coordination and in the wider area of its contractual and noncontractual relationships with groups of interests that make contributions to and assert claims upon the corporation.

By "principles" in this definition we mean the settled rules of action. The principles embraced are fundamental in that they refer to rules of action that are of superior validity as contrasted with the numerous detailed rules and regulations derived from them. They are fundamental also in that they refer to the *structure* of authority rather than the detailed way in which authority is exercised.

"Authority relationships" refer to the dominant expectations [20] among participants in the organization that certain persons (or bodies) with generally acknowledged qualifications will be legally or otherwise competent to make certain kinds of decisions in accordance with certain procedures and certain norms. "Power relationships" refer to expectations that decision processes will be controlled in some way that is not necessarily authorized by law or established rules of formal procedure. Authority relationships are *ipso facto* subject to the restraints of ground rules; power relationships may not be, but custom and practice tend to establish constraints on power, and it is these constraints, primarily, that one looks for in the "unwritten" corporate constitution.

The "participants" include not only the members of the formal organization at the core of administrative coordination, but also those outside this area who, in various ways, are able to exercise a substantial influence on decisions made at the core, whether they are authorized to do so or not. There is in every large industrial corporation an aggregate of "external" participants who are normally expected to exercise influence of this kind—whether in contractual relationships or by custom and convention.

The persons (or bodies) who, at the administrative core, make important decisions are ordinarily identifiable as directors, or executive managers, and their "competence" is established by their official status. Status ordinarily predetermines the kinds of decisions one may make and the norms and procedures required in the decision process. This is not necessarily true of other participants at the periphery, whose status is often determined less by formal rules than by business practice, business ethics, custom, and convention.

By the "core area of administrative coordination" we mean the organizational structure at whose peak is the board of directors and proceeding downward, by hierarchy, through executive and other managerial levels. It does not include the body of stockholders, although it might, by definition, be made to do so. For the purpose of constitutional analysis, however, it is better to place the stockholders in the wider area of contractual and noncontractual relationships with the corporate entity. One reason for this placement in analysis is that it aids in distinguishing the more usual field of "management science" from the field of stockholder-corporate relationships. Most of the current rational-legal-model analysis of corporate organizations has to do with the core area of administrative coordination as defined here. The real problems of constitutional analysis lie beyond this area and, first and foremost, in the immediate outer layer of stockholder relationships.

This latter area, in the first peripheral layer, is of course the subject of much legal analysis, but of a character entirely different from the organizational analysis usually encountered among writers on the science of management. Despite the vast amount of writing on the "separation of ownership and control," there is no well-developed *model* for describing stockholder status in the larger organization; and it is perhaps significant that in many companies the stockholders are regarded—for organizational purposes—as outsiders, though for hortatory purposes they are always greeted as the "ultimate owners" of the business.

As one proceeds outward into further peripheral layers of the larger organization it is even more obvious that no model has yet been designed to account in a systematic way for the remaining participants. Perhaps some initiatory steps have been taken as to management-union relationships. The first groping inquiries into "public relations" have been made, too; but a usable model for bringing the whole structure of authority relationships within a common framework is obviously lacking.

It cannot be assumed, of course, that a single model would pattern the relationships of all businesses. One of the first issues to be faced is whether or not there are distinguishable types of organization for each of which there may be an ideal model. Peter F. Drucker has proposed two essential organizational forms: *federal decentralization* and *functional decentralization.* If, organizationally, these are the two simple root forms, and if each of these—as Drucker proposes—is appropriate to some types of business and necessary to others, then model construction might well start from such a base. For example, this could mean that businesses providing services would probably have constitutional governing problems different in kind from those faced in businesses supplying goods to the economy. And it could be hypothesized that businesses whose core activity is research or engineering would be related to models different from those businesses whose work is manufacturing or those whose work is mainly distributive. At the same time, it is plausible that a model of authority relationships for a service company may essentially resemble a model of authority relationships for a research-and-development company.

The complexities of these considerations arise out of the requirement to take into account not only the economic role of the business, its functions, and the character of talents assembled, but also the markets and customers it serves. Such complexities, coupled with the fact that any corporate constitution will have to be a unique instrument, suggest some of the reasons why inadequate attention has been given to this issue.

If it be objected that "organization" is used here in too loose a sense because it brings in participants who are not members of the administrative core, the answer must be that no better term seems applicable, though it has been suggested here that "corporate community" and the "constellation of corporate interests" might suffice. Organizations, as we use the term, are not isolated monads with territorially defined jurisdictions, like states. They interpenetrate each other because of multiple participation by nonmembers as well as members. The danger of confusion here is overweighed by the necessity for inclusion. It is often not *whole persons* but *particular interests* of persons—in their role as stockholders, customers, suppliers—that participate in the corporate organization broadly conceived. And unless such participation is accounted for in the corporate constitutional structure, we are left with a meaningless, if neat, nucleus of whole-person members of the core administrative organization, few of whom may have any "ownership" interest in the orthodox sense. Such an exclusion of the relevant groups of interests in the total corporate constellation would lead to arid conclusions about its true constitutional structure.

We now turn to the two major aspects of corporate constitutionalism: the adequacy of power in the corporate polity to get done the things that have to be done for functionally defined reasons, and the necessary and workable constraints on that power in order that it be properly channeled and exercised. In the discussion of these problems we need to bear constantly in mind the two areas of codification just referred to, and to avoid the elementary error of looking at the corporate constitution as a definitive written document remarkably "produced by the human intellect at a single stroke." It is a living thing in the process of growth.

CHAPTER *6*

Functional Bases: *Traditional Views*

THE BASIC ALLOCATIONS of authority among various groups of persons in a business corporation and the operative limitations of the powers exercised by various participants in the organization—in short, the corporation's constitutional rules—are related in some way to the corporate function. The authority structure may be clearly functional. But it may also be nonfunctional or even dysfunctional.

By the corporate function is meant here those purposes [1] which the organization serves in fact, though not necessarily in theory. The concession theory of the corporation,[2] for example, tells us very little about a given corporation's role in the economy or what purposes it actually serves for those related to it as investors, managers, employees, suppliers, customers, and so on. Thus, a company that manufactures chemicals, for example, is, like all corporations, a "creature of the state" in juristic theory, but this definition tells us nothing about its real function in the economy, or about its significance to the range of participants just mentioned. The relative position of these groups of participants in the company's authority structure cannot easily be discovered by reference either to the corporate charter or to corporation law. Nor would any extant economic theory provide the clue, though in institutional economics one comes closer both to the real functions and to the real constitution of business organizations.

The Real Functions of Organizations

CORPORATIONS, like other organizations, are functional instruments of their participants [3] if among the participants we include not only the "members" of the formal administrative apparatus but also outsiders whose relations with a company in one way or another tend to shape its functions. The real functions of any organization, either as an instrument of the common purposes of its participants or as an instrument of some larger social purpose, are difficult to define in scientific language.

Most organizations are the result of nonrational as well as rational effort, of historical experience and political compromise as well as the neat blueprinting of nicely calculated means to obvious ends. Thus, for Edmund Burke the British governmental system grew out of the slow processes of time and change to which countless individuals had contributed. It was shaped not by any upstart constitution-makers but rather by "the certain march of veiled destiny." [4] From the standpoint of French and American constitution-drafters, Burke greatly underrated the possibilities of organization blueprinting. Yet as one surveys the growth of the Commonwealth of Nations, headed today by the person of the British monarch, one sees the force of Burke's observation. The Commonwealth, as has been pointed out, was never deliberately designed; it is a historic growth rooted in centuries of constitutional development by the English-speaking peoples—not excluding our own part before and after the Revolution. Even today it is hard to define either its purpose or the basic authority relationships in what is nonetheless an influential organization in international affairs.

Similarly, the real functions of the business corporation and the relevance of its basic constitutional pattern to those real functions may be elusive. Its supposed goals, as conceived by business leaders, economic theorists, jurists, philosophers, and stockholders, may be at odds with the functional realities. The received doctrines of corporation law and certain theories of the firm express debatable conceptions of the basic authority relationships in business corporations. The idea that a business corporation is a company of property-owners which acts as a legal person through its board and their employed "agents" is an example of this. According to this theory, ultimate authority resides in a constituency of stockholders, and the line of responsibility for all decision-makers in the organization runs back to this constituency, for whom profit maximization is an "ideal" objective.

But this is hardly an accurate description of the full functioning of any given business corporation. The so-called apologists of managerialism [5] take a different position of the ultimacy and exclusiveness of stockholder authority. They talk of "balance of interests," "equitable" treatment of all who have a stake in the business, and "adequacy" of return on investment. It is not clear whether these managerialists have in mind any basic alteration of the received doctrines of corporate constitutionalism. The managerialism which the traditionalists denounce [6] could hardly be translated into a fully articulated constitutional law of the modern corporation without radical departures from the traditional pattern of authority relationships in the corporate organization. The arbitral functions of managers, as conceived in the "balancing of interests" idea, would be difficult to reconcile with the older and established legal status of corporate executives. It is nonetheless true that managerialism does indicate a real trend in corporate practice and points, perhaps, to a new and emergent principle of corporate function.

Functional Patterns of Authority in Nonbusiness Organizations

ORGANIZATIONAL FUNCTION and the basic pattern of authority in the organization are correlative. This appears perhaps more clearly in certain nonbusiness organizations.

Let us take, for example, Company A, part of a military organization with a simple hierarchical structure of authority relationships internally and externally with respect to the superordinate chain of command. Its authority relationships with coordinate organizational military units are set within a larger hierarchical pattern, and the armed forces as a whole serve a definitive purpose in the organized political community: defense of that community, organized as a nation-state. Members of the armed forces are specialists in the use of weapons for purposes that are constitutionally determined, and the authority structure both within the armed forces and in their relations with outsiders is determined mainly by this protective purpose. The nature of warfare in constitutional societies—the fact, for example, that it involves the use of force through weapons systems that change with technological change—sets certain requirements for this authority structure.[7] Some of these requirements are constant for all regimes, from free societies to dictatorships. There is little room for "free enterprise" and elaborate checks and balances within any nation's armed forces. Peril ignores persuasion when automatic obedience is a prerequisite for protection. On the other hand, the subordination of the military to civil authority is supposed to assure the protection of the community against its own specialists in violence. The authority relationships here are obviously dictated by functional considerations.

Take another example: the authority pattern in the transient and less formalized organization of a cruise ship en route.[8] The perils of the sea require hierarchical command, certainly among the crew, but not less so for the entire ship's company in any emergency. Sufficient centralization of control is needed to get the ship safely to its destination, but control with enough permissiveness for passengers to induce their custom as paying guests. There is a basic constitutional structure for this "going concern" during the voyage which derives essentially from the physics and the economics of the situation as well as from the more formal constitutional structure of the society under whose laws a ship is registered and under the international law applicable to nonpublic vessels.

Or let us consider the parish church as an organized religious unit within a larger—regional, national, or world-wide—religious society. The authority relationships among the communicants of the local church, between these communicants and their local leader(s), and between the local church and the larger organization will all reflect to a high degree the religious function of the local organizational unit. These authority relationships, reflected in the polity of the church as a whole, will be derived in part from its doctrinal premises and in part from nondoctrinal determinants such as the "charisma" of leaders and the social, political, and economic conditions in the general environment. Congregational, synodal, and episcopal types of church polity [9] are all deeply rooted in doctrine, but they are also traceable to historic forces such as those which shaped the development of Lutheran and Calvinist political theories in the sixteenth century. The economic welfare of members, their educational indoctrination, and their adjustment to social conditions will also be recognized by careful observers as determining factors in the constitutional development of church governments everywhere.

Examples can be multiplied from every area of human activity. Political governments, from the Greek *polis* to the modern nation-state, have been the focus of most of the historical inquiry into the functional bases of authority relationships. The comprehensiveness of the political function in most political theory and the claims of modern sovereignty in ultimacy of authority within territorially defined communities both tend to overshadow the significance of more specialized authority systems. Yet the organizational purposes of private associations should lend themselves better to functional analysis of authority patterns because their functions are presumably fewer. This is especially the case with defined human relationships of association in which authority structure may be thought of as closely correlative with the function of the particular association. The apparent simplicity of the inquiry is nevertheless an illusion.

In that most basic of all relationships, for example, the familial, one might expect to find a functional element that gives one a clue to the authority pattern in the family. Yet anthropologists report great diversity in forms of family government,[10] and no one could deny that even in our own culture the authority of parents has undergone considerable change during the past fifty years. Nor is this necessarily the result of any youthful revolution. It may be due as much to the independent development of other authority relationships in which the young are governed by functional authorities in school, church, club, fraternity, team, army, welfare agency, and a host of other competing or complementary organized entities. The locus and scope of authority over a young person is difficult to define because there are so many functional authorities that have an impact on his life.

When a family relationship is extended into the business arena, do we find that either business functions or familial relationships take precedence, or that combinations of these two forces are regularly integrated in superior forms? The history of such interrelationships is replete with examples from the Middle Ages. In the medieval guilds the master craftsman was accorded more respect than his relatives whose skills were not so highly rated. A son and a nephew, apprenticed to a master craftsman, might develop unequally. The nephew could well surpass the son in the trade. Authority, of course, would devolve upon the nephew to such a degree that, lacking the wealth inherited by the son, the nephew would nevertheless be able to earn a higher order of deference in his community.

In a family business, in modern times, competitive individuals within a generation may settle the issue of succession mechanically—as the right of majority ownership. But when managerial talent is wanting in the successor who takes authority as the right of ownership, the corporation's life may be shortened or its health may suffer.

Or consider the problem of private government in hospitals, prisons, and other custodial institutions where a more or less authoritarian system prevails, presumably for clearly definable functional reasons. The locus, nature, and scope of authority over patients and inmates is presumably derived from the custodial objectives of the institution, as are also the authority relationships among the custodians themselves—doctors, nurses, wardens, guards—and their relationships with governing boards, executives, legislatures, and so on. Lack of consensus about the real purpose of custody in such institutions results in considerable ferment today with respect to what we may call the constitutional theory of these governmental systems. The received theories of command-obedience relationships are increasingly questioned on therapeutic and criminological as well as humanitarian grounds.[11] Revised analysis of function will point to revision of authority structure.

The functional basis of organization in its constitutional aspects can be studied, comparatively, in the widest possible range of human associations [12] from the magisterial state to those multifarious types of illegitimate society in which there prevails a kind of "law among the outlaws." [13] The science of comparative constitutional development as applied to all kinds of human association is in its infancy, but the raw materials are there for those who have the will and the imagination to explore. The source materials include the facts about not only public governmental systems but also large untouched areas of private control systems.

Many licit associations formerly maligned have risen to legitimate status as established organizations, while others, formerly licit, are now banned. Partisan political associations, once suspect as divisive "factions," have become legally recognized parties. Labor unions, once banned as conspiracies, are not only protected by law under the right of associations but, as institutionalized control systems, they are required to conform to certain norms of democratic government. Joint-stock companies and corporations, once regarded as dangerous combinations in restraint of trade, are now admitted to the company of licit and indispensable business entities. For the student of authority structures, all organizations, licit and illicit, are grist for the mill: they all display certain functional bases for their own internal control systems. The same is true of transient, amorphous, and formally unorganized types of association which exhibit some elementary kind of control system with patterns of authority relationships worthy of careful study. The absence of formal organization may delude the unwary into believing that no authority patterns exist in such associations.[14]

The factor of function as a determinant in the authority pattern of any kind of human association can be studied, then, whether the association be transient or permanent, organized or unorganized, licit or illicit, public or private, and whether the common purposes of those associated be economic, political, religious, scientific, educational, familial, filial, humanistic, predatory, or whatever. Our focus here is upon the relatively permanent, organized, licit, and nonstatist type of association known as the business corporation, in which the common purpose is primarily—but not exclusively—economic.

Profitable Business as the Corporate Function

IF A CORPORATION's constitutional structure reflects first and foremost the *business* purpose of the organization, one must first define that purpose and then show how the business objective requires achieving of a certain kind of authority pattern in the organization.

"Profit making" as a business purpose today needs qualification. How much profit, how calculated, for whom, and whether "long-range" or "short-range" profitability—the answers to these questions may so modify and qualify the "profit making" purpose as to convert it into a very different one. Profit and profitability may be a major test of business performance, and perhaps the only reliable test in marketing, innovation, and productivity aspects of corporate enterprise. But "buying cheap and selling dear" does not describe the profit goal of most large industrial corporations as they operate today. When businessmen define their goal as not maximization of profit but rather the avoidance of loss, the assurance of a "required minimum profit" to cover future risks, to attract equity capital, and to guarantee corporate survival, we are obviously in the presence of ends to which profitability may seem to be secondary.

Yet one does not easily dismiss as an "old crude fiction" the idea that the corporation is "nothing but the sum of the property rights of the individual stockholders" on the ground that it is instead "an instrument for the organization of human efforts to a common end" in which the going concern is more important than "the individual rights of stockholders, creditors, workers, and, in the last analysis, even of consumers." [15] Profit for the holders of common stock *is* widely held to be the purpose of an incorporated business despite the trend toward more advanced doctrine among the proponents of managerialism.[16]

In some American industries there has been continuous experimentation toward the end that corporations are maintained "in business," let the profits fall as they may. Public transportation companies, for example, may declare bankruptcy without ceasing to provide their services to the community. Or, in other cases, franchises of unprofitable transportation companies are extended in scope so that they "share" customers of profitable companies—often with the outcome that the profitable become unprofitable. Or, again, in the realm of companies whose activity is largely in service of government contracts, contracts are allocated with a view to keeping in being some companies whose profitability may be negative but whose organization contains promise of performing vital service at some *future* date.

But here arises a fundamental issue with respect to the

corporate constitution: does the basic pattern of authority in most large industrial corporations today effectively implement this basic function of profit making for stockholders? A long line of critics before and after Berle and Means [17] testifies to the contrary. The "control" has moved out of the hands of the stockholder constituency into, first, the hands of managers who are not the legal owners and, now, we are told, increasingly into the hands of trustees who are hardly "owners" of the corporation in any traditionally understandable sense.

In the process there has been a shift of control into the hands of government "regulators" and administrators. This trend has also been associated with an increase of control in the hands of organized wage-earners. In fact, trade-union pressure to get recognition as a prior, or at least primary, claimant upon the revenues of a business has been exerted in many industries, not alone in the highly dramatized case of the automobile industry. Ocean-shipping lines, for example, are entangled in a web of controls and regulations which literally make it impossible for the shipping lines to make a profit, while government "subsidy" covers the losses. Analysis of the authority structure of the subsidized companies strongly suggests that control is in the hands of the trade unions *and* the government regulators, not in the hands of the managers of the business. Analysis of this issue by the Transportation Center of Northwestern University supports the proposition that the policies imposed by trade-union and government regulators—antagonistic to profit making—have kept in being a merchant-marine service whose economic value is highly questionable as presently organized and operated.

In the coming "paraproprietal society" the very nature of property may be changed, and with it the old idea that ownership means control of things or even incorporeal property. The corporate property, as physical plant and financial assets, was, of course, never in the control of the holders of mere stock certificates. But presumably these "share-owners" in the business had reliable agents or representatives [18] at the controls who would manage the property on behalf of the "ultimate owners"—that is to say, the shareholders.

But, in practice, the governmental system of a corporation with widely dispersed stockholding presents no such picture, whether in terms of agency, representation, or fiduciary relationships. All these theories of the relationship between the "ultimate owners" and those who actually run the corporation fail to take into account the dynamics of corporate governance. The living and working constitution of the large industrial business corporation with widely dispersed shareholding is something quite different from any ideal formulation based upon theories of representative government, agency relationships, or fiduciary responsibilities. Berle and Means, in their concept of "the separation of ownership and control," made a fresh start on the more realistic analysis of the corporate constitutional system as it actually operates. But, as James Burnham [19] pointed out a few years later, that analysis left something to be desired to the extent that "control" is an ambiguous term.

Control of What—by Whom?

WHO DOES ACTUALLY *control* the affairs of an industrial corporation, asked Burnham, and how is it done? His answer was: the "real" managers. The real managers are those who operate the productive mechanism and have interests potentially at odds not only with the share-owners as passive receivers of profit-cum-dividends, but also with those pseudomanagers who are in effect the "finance-executives" and the "finance-capitalists," pursuing quite another end than productivity. Burnham overstated the case in arguing that the latter two groups were interested only in profit, selling, financing, and the preservation of the capitalist system, to the exclusion of a corporation's essential productive processes.[20] His analysis nevertheless pointed to some basic difficulties in the authority structure of large enterprises as that structure is ordinarily contemplated.

The real managers, Burnham declared, tend to think about coordinating and organizing the actual process of production in terms of the social and political problems involved, and in terms of what more recently has been dubbed the "human relations" side of business. The nonmanagerial executives "think of society as a price-governed profit-making animal" while "the finance-capitalists think . . . in terms of what happens in banks and stock exchanges and security flotations." The stockholders see in the economy "a mysterious god who, if placated properly, will hand out free gifts to the deserving." [21] For Burnham, it was meaningless to talk about "the separation of ownership and control" as though that were the decisive element in assessing the present and future of governance of the economy or of the corporate units in the economy. "Ownership *means* control," he insisted, and "if there is no control then there is no ownership." [22] The "ruling class" he defined as "the group of persons which has (as a matter of *fact*, not necessarily of law, or words, or theory), as against the rest of the population, a special degree of control over access to the instruments of production and preferential treatment in the distribution of the products of those instruments." [23] Not only were these two rights the fundamentals of ownership; the first was determinative of the second.

Of the four groups he discerned in the corporate constellation of interests—the shareholders, the real managers, the "finance-executives," and the "finance-capitalists"—Burnham thought that, while all to some degree share in control, at least in controlling preferential treatment in distribution, the ownership rights of the bulk of stockholders are of a very subordinate kind. He reinterpreted the Berle and Means thesis to mean "separation of control over access from control over preferential treatment in distribution" [24] and drew the conclusion that income and power thereby had become unbalanced, with far-reaching consequences for the real constitutional structure of the corporation and, more particularly, for the economy as a whole:

> Those who receive the most preferential treatment in distribution (get the biggest relative share of the national income) have, in differing degrees in different nations and different sections of the economy, been losing control over access. Others, who do not receive such a measure of preferential treatment in distribution, have been gaining in the measure of control over access which they exercise.[25]

The absence of correlation between the two kinds of control—and therefore of the two basic rights of property—seemed to Burnham to be an unstable situation. Control over access was decisive, he thought, and when that kind of control was eventually consolidated through the "managerial revolution" it would carry with it control over preferential treatment in distribution. It would, in other words, "shift ownership unambiguously to the new controlling, a new dominant class." [26]

The current spate of studies on the larger social significance of the modern corporation [27] can better be seen in perspective when one looks back at these earlier views of Berle and Means and of Burnham. For it is obvious that the profit-making function of the corporation, as a determining factor in its constitutional structure, has undergone penetrating analysis for many years, and this analysis leaves one in serious doubt about the presumed "sovereign" status of the shareholding constituency. The constitutional crisis has been long in the making, and its prophets have been many. But they are not in agreement on the essential nature of that crisis. Clearly, there are competing groups in the struggle for "control" of the corporate organization, but there is little agreement on what "control" means, and especially on what its purpose should be: control over the distribution of earnings, for example, or control over access to the productive mechanism?

Nor is there agreement about the range of the competing groups in the struggle for control. The identification of these groups, in analyzing the corporate constitutional crisis, will depend to a degree upon the relative emphasis put by the analyst upon the profit-making function as contrasted, say, with that of consumer satisfaction.

The Traditional View of Business Function

THE REAL PURPOSE of a business, it is sometimes urged, is "to create a customer" and thus, by derivation, to perform the basic functions of marketing and innovation—the "entrepreneurial" functions,[28] which are clearly distinguishable from the simple, profitable business of "buying cheap and selling dear." The entrance of the consumer into the picture further complicates it, for here we have another contributor-claimant. Does the consumer deserve a place at the table of power in corporate affairs, or is the "consumer interest" adequately cared for by those exterior control systems, the market and public governments?

Add to this the complication of "public representation" [29] on boards of directors in order, so it is said, to assure recognition of the outsider's point of view and a proper respect in corporate management for the "public interest," and you have still more confusion for the straightforward traditionalist who sees the corporation simply as an organizational instrument for maximizing profits for the stockholder. To him it is anathema to suggest that the *business* of the corporation embraces diffuse public responsibilities. The simpler the concept of "business" the better, in his view, and no nonsense about the variety of contributor-claimants or the "arbitral" functions of management in a "major social institution" that longs to become a kind of *societas perfecta.*

Business, from this viewpoint, is the honest and candid practice of the acquisitive art, the activity by which private persons—through organizations increasingly in corporate form—accumulate wealth for their own personal use as private property. Its ultimate purpose is not the acquisition of wealth for advancement of the arts, of science, or of social welfare. The governance of the corporation, then, must be government of a profit-making organization *for* the stockholders if not *by* the stockholders; the traditionalists are seldom "corporate democrats" in the Gilbertian sense.[30]

"The motive of business," wrote Veblen, "is pecuniary gain, the method is essentially purchase and sale. The aim and the usual outcome is the accumulation of wealth. Men whose aim is not increase of possessions do not go into business, particularly on an independent footing." [31] "Industry," he believed, "is managed on a business footing, in terms of price and for the sake of profit," [32] and not in terms of industrial efficiency as a primary goal, or for purposes of social welfare. "Business enterprise . . . is swayed by considerations of nominal wealth rather than by considerations of material serviceability." [33]

The traditonalist would hardly disagree with Veblen, though he would reject this ethical evaluation of the business system and would not accept so dogmatically the mutual exclusiveness of industrial efficiency and profit seeking, which could go hand in hand. Nor would he perhaps disagree with Veblen's belief that "a constitutional government is a business government" in which "the budget is voted with a main view to its expediency for business ends," though he would cavil at the dogmatic statement that "representative government means, chiefly, representation of business interests." [34] But when the problem of government is turned around, when the question of *corporate* constitutional government is raised, the traditionalist emphasis on the meaning of business in Veblen's sense would certainly exclude representation of nonbusiness interests in the corporate polity. And by that would be meant the exclusion of representatives (on controlling directorial and managerial levels) of those whose incomes from the enterprise derive from wages and salaries alone. They are not the risk-bearers, the capitalists who are entitled to profit as a reward for insecure venture, but the servants of these shareholders. They may, perhaps, be rewarded—if not as entitled to a certain measure of "entrepreneurial profit" as "a surplus over costs," [35] then as determined by board action reflecting the primary interests of the shareholders.

But the vested interest of the professional in any line is his educational training and the skill developed in practice. Essentially, the large business enterprise would be hopelessly insecure without the professional services of its managers—and the manager's career is itself at as much risk as is invested capital unless his decisions strike a balance between vision and optimism on the one hand and practicality and prudence on the other.

CHAPTER 7

Functional Bases: *Recent Trends*

IT IS CLEARLY THE OPINION of many business leaders today that the traditional view of the business function of large corporations is far too narrow a view for purposes of translating corporate function into corporate polity. One may take the position that businessmen are those who are entrusted with the economic process in a capitalist society, or with the most substantial part of it. Or one may take the modified position that in a mixed economy businessmen are still entrusted with important elements in the economic process. Still "business" as a function of corporate enterprise involves much more than profit seeking for anybody, much more than the marketing and the innovation that "creates a customer," and more than "managing" (here with reference to Burnham's strictures on the pseudomanagers) the productive mechanism of nonpublic going concerns. This is because it is conducted by men whose aims, regardless of their affiliations, are various—and even, at times, in conflict with the ends of organization. Their aims, especially as managers of large industrial corporations, embrace such a wide range of interests that corporate polity must now be given new forms and governing processes to meet revised functional requirements.

The Businessman and the Business Corporation: Separate Functional Entities

THE ORGANIZATION OF AUTHORITY relationships in a business in corporate form, as these relationships stand today, may not be adequate to take care of the nontraditionalist business functions indicated by Schumpeter's view of the businessman's role.[1] Could this be because the business *man* and the business *corporation* are distinguishable entities in the economic process, with differentiated functions? Surely they are not distinguishable merely because the corporation is an organization, a collectivity of effort. The very size of the larger industrial corporations tends to emphasize their power, and hence their responsibility, in the economic process. As leaders of large organizations, businessmen are confronted daily with quasi-political problems, and with the necessity to make decisions that have an impact on the whole economy and not merely on the business as a unit in the economy. Corporate polities may not be well designed to carry out either such "economizing" and quasi-political functions or the narrowly conceived profit-maximization function of the traditionalist.

One cannot leave aside due consideration of the nonprofit functions of the corporation. Let it be emphasized that one cannot escape the caveats of the traditionalist; the corporate constitution as it stands today cannot *neglect* the stockholder constituency, and if the interest of that constituency are not to be protected by some kind of corporate constitutional reform initiated within the organization, then reform may be imposed from the outside. That can only mean the intervention of public government in the affairs of the corporation. The efforts of the "corporate democrats" to increase access of the shareholders to decision-making power have not been impressive. Nor can it be said that legislation seeking to protect security-holders' interests vis-à-vis those of other groups in the constellation of corporate power has gone very far toward corporate constitutional reform. Not much more can be expected by way of public law to restore to the stockholders the kind of authority over corporate affairs that the traditionalists demand. Public policy on corporate constitutionalism is not likely to be crystallized in the mold of traditionalist formulas.

The demand that corporate "business" be interpreted solely or even mainly as profit maximization for stockholders is not, in other words, likely to be translated into legislation. But this does not necessarily mean that there will be no external pressures to revise the present pattern of power allocation in the corporate constitution. Such pressures, on behalf of the stockholder interest, could come from the large institutional investors who now occupy a somewhat quiescent and anomalous position. They could, if they chose to do so, exert considerable influence on corporate affairs; but if they do decide to activate their dormant function, new problems will arise for legislators. The question of power concentration in merely titular holders of stock, such as the pension trusts and cognate financial institutions, would undoubtedly receive an airing—with outcomes of public policy that are hardly predictable at this time. But it is difficult to see how any outcome would strengthen the voice of the individual small shareholder who insists only that the corporate business be profitable for him.[2]

Corporate business, even when conceived in the relatively narrow terms of stockholder returns, is so *complex* a business of production and marketing of goods and services and so caught up with the *organizational* aspects of enterprise on a large scale that the many people involved in it—with a great variety of roles to perform—cannot be expected to polarize all of their thoughts and actions around the single goal of profitability. And even if they could do this, profit would be thought of in relation to risks. The risk-takers in a large industrial corporation include many people besides the stockholders, and not least those who, as employees, commit themselves to careers in the business. Hence the widely held view that "the fundamental test of any business is whether it serves our society well—whether it provides in its products increasingly good values to consumers, whether it provides good, well-paying jobs for employees, and whether it yields a profit to owners commensurate with the risks involved."[3]

Production as the Corporate Function

THIS MORE COMPREHENSIVE VIEW of the function of a corporate business has interesting implications for corporate constitutionalism that are seldom drawn explicitly. The constitutional implications of the traditionalist view—that the corporation is the instrument of stockholders' profit-making interest and nothing more than this—are fairly clear, though not followed through in practice. The constitution of the traditional corporation would vest in the stockholder constituency enough authority to guard that interest. But this is not the situation in most large industrial corporations with widely dispersed shareholding.

The reason for this discrepancy between fact and theory is that there are really competing theories about the corporate function, the most influential perhaps being the theory that an industrial organization exists for the purpose of producing material goods or services, and, even then, not by methods that emphasize the productive goal alone. Chester I. Barnard, for example, has specifically denied that the purpose is profit, "notwithstanding that business men, economists, ecclesiastics, politicians, labor unions, persistently misstate the purpose."[4] He was not denying that a business ought to be profitable, and surely as president of a large utility company he had sought to make his a profitable operation. But what impressed him, as a careful student of organizations, was the necessity—from an executive's point of view—of finding a workable "balance of incentives"[5] in any cooperative system, whether it be industrial, political, religious, or other. The executive must find ways to provide net satisfactions that will induce people to contribute their efforts to the organization, and these net satisfactions will result from the positive advantages to them as against the disadvantages of cooperating.

What were the kinds of incentive, Barnard asked, that would produce such a result? The answer was: objective incentives (not limited to material rewards) [6] and the changing of subjective attitudes by processes of persuasion.[7] The latter method was usually thought to be the characteristic method of producing a favorable balance of incentives in political and religious organizations, while commercial organizations were assumed to have relied on "objective" incentives and especially material rewards, but Barnard's experience pointed to a different conclusion. Both methods, he insisted, were used in all types of organization, including industrial corporations.

In religious organizations, according to Barnard, "intensity of faith and loyalty to organization" are the fundamental contributions required of their members, and ideal benefactions and the communion of kindred spirits are the predominant incentives. But "inferior" incentives are also effective, and these may include coercion of sorts, while "the material aspects of religious organizations have often been prominent and always inescapable." [8] Political organizations, too, require the use of inferior incentives of a decidedly materialistic kind along with ideal benefactions and community satisfactions. In both these types of organization, as in all cooperative systems, a balance of incentives is a necessity if the cooperative effort is to continue.

In an industrial organization, Barnard observed, material inducements alone will not in practice produce those net satisfactions to the cooperating members which guarantee its survival and success. The price paid for their services cannot elicit from them the required contributions in the absence of certain environmental conditions, effective organizational effort, and internal efficiency in the organization itself. More recently and in retrospect he declared that "every formal organization is a social system" far broader than a mere economic or political instrumentality for some fictional purpose, and that "as social systems, organizations give expression to or reflect mores, patterns of cultures, implicit assumptions as to the world, deep convictions, unconscious beliefs that make them largely autonomous moral institutions on which instrumental political, economic, religious or other functions are superimposed or from which they evolve." [9]

It might appear from such observations as these, with which many experienced executives would agree, that Barnard had lost sight of the *production* objectives of a corporate enterprise. He certainly did reject the conception of organization as comprising a definite group of people whose behavior is coordinated with reference to some explicit goal or goals,[10] for he thought of it rather as "an integrated aggregate of actions and interactions having a continuity in time," including, however, "the actions of investors, suppliers, and customers or clients," and not simply the interactions of employers and employees.[11] An act of purchase by a customer was a part of the organization of the seller: "we may think of the department store as a group of employees, as a physical plant, as a stock of goods, but it nevertheless remains a store because of the cooperative act of customers." [12]

Similarly, one may think of the industrial corporation not as the legal entity of the lawyers or the limited, hierarchical formal organization of managers and nonmanagerial employees, but rather as a behaviorally defined "aggregate of actions and interactions" among the more extended categories of people who determine—by these actions and interactions—the range of the organization's functions in practice. In this sense, the systematic coordination of the acts of all those persons constitutes the industrial corporation as an organization for production because of the consumer orientation.

This is what Drucker had in mind when he said that the purpose of a business is "to create a customer." But Barnard's analysis of the business organization as "a composition of cooperative acts," [13] including the actions and interactions of customers, carries one further toward an answer to this question: how does the *structure of corporate polity* reflect this productive function of the organization? The objection will of course be raised that customers are no part of the organization and therefore have no place in the basic pattern of authority relationships in an industrial corporation. But is this in fact the case?

Customers are of course not within the area of administrative coordination that describes the boundaries of the firm, or within the field of "authoritative communication" [14] that is ordinarily thought of as the corporate organization. But Barnard was right in extending his analysis of the larger organization to include customer relationships and supplier relationships as well. Any executive knows that they are vital elements in the enterprise even though such relationships are obviously not governed in the same way as the employer-employee relationship in the typical hierarchical structure of authority relationships. For the student of corporate constitutionalism, however, these "external" relationships are of considerable importance. It is not enough to say, simply, that these external relationships are governed by the impersonal forces of the market.

The production process embraces all of these relationships, and the corporate *formal* administrative organization standing as a hierarchical system at the center of this process is only a part of this more extensive, *informally* organized process. What is the allocation of powers among the persons and groups who participate in this more widely conceived process? As Charles E. Lindblom has pointed out, the price system operative here is "a political system something like a government" (or, as we should prefer to say, a nonstate governmental system) in which "certain powers lie in the hands of a small active decision-making elite called businessmen" who "decide directly both how much is to be produced of each good and what combination of labor, equipment, and other factors of production is to be used." [15] In the large corporation, business executives thus coordinate a productive process *hierarchically* within the area of administrative coordination; but beyond this area, through bargaining and other nonhierarchical techniques,[16] there is another species of coordinative effort that is not easily reducible to descriptive constitutional terms.

A currently popular method describes this coordinative production process in the peripheral reaches beyond the formal organization in terms of "market voting" by consumers, the consumer "vote" thus becoming an important determinant in the productive process. As Lindblom suggests,[17] however, the market electorate is double-headed: executive managers at the center of the formal corporate organization compete not only for the consumers' dollars but also for their productive services. Supplier sovereignty is as significant as consumer sovereignty in constraining the corporate executive's decisions; the businessman's "electorate" is both a supplier and a demander. If we include among suppliers the suppliers of labor and equity capital, it would appear that the corporate executive has many kinds of electorate to appease.

These analogies of the production process with political models are admittedly suggestive only and not definitive. In the production-distribution process a distinction can be made between the hierarchical system *within* the corporate formal organization and the nonhierarchical system in the larger area of coordination. But industrial democracy is not necessarily absent within the formal structure of authority; nor would the presence of monopolistic conditions in the market exclude hierarchical controls in consumer and supplier relationships. There is, for the whole, a certain unity in authority relationships. The way the powers over the production process are allocated to such disparate loci of power as stockholders, boards of directors, executive managers, labor unions, suppliers of all kinds, and customers of all kinds (dealers, distributors, retailers, the "ultimate consumer" in household[18] units, for example), if accurately described, would give one a fair picture of the corporate constitutional structure. No such comprehensive pattern of authority allocations has yet been formulated for the corporate organization in its extended reaches, nor is it likely to be until the ruling dogmas in corporation lore are set aside.

But even then the problem of tracing the grand outlines of the corporate constitution as a production-oriented pattern of authority allocations would be far from simple. In the first place, one needs a comparable picture on a much larger scale of the constitutional structure of an entire political economy in terms of production-distribution processes. A particular corporate constitutional pattern is an integral element in this larger picture. The other trouble is that a corporate constitution obviously is not merely a *production*-oriented pattern of authority relationships.

The powers that focus in corporate executives, together with the limitations on those powers—powers and limitations that arise through practice and not alone from legal norms—are by no means fully explicable as the limited powers of production-oriented organization leaders. The modern corporation is a many-faceted organization, with a multiplicity of purposes. Some of these purposes are economic, but others would be hard to subsume with accuracy under that rubric. The polity of business corporations was undoubtedly fashioned historically by the dominating economic purpose (whether profit seeking for stockholders or production for consumers), but there is plenty of evidence [19] today that other purposes are strongly operative. But even if we assume, as seems appropriate, that the economic functions will continue to predominate in one form or another, it by no means follows that the constitutional pattern of the modern corporation will remain fixed as it now stands.

It makes a great deal of difference, in any ideal allocation of powers among the various contributors to the corporate enterprise, (A) whether the claims of one or another of these groups of contributors (such as capital-suppliers, managers, non-managerial employees, or customers) are to be recognized as having priority over all the others, or (B) whether the economic function of the organization is so conceived that the organization becomes the instrument of the whole political economy or only of some segment of it.

Service to the National Interest

AS TO THE LATTER POINT, it is often charged that managerial power is irresponsible, that it is exercised in ways that fail to meet those material requirements of society which it is the main task of business to meet, and that in important respects "business values and business attitudes are dysfunctional in meeting our national needs" [20]—both domestically and in our relations with other nations. From this point of view, a reconstruction of the corporate constitution is called for as one way of harnessing the business corporation to the higher economic, political, and security goals of society as a whole.[21]

As American businesses extend their activities overseas, as the marketing frame of reference of American businessmen takes into account markets both abroad and at home, the benevolence of the free society toward pluralistic business comes to be appreciated as fundamental in importance to business. The costs of business in a closed and planned society can be compared directly with the costs of business in an open and pluralistic setting. When this comparison is made coolly by Americans, grave urgency is usually felt as regards maintaining our advantages. At this base level of analysis most American businessmen can conclude that *their* businesses, and business as they know it, would cease to exist if the nature of our political economy should be changed in kind.

Beyond this simple view there are stirrings of more complex evaluations. Frank Pace, as Chairman of the Board of General Dynamics, was reported to hold that the major competitor of General Dynamics was the Soviet Union. With such a conception in mind the most dramatic implications can be inferred. Can the national government rely upon weapons-development work of the corporation as sufficient safeguard to national security in that field? Is the position of our government sound if it relies upon a number of corporations to compete among themselves in such work while they equally compete with the work of foreign governments? Is it possible for the chief executive officers of such corporations to assume, within their respective domains, authority as large and as specific as that of the president of the United States, in order to get the job done? If weapons development, in the end, must be put out to bid among the competing companies, can a fully committed corporation which loses key bids survive? What authorities other than those within the corporate domain proper are required to meet a commitment such as Pace is reported to have assumed? For example, can a corporate chief executive demand military intelligence from the intelligence arms of the government? And what about raw materials or scarce talents: can a corporate executive undertake to engage in economic warfare for these, competing with the Soviet Union?

The issue, finally, turns on the question of objectives and responsibility and authority. If the governmental objective is to maintain our open society and to encourage the creation of others which are essentially open, can a corporation engaged in weapons development accept as large a goal? If "yes," how does one distinguish between government and corporation? If "no," would it not be more plausible to believe that a weapons-development company, for example, could responsibly accept research goals, establish standards, mark out fields of activity—and establish its corporate constitution in these terms?

Service: Means or End?

FUNCTION WILL in the long run determine the form of the corporate polity. If it is an economic function primarily, there will still be room for considerable diversity of authority structures, depending upon the relative emphasis given by men and events to the choices just indicated. As noneconomic functions enter in, the corporate polity seems destined to undergo certain changes that reflect these new functions, too.

Take first the predominantly economically oriented corporation in various constitutional forms. If the economic purpose centers on stockholder claims, there will be renewed emphasis upon the reallocation of authority in favor of that group of claims, to the relative disadvantage of managerial, union, and customer interests. No such radical change in corporate polity as that foreshadowed by Kelso and Adler in *The Capitalist Manifesto* would necessarily occur. They call for "a radical reformation of the relation of the owners of capital to operating management" and the "adoption of legislation designed to require mature corporations to pay out 100 per cent of their net earnings to their stockholders." [22] Nor would the stockholder-oriented corporation necessarily be a kind of cabinet-parliamentary system with the fulcrum of power lodged in a shareholder constituency.

What might emerge instead is a far more aggressive legislative program (at both state and federal levels) for the revision of corporation law and securities acts which could lift the investor in common stocks to a new level of governing power in "his" companies. The stock exchanges might simultaneously greatly extend their surveillance function over the companies they list, and might institutionalize the trend toward guaranties against fraudulent dealing in the securities of these companies. The campaign to establish a "people's capitalism" through ever widening small-investor participation in corporate enterprise could conceivably lead to popular demand for more than the passive ownership now so widely regarded as a permanent characteristic of stockholding. The way might be led by legislation concerning the large pension and investment trusts.

But all this is highly speculative. The emphasis on economic function of the modern corporation could continue without any corporate constitutional "reform" at all. The changes likely to occur in the basic patterns of authority are changes that develop mainly through practice rather than through legislative enactment. Some of these changes are on the way, and are not always perceptible to the contemporary observer. If we think of the corporation not too strictly in terms of the formal organization alone but rather in terms of all of the internal and external relationships with managers—thus extending the scope of the constitutional structure beyond the "area of administrative coordination"—it is possible already to observe some of these changing trends. They can be seen, for example, in the "encroachment" of a number of interest groups on managerial authority.

Labor unions, as participants in the corporate constitutional processes, appear less as successful claimants of a larger piece of the earnings pie than as increasingly institutionalized participants in the judicial processes of corporate governance at shop levels.[23] Another example is the larger voice that dealer-distributors demand in the marketing policies of primary manufacturing companies, or, alternatively, greater freedom from control through those policies. A third example is the appearance, just around the corner, of institutional investors as parties with immediate interest in the scope and substance of managerial decisions. Most pervasive of all is the steady march of the largest consumer of all—the federal government—into the private bailiwicks of corporate managers in the persons of procurement and industrial-security officers.

In these and other ways the nature of the corporate constitution gradually becomes modified—in practice if not in legal theory—so that the basic authority relationships reflect new functional directions for the enterprise as a whole. But quite aside from these trends in the political economy itself and their impact on the authority structure of corporations there are certain developments within the formal administrative organization which have implications for corporate constitutional development that seem to have attracted little attention outside a relatively small group of specialists on organization theory.

Function and Dysfunction in Administrative Organization

THE SYSTEM OF DIRECTION and control within the formal organization of large enterprises tends to be shaped to some extent by efforts to overcome "pathological" processes and dysfunctional arrangements in the authority structure. Among those who have studied these trends [24] one may note particularly Merton, Selznick, Gouldner, March, and Simon. They have not drawn conclusions about corporate constitutional development in the broad terms we envisage here, but their hypotheses and empirical work on organizations generally indicate the possibility of significant changes in administrative structures.

Weber [25] showed much earlier that modern bureaucracies provide a rational solution to the complexities of administering large enterprises, public and private, through well-defined methods [26] of organization and procedure that yield efficient organizational instruments (efficient, that is, with respect to the goals of the formal hierarchy under a given policy directorate) which achieve certain highly desirable results. Among other advantages, bureaucratic organizations "overcome the decision making or 'computational' limits of individuals or alternative forms of organization." But the "dysfunctional consequences," as March and Simon have shown in reviewing more recent studies of organization theory,[27] are probably less understood than the obvious advantages of bureaucratic rationalization as it is widely practiced in government and industry. Nor is there yet much literature on the implications of these dysfunctional consequences for corporate constitutional theory.

One might expect eventually to see the systematic analysis of this latter type of problem in comprehensive treatises on the corporate constitution. This kind of scholarly enterprise still awaits the appearance of adequate hypothetical constructs and empirical work on large numbers of corporations. In the meantime, we may perhaps anticipate elements in the constitutional theory to come. Some of these elements involve changes in the authority pattern of the *formal administrative structure* of corporations, while others will deal with the authority structure for *the larger, less formally organized* corporate constellation embracing all relevant participants.

As the formal administrative structure, the hypothetical constructs for a theory of corporate constitutionalism will be built in part upon what March and Simon call "classical" organization theory stemming from the work of Frederick Taylor, Haldane, Fayol, Mooney, Reilley, Gulick, Gantt, Urwick, Sheldon, Gilbreth, Hopf, and others,[28] and partly upon theories of bureaucracy[29] stemming from Weber. March and Simon's *Organizations* is the most systematic attempt to date to point up the theoretical and empirical requirements for future development from these classical foundations. Though they do not focus primarily on the constitutional problem we deal with here, their observations provide stimulating commentary on some unanticipated consequences of bureaucratic organization. These include dysfunctional organizational learning, rigidity of behavior as an unintended result of managerial emphasis on reliability, deflection from organization goals resulting from delegation as a technique of control, and the dysfunctional[30] effects of some reward systems and incentive schemes, as well as of the implementation of the "machine" models of classical scientific management theorists. All of these matters are of considerable significance to the student of corporate constitutional structures.

For the formal administrative structure alone, there are possibilities of change in theory and practice not precluded by any supposed fixity or maturity of doctrine in the field of management science. Nor will change be limited necessarily to reshuffling of organizational diagrams. When one turns to the broader corporate structure, embracing all of the relationships with shareholders, financial institutions, customers, suppliers, competitors, governmental agencies, and so on, the dysfunction in the total authority structure is somewhat more obvious. Most of the contemporary debate about the modern corporation, in fact, lies in this area of corporate constitutional development rather than in the more limited area of the formal administrative structure.

Yet the lines of this more general development remain unclear because the problem areas are still treated discretely. No one has been able to assemble all of these problem areas into a single grand design for systematic study of emergent corporate constitutional patterns. What we can conclude at present is that the modern corporation, like all organizations, can be viewed as a functional instrument. The functions of this corporate instrument are not necessarily clarified in the stated goals of a given company or in current corporation theory.

Corporate constitutional patterns can be regarded, from the functional point of view, as a structure of authority relationships in the total constellation of competing and cooperative interests that together present the realistic picture of a large industrial enterprise. Organizational function tends to shape the nature of the polity of any organization, business or nonbusiness. A uniform and universal pattern of authority relationships is not in practice imposed upon all public and private organizations. That the public philosophy is essentially democratic, for example, does not necessarily mean that democratic forms of polity will uniformly pervade the social structure. There are organizations of many different kinds with widely divergent constitutional structures which contribute in many different ways to the ongoing pluralistic democratic society. Some of these organizations have, indeed, quite undemocratic constitutional patterns. The explanation for this is partly that as *rational* instruments of their participants some organizations are designed for efficient achievement of purposes that are not attainable by a democratic internal system of governance. But the structure of authority in an organization is seldom determined solely by cool means-ends reasoning; it is also a precipitate of historic experience and custom, shaped by nonrational as well as rational forces.

Dysfunction in an organizational structure is discernible in tensions and dissatisfactions that may mount to the level of crisis in the organization. The constitutional structure—the basic pattern of authority relationships—then fails to reflect the organization's functional requirements. The disparity between means and ends becomes especially obvious in organizations which are widely regarded as essentially rational instruments for known purposes.

The modern corporation in our culture gives high priority to rationality in business decisions and especially to the role of rationalization within the corporate organization. Rationalization of the economy as a whole is widely resisted on the ground that general collectivization and national planning are somehow beyond the capabilities of men, and even subversive of freedom. The rationalization of less comprehensive collectivities such as business corporations is generally accepted as normal and possible. The burden of much of the contemporary criticism of Big Business is that the modern corporation as an instrument for this more limited kind of planning leaves something to be desired. But the corporate dysfunction noted in this critique is not limited to the inadequacy of the internal administrative arrangements of the corporation. The authority relationships in the larger organization, with its multiplicity of "external" relations and a wide range of participants, are also increasingly commented upon as dysfunctional, both as to the specific goals of the corporation as a business and its function with respect to "national purpose," the aims of the economy, and so on.

As we have seen, the functional basis of the corporate constitution is to be sought quite as much in these external as in internal authority relationships, though it is chiefly the latter which have occupied the attention of most students of management science and organization theory. The necessity for broadening the scope of our inquiry to this more comprehensive informal organization is pointed up by posing the question: what is the real function of the modern corporation? Is it the conduct of a profitable business or is it something more? If profitability is the test of business success, how is profitability measured, and who are the profit-seekers of which the corporation is a rational instrument? If the end sought is something else, such as contribution to the whole production-distribution process of the economy, does the corporate instrument serve that function with its present constitutional pattern?

If one is to assess managerial performance in terms of earnings, managers must have powers adequate to yield those earnings. Boards seldom hesitate to delegate enough authority to match that responsibility, nor do they hesitate to withdraw the authority if the responsibility is not met. Boards, in turn, seek from stockholders and from society generally a scope of authority to match their responsibility as profit-makers by delegation. Where authority—as legitimized power—is lacking they may be expected to, and often do, create power for the purpose in hand and seek to legitimize the necessary decisions.

Critics of the "vast power" of the modern corporation often fail to deal with this fundamental fact of life in the business world, though they frequently are willing to concede to public governments vast powers to do those things which modern nations must obviously undertake. The inarticulate major premise in much of this criticism is that all corporate power to administer human and material resources should be taken out of the private sector of the economy and handed over to the state. This position is not a logical one. It runs counter to the pluralistic preferences of most Americans, however attractive it might be to thoroughgoing state-collectivists. Given the necessity for large industrial organizations to get the world's work done, the only alternative open to us is the empowering of private collectivities to get a large part of it done.

Part III

THE POWER TO GOVERN

CHAPTER *8*

The Powers of Constitutional Corporations

The Corporate Constitution as a System of Controls

A BUSINESS CORPORATION, like every other cooperative human effort, requires some system of controls. What is the nature of the control system in a corporation? What kinds of power must be lodged with what persons to be exercised in what way and under what conditions in order that the cooperative effort to run a business in corporate form will be successfully carried through?

These questions refer to an aspect of corporate constitutions that is often overlooked. The tendency is to emphasize restraints rather than the requirements for corporate functions. In the discussion of corporate constitutionalism, this special emphasis on limitations and restraints is a natural corollary of the traditional emphasis on restraint of public governmental power in Western constitutionalism. When contemporary critics of the modern corporation urge that business corporations be "constitutionalized," they usually mean the introduction into the corporate organization of certain analogues to constitutional devices found to be effective in limiting power in public governments.

Reactionary constitutionalism goes further than this and insists upon the radical diminution of all governmental power. But in all constitutionalist regimes it will be observed that the powers of public governments have expanded in response to the demands made upon them, and that "constitutional limitations" do not in practice take the form of shrinkage of governmental functions. Rather they reflect a continuous search for practicable methods to channel and direct indispensable powers to legitimate ends. So it is in corporate constitutional development. The modern trend is not toward limiting the power to govern within corporations, but rather toward devising systems of control that can be legitimized, with a view to consolidating that power.

The Power to Govern

THE ADEQUACY OF GOVERNMENTAL POWER is thus quite as important an issue in the corporate polity as it is in public polities. That this is seldom recognized results in part from the failure to discern the common denominators in public and private governmental systems, but more particularly from the businessman's aversion to the very concept of power as applicable to a business organization. To see in the business corporation a system of private government in which adequate resources for control over human beings are indispensable is to raise the specter of policing functions that are ordinarily consigned exclusively to the state. Coercion is regarded as the necessary, if evil, function of public but not of private organizations.

Coercion, power, the police—these are undoubtedly trappings of the state, though, among the wide spectrum of human organizational forms, certainly not of the state alone. Nor does the state rely exclusively upon the techniques of naked power to achieve a system of controls within its jurisdiction.

4

cuf

Smith, Kenneth L., 1925-
Search for the beloved community : the thinking of Martin Luther King, Jr. / Kenneth L. Smith, Ira G. Zepp. -- Lanham, MD : University Press of America, c1986.
159 p. ; 22 cm.
Bibliography: p. 153-159.
ISBN 0-8191-5718-X (alk. paper)

1. King, Martin Luther, Jr., 1929-1968. I. Zepp, Ira G. II. Title

Like all other organizations, states must rely upon all of the basic control techniques to achieve their purposes. There are relatively narrow limits within which public officials can command obedience; they must depend to a far greater extent than is usually conceded on the techniques of "spontaneous and manipulated field control" and on reciprocity.[1] The state is the outstanding example of an organization that depends upon an adequate system of rewards and penalties as a necessary condition of effective control. But other organizations also require such a system, and, like the state, they depend as well on the congruency of goals of governors and governed. They depend also on the "surrogate control" system of rewards and penalties internalized in the conscience of the governed, and on the identification of the governed with the governors in their perspectives and aspirations.[2]

In a proper assessment of the corporate constitutional system as a whole, one needs to face candidly the necessity of control systems in all organizations, the business corporation not excepted. In an objective analysis, the bias against "power" and the "powerful," or "influence" and the "influential," cannot be allowed to obscure this necessity. We may hasten, with Rousseau, to say that "the strongest is never strong enough to be always the master unless he transforms strength into right, and obedience into duty." [3] But the yearning for the legitimacy of power assumes the fact of power and the necessity for it. A condition of anarchy excluded, some power to govern in any human association is elementary. But power of what kind and for what purposes?

Power as a Range of Capabilities

THE POWER TO GOVERN in any human association is a kind of *capability*. It is one of those resources without which coordinated effort on a large scale is seldom possible. It is one of the necessary means of getting things done collectively. The system of control over both human and physical resources in any coordinated effort does entail, indispensably, unique capabilities in a relatively limited number of persons.

Political scientists do not speak in unison on the definition of power. In the Hobbesian formulation "the Power of a Man . . . is his present means to obtain some future apparent Good." [4] The means are numerous and the "Goods" are various. "Power," as Arnold Brecht has pointed out, "always designates the ability to get one's own will done and opposing wills frustrated." [5] He has objected to the use of the term as a basic symbol in political science because "it fails to express unequivocally by what means and to what purposes this ability is desired and used." Power, he observed, is a capability traceable to such diverse sources as "brute force, or threat of its use; prestige or authority, legal or otherwise; pecuniary means that give their owner the 'power' to buy what he wants in the market; or personal attraction, fascination, charisma, love—phenomena that, in turn, may have their origin in highly divergent factors, such as external gifts, like beauty; mental qualities, like wit; popular actions, like heroic deeds or prominence in sports or arts; that particular something, called personal charm; or, finally, as with Buddha, Jesus, or Gandhi, humility and altruistic modes of life." [6]

Brecht thus concluded that the term "power" requires symbolic subdivision for precision in scientific use, since the term is applied to capabilities ranging all the way from physical force to Whitehead's usage: "The power of God is the worship He inspires." Brecht would use the symbol "P" to designate legal power to set juridically valid norms, and the Greek letter π to designate the "factual power" to influence the use of that legal power or to interfere with the norms set by it. There might be many different symbols to designate specified power concepts.

Power as "Limited Possibilities"

BUT BRECHT DID NOT PROCEED in this way in his own analysis of power. Instead, he introduced the concepts of "positive and negative necessity," the latter being another term for "impossibility." Some proposed actions are impossible—not perhaps logically, but practically so in that they are only *limitedly* possible within narrowly confined conditions that prevail. Many things of practical importance, on the other hand, are quite impossible and cannot be made possible by persuasion or force.[7] A great number of logical, physical, biological, psychological, and legal impossibilities stand in the way of reaching goals of the imagination.

Corporate power, in the Brechtian sense, thus could be stated in terms of the "limited possibilities" open to corporate decision-makers. A corporate government, like any other government, is always confronted with certain kinds and degrees of "negative necessity" in carrying out projected plans of action, and its power is to that extent a limited power. The possibilities open to it are not defined by its "powers" *de jure* or the "just" courses of action, but rather by those which—in all governments—are discoverable by the "art of the possible." The art of the possible in corporate as in public affairs requires due consideration of the necessary and sufficient conditions for policy. Some of these conditions undoubtedly refer to the authoritative as well as nonauthoritative elements of power.

To set up a business in corporate form, for example, it is necessary to have the coordinated effort of a number of persons and the assembling of minimal physical resources for unified action to produce and sell goods and services. It is also necessary, but not sufficient, to obtain a charter if the business is to be incorporated; the insufficiency of this formal authorizing act in creating a viable concern is obvious. Viability of organization may occur before the charter is granted, and it may end before the firm has expired as a legal person. The birth of power in corporate governance depends on the presence of people who are in control of persons and things. Public authorization enhances this control but does not create it.

Similarly, once the firm is established, there is a formal organization with ritualized control systems. But, in addition, a number of informal organizations exhibit techniques of control not necessarily contemplated in the formal polity and perhaps inconsistent with the authorized rituals.

Formal and Informal Governing Power

THIS AGGREGATE EFFORT, which is the result not so much of formal authorization as of actual coordination of resources (human and physical), is both a result of power exercise and the cause of it. People acting together as individuals can create a pool of power, but the pooling of power in an organization leads to an apparently independent *organization* effectiveness in business performance. No mystical entity or "group mind" is involved here; but the power of an organization *per se* is separable for analytical purposes from the sum of the individual efforts of the organized.

It is said that the real governors of society are undiscoverable, and that in any case they are unlikely to be discovered within the *formal* structure of the polity. The prime movers in corporate as well as public governments may not be the bearers of formal authority, and the causal factors in the exercise of governing power may be obscure. If we fix our attention solely upon the authoritative sources, we can observe some, but probably not most, of these factors. The things that are done to advance organizational effort are done by real persons who may not wear the official *persona*. Power as capability may be traceable also to aggregate efforts or collective action carried out within certain "areas of coordination" —whether these areas be defined by law or otherwise.

Thus a species of power-to-govern originates in a pattern of co-action [8] that may or may not depend very much upon formal charters, legal authorizations, or official policies and directives. A formally decentralized firm may reveal, on close observation of practices, a high concentration of controls in central components. Such power may not show up as the authoritative center of command on the organization chart. Conversely, there may be a considerable diffusion of the power to govern the firm despite an apparent centralization of authority.

The power-to-govern thus refers to a special kind of capability: participation in the making of important decisions, decisions which affect a relatively large number of persons and are enforceable in some way. Those who make such decisions may or may not be formally authorized to do so, though the absence of formal authorization does not necessarily imply illegitimacy of the action. There is a difference between *un*-authorized or nonlegitimate exercise of power and the non-authoritative exercise of it. No large corporation could be run without the making of some important decisions in non-authoritative centers. Recommendations of policy often originate in noncommand centers, sometimes outside the formal private governmental structure of the corporate polity. Such recommendations are normally given official imprimatur before they are promulgated. This formal authorization undoubtedly lends weight to the command as issued. It does not by itself assure enforceability.

Authority as an Element of Power

AUTHORITY AS THE RIGHT TO COMMAND, however, does become an important ingredient of power and an indispensable one in any organization. For authority is recognized power—"the expected and legitimate possession of power." [9] More specifically, authority is "the structure of expectation concerning who, with what qualifications and modes of selection, is competent to make which decisions by what criteria and what procedures." [10] Competence, or authority of knowledge, the capacity to make authoritative decisions, is thus distinguishable from control, whether authorized or not, as an effective voice in decision.

Fayol once defined authority as "the right to give orders and the power to exact obedience" [11]; but this formulation confuses authorized and unauthorized control. The power to exact obedience may in some instances amount to naked force or the threat of its use. But authority can also mean—in Jouvenel's apt phrase—"the faculty of gaining another man's assent" and is thus "the efficient cause of voluntary associations." [12]

The legitimacy or "rightness" of control is not always articulated through logically constructed norms that have been deliberately formulated in legal or other codes. It may rest rather on "the less conscious, more incoherent norms with less logical structure and abstract theory, the 'feeling' of what is right or wrong in a given instance." [13] Thus Krabbe [14] speaks of the *Rechtsgefühl*, or the sense of right, as the true source of law rather than the mere command of the sovereign.

Nor is authority always correctly conceived of as coming from on high, as in a structured "pyramid of power" with essentially vertical dimensions. As Miller [15] has shown in his study of Fox Indian communities, our "European" approach to authority structures is parochially and historically biased in its emphasis on the superordination and subordination of roles as distinguished from interpersonal relationships horizontally conceived. It is also biased in its theory of "empowering" status-holders to direct the actions of others who are "obligated" to obey. We normally associate authority with a complex of prestige and functional differentials assignable to persons in the pyramid, and with the idea of tenure of role positions over extended periods of time. Miller found little of this in the Fox conception of authority, where the possession of a pervasive power *manitu*, accessible to all, was temporary and contingent and never located as of right in a hierarchical structure.

While the Fox conception of authority was adaptable to small communities without any high degree of division of labor, even in our highly organized society recent commentators on authority tend to stress voluntarism in industrial organizations rather than chains of command. This raises basic issues concerning the nature of corporate polity, not only as to the governance of the area of administrative coordination but also in the more extended constitutional framework.

The "Force" of Authority

VOLUNTARISM IS of course the most necessary ingredient of authority in a corporate government when it deals with centers of power that lie beyond the administrative core of the organization. Most of the "external" relationships of a company—relations, that is to say, with persons and groups outside the board-manager-employee hierarchy—are contractual in nature. These relationships become in some cases so highly institutionalized (as in the web of rules of developed "industrial jurisprudence" through collective bargaining agreements) that they establish an extended framework of corporate constitutional government that is essentially voluntaristic.

But even within the hierarchical administrative core of corporate governments a high degree of voluntarism normally prevails. This becomes obvious when one asks how the important decisions are made and enforced at the core. What sanctions are available to decision-makers? The legal sanctions, to be sure, which involve enforcement agencies of public government; but not primarily these. Force must not be ruled out, since it is always in the background and may be invoked through courts and other public agencies on occasion; but it is seldom invoked in the day-by-day operations of a corporate polity. Inducements and incentives are generally more useful to the administrator than negative sanctions or threats of punishment, internally or externally executed. Direct or indirect coercion is a disruptive and not an integrating method of producing the kind of cooperative effort required in the firm, as C. I. Barnard has observed. This view of the nature of organization appears clearly in his definition of authority as "the character of a communication (order) in a formal organization by virtue of which it is accepted by a contributor to or a 'member' of the organization as governing the action he contributes; that is, as governing or determining what he does or is not to do so far as the organization is concerned." [16] Authority, for him, does not reside in "persons of authority" at all; it arises in consent, and lies with the person to whom the order is addressed. A communication becomes "authoritative" only "when it is an effort or action of *organization*" and not that of an individual acting outside the area of coordination.

While this is a rather specialized interpretation of the term "authority," Barnard's emphasis on the "willingness and capacity of individuals to submit to the necessities of cooperative systems" [17] as the most important basis of coordinated effort is increasingly recognized as sound. When he wrote (in 1938) of the requirement of "loyalty, domination by the organization personality" [18] as a qualification for executives, we had not yet heard about the recently discussed Organization Man. But we can still agree with him that corporate governors (his "leaders or executives in formal organizations") can seriously disrupt the equilibrium of cooperative systems such as corporate polities by "false ideologies" in guiding organization practice. Among these he mentioned dogmas of formality (excluding the fact and necessity of informal organizations), false notions of authority, and the confusion of morality with responsibility.

In recognizing the significant fact that "cooperation among men, through formal organization of their activities, *creates moralities*" [19] and that the government of an organization involves far more than the imposition of sanctions for violations of its own code, Barnard formulated an old principle into a new theory of corporate governance. That contribution lay mainly in his discussion of "the economy of incentives" and other economies or "systems of utilities" which he thought had always been taken into account by people skilled in the executive arts but never explicitly stated as principles of organized action.

Search for the elements of authority in the corporate polity thus has led men of wide experience in managing large organizations to discount many popular clichés about power and to pave the way for a new theory of corporate polity. The admonition of Mary Parker Follett [20] that authority is power with people, not over people, becomes, in Barnard's analysis, a specification in detail:

> Authority is the character of a communication (order) in a formal organization by virtue of which it is accepted by a contributor to or a "member" of the organization as governing the action he contributes. . . . The decision as to whether an order has authority or not lies with the persons to whom it is addressed, and does not reside in "persons of authority" or those who issue these orders.[21]

Similarly, in Herbert Simon's formulation, authority "involves behaviors on the part of both superior and subordinate" since "the superior frames and transmits decisions with the expectation that they will be accepted by the subordinate," while "the subordinate expects such decisions, and his conduct is determined by them." [22]

That this acceptance of decisions is not necessarily along hierarchical lines in a "pyramid of power" is indicated by Simon's further observation that authority is "a relation that secures coordinated behavior in a group by subordinating the decisions of the individual to the communicated decisions of others," and that there is thus "a subordination of specific to general decisions." [23] One who accepts the general decision as guidance for his specific decision is not necessarily an inferior, either as to role or as to personal quality. It is only necessary that he recognizes, regardless of his status, the legitimacy of the decision in the situation at hand and with respect to a given subject matter. He may, in fact, guide his actions according to the general decision not on the merits of that decision but because of a felt need for compliance in order to sustain the whole cooperative effort.

Authority, as a necessary ingredient of power in the governance of corporations, is thus to be understood in not too narrowly juristic terms. The "right" of decision-makers in corporate polities to make decisions that influence the lives and property of many people is only partly codified in law. The law is in this respect a laggard; it only slowly recognizes the real authority structure. The real authority structure is a product of evolution. The locus of controls is a matter of adjustment to the internal and environmental conditions in running the business.

Barnard's acute observation with respect to the multiplicity of "created moralities" in any large organization applies not only to the nature and structure of authority at the administrative core but also to authority structures in the extended area of the corporate constitution. Even within the orthodoxly conceived corporate organization there is no agreement among contemporary writers on the "correct" authority structure and the codes that should guide decison-makers in governing the actions of their subordinates: the much-debated issue of "human relations" in industry is one indication of this. But in a company's external relationships the problem is even more confused. In such areas as stockholder rights, dealer relationships, competition, and relations with plant communities, the received patterns of corporation law provide inadequate constitutional blueprints for executives. The conflict of moralities in these areas is seldom candidly recognized for what it is: an indication that for the larger framework of corporate authority we have only an inchoate corporate constitutional law.

The Requisite Power

AGAIN, THIS POSES THE PROBLEM of adequate power to govern the modern corporation as distinguished from the problem of restraint in classical constitutionalism. The requisite power (capability, controls) to run the business and the allocation of power to various loci in the corporate constellation both depend upon corporate purpose and the functions that a given company has to perform. The power to govern the affairs of a business corporation tends to become congruent with the assignments and responsibilities it has. The scope and nature of this power have to be sought not so much in the law as it stands as in the configurational analysis of the individual firm.

This is clearly shown in the early studies by Henry Varnum Poor of railroad corporations.[24] Writing even before the Civil War, he and his contemporaries saw the problem of control separated from share ownership. But, unlike most of his contemporaries, Poor discerned that this was not simply a question of the proper nexus between stockholders and corporate directors. Without a carefully structured administrative hierarchy in railroad operations there could be no real accountability to the share-owners. Channels of accountability, communication, and information must run from every branch of field operations in carefully defined ways up to the board and thence to stockholders. Poor observed that "the employers must be responsible to an intelligent board of directors; and those in turn to an intelligent board of stockholders. If either link in the chain is wanting the road will fail. Nobody can be trusted without exacting such responsibility."[25]

The argument is familiar to every student of scientific management today, and it leads to the conclusion that where such responsibility rests there must be commensurate authority to act. The argument leads, in other words, to a unified theory of corporate governance in the traditional[26] corporation, in which the stockholder-board-management relationships are keyed to profit maximization through an authority structure of relative simplicity. The decisional authority is so patterned as to permit enough discretionary action on the part of boards—and delegated so far as possible by them to a bureaucratic management and so on down the line—to get the profit-making job done to the satisfaction of the share-owners.

The scope of discretionary power is often very wide at the levels of both directors and top managers simply because the capacity to govern the business operation must be great enough to meet all contingencies of a large, complex, and profitable enterprise. The capabilities of the organization—in the sense that we now speak in military terms of the capabilities of a nation—must always be adequate to deal with "the competition." But they must be more than that. They must measure up to the exacting requirements of intractable situations in the environment, immediate and remote. Factors of production must be assembled and organized productively. Share-owners are seldom inclined to question the demands of management for adequate capabilities—in material, financial, and human resources, as well as decisional power in respect of these—to do the job, if there are indications that the job will be well done. That is why one sees little application to corporate governments of the *public* philosophy about good government governing least. A *corporate* government may govern much and even despotically, without a whimper from the most Jeffersonian shareholder, so long as the business prospers. The corporate polity that boasts an *internal* system of government along Jeffersonian lines could never be armed with adequate powers (capabilities) to meet its responsibilities to the shareholders.

The "fields" in which corporate governance will be exercised will overlap as one moves out toward the periphery from the more formally organized administrative orbit. This is inevitable in a pluralistic society. Adjustments of competing claims of jurisdiction of the respective overlapping fields will entail a variety of devices ranging all the way from voluntary agreement to public governmental regulation. But it will be at the penumbra of these extreme zones that the most striking creativity in public-private governmental mechanisms will be exhibited by imaginative business executives and public policy-makers. The absolutists of extreme statism, on the one hand, and of unfettered "free enterprise," on the other, will not make useful contributions to the solutions of such problems.

CHAPTER 9

The Multinational Corporation

IT IS ALREADY TAKEN FOR GRANTED that the multifunction, multiproduct corporations of the future will also be multinational. David Lilienthal predicts that "the wholly American company has no future on the international scene,"[1] since competition in international markets will require it to put down local roots in every country it enters. The powers (capabilities) of these multinational corporations will bear little resemblance to those of the traditional corporation doing business that is merely continental in scope. Their managements will be required to maintain relations with numerous foreign governments as well as governmental agencies at home. They will need the services and the protection of these governments and will often have to work intimately with them in co-partnership[2] arrangements hitherto unknown to managers of the traditional domestic corporation. One need not assume that these multinational corporations will sacrifice the discipline of the balance sheet and the search for profits as they take on the roles of co-developers of growing economies and absorb new social responsibilities. But the nature and scope of the power to govern such organizations are certain to be novel in many respects.

One sees this in Mr. Lilienthal's listing [3] of the important problem areas that will confront the "multinational" managers of these new multinational corporations: relations with foreign governments and regional organizations like the European Free Trade Association, the European Economic Community, and the Organization for Economic Cooperation and Development; taxation in many different jurisdictions abroad; antitrust both at home and abroad; labor and union relations in widely varying cultural contexts; relations with foreign as well as domestic stockholders, including governments as investors; intercultural problems; and business relations with state trading organizations within the Soviet bloc and China.

Corporate Powers in External Relations

THE SCOPE OF MANAGERIAL ACTIVITIES in this list indicates the varied capabilities required in the corporation of the future. These capabilities include quasi-diplomatic powers to negotiate with public and private bodies. The list shows clearly the growing importance of so-called external relationships. It indicates the necessity of recognizing a frame of reference for the corporate constitution larger than the core area of administrative coordination which, with stockholder relationships, has been conventional. Many new loci of authority and power must be included in any realistic view of authority relationships that regularly command the attention of corporate managers.

Here Barnard's conception of organization as "an integrated aggregate of actions and interactions having a continuity in time" [4] is relevant. He rejected the view that it is "a rather definite group of people whose behavior is coordinated with reference to some explicit goal or goals." So he included in organization the actions of investors, suppliers, and customers or clients, since "the material of organization is personal services, actions contributing to its purposes." The "bringing of persons into cooperative relationship with the organization" and "the eliciting of the services after such persons have been brought into the relationship" [5] referred not only to those who had traditionally been regarded as "members" of a firm, either as investors or as personnel at various levels of "scalar status," but also to persons who from other points of view would be regarded as outsiders.

In the multinational corporation this broader conception of organization would clearly be necessary, even if it had not already been proved to be so even in the operation of large, domestically confined industrial companies. The corporate polity can no longer be regarded realistically as the hierarchical structure of classical theory, but rather as a kind of governance in which one can see all of the four central sociopolitical processes described by Dahl and Lindblom.[6]

These four processes are: the price system, hierarchy,[7] polyarchy,[8] and bargaining. All industrialized economies combine these four central processes, in various ways, for the purpose of economizing: calculation and control with respect to the use of all resources in production, the distribution of claims, the choice-allocation processes, stabilization, and resource output and development. The price system and bargaining characterize the more decentralized economies, while hierarchy and polyarchy become the methods for more centralized direction of economic life in other countries. With the rise of modern, large-scale, incorporated industrial enterprise, the trend is away from the highly decentralized price system and toward rational calculation and control of the economizing process.[9]

In the American business system this trend stops far short of inclusive or comprehensive national planning. Still, there are significant—and significantly large—nuclei of rational calculation and control over substantial parts of the domestic economizing process, and these nuclei are precisely at the administrative core of a few hundred of the largest corporations. Many attempts have been made to explain why such "concentrations of power" are, or are not, basically at odds with the constitutional principles of a free society. Few attempts, on the contrary, are made to show that these nuclei of decision making for the process of economizing at the corporate level are organically related to their environing nuclei at the national and transnational levels.

The corporation of the future will eventually be seen in an enlarged constitutional framework that accounts for this organic relationship of the firm to the several economies to which its destinies are tied. The co-partnership arrangements now being worked out abroad by American and European multinational corporations operating in newer countries at various stages of economic growth are likely to provide the most useful examples for the study of this organic relationship. In the multinational corporation the problem of corporate *governance* is more likely to be met on its own terms for reasons that Lilienthal has indicated: the multinational manager is by force of circumstance thrust at once and without equivocation into quasi-diplomatic activities in countries where the spheres of "business" and "government" are not so dogmatically circumscribed. The management of large enterprise in countries like India, for example, is not regarded as a dilemma of "business" management *versus* bureaucracy. The problem is to get big jobs done somehow.

In such situations the executive who abhors the thought of governing power in the so-called private sector will find it difficult if not impossible to tackle the job in hand. The executive, on the contrary, who masters the political arts within new and wider authority structures that include his own business operation will have more chance of success.

Types of Power at the Administrative Core

WHEN ONE TURNS from a consideration of the external relations of the corporate polity to the question of types of power at the administrative core of the firm, some difficult issues of classification arise. It is of limited usefulness to adopt the tripartite classification of governmental functions ordinarily found in the political scientist's analysis of public government. Legislative, executive, and judicial functions are certainly distinguishable in private as well as in public governments; and the separation of these "powers" may be equally important in both. But this classical eighteenth-century method was motivated primarily by a desire to minimize abuses, and not to strengthen the hands of public officials. When we come to the question of corporate justice it will be time enough to ask whether separation of powers along the classical lines is a wise method of corporate constitutionalism.

Here our purpose is different: to see where the search for adequate power to govern the corporation leads us. What we need to ask is whether there are enough of the essential kinds of power to carry out the corporate purpose. This task calls for relevant theory about the basic functions of a business firm. Here a comparative approach is the most useful one.

In their comprehensive study of managerial systems in many parts of the world, Harbison and Myers [10] distinguish four important types of function, each of which can be taken as a point of departure in classifying the types of power required at the administrative core of the corporate polity:

1) the undertaking of risk and the handling of uncertainty
2) planning and innovation
3) co-ordination, administration, and control
4) routine supervision

The first two involve "entrepreneurship"; the latter two are more "administrative" in character. To carry out these four functions, differing systems of authority appear in firms here and abroad. The risk-taking function, for example, tends to make the risk-taker a rule-maker; "he seeks control over any of the factors which must be coordinated in the planning-production-selling process," [11] and is frequently disinclined to depart from the "sovereign rule" of primitive paternalism in favor of less highly centralized and authoritative systems of business polity. Subordination, loyalty, and productivity are the responses he seeks from the work force.

Harbison and Myers distinguish four major types of managerial philosophy with respect to the governance of the workplace: (*1*) dictatorial; (*2*) paternalistic; (*3*) constitutional; (*4*) democratic and participative.

The "constitutional" type of management, in their usage, is one in which the rule-making power of employers is shared with other agencies. There may be public governmental intervention to regulate terms and conditions of employment and to protect or encourage the growth of labor organizations "which themselves challenge management's authority." Collective bargaining and other means lead to a kind of "constitutional framework within which management must exercise its functions." [12]

The democratic or participative type of management, on the other hand, greatly broadens the areas within which workers participate in the process of decision-making on matters that directly affect them. It is a type that is rarely found in practice. But they believe that during the past quarter-century the "managerial authority system"—both within the managerial group and between this group and wage-earners in the firm—has undergone significant changes. "The shift from corporate centralization to decentralization and the sharing of managerial authority with trade unions and [public] government are the most notable developments." [13]

Clark Kerr's view [14] that the American economy has a power structure that has changed "from monism to pluralism" is related by Harbison and Myers to the trend toward what they call "constitutional management"; and they conclude that "increasing numbers of American managers are doing a good job both in the advancement of economic progress and in the enhancement of the dignity and worth of the individual as a citizen in a political and industrial democracy." [15]

The emphasis in Harbison and Myers' analysis is on the "administrative orbit" of the firm, and on the functions therein performed. One is left with a question: what of the essentially "entrepreneurial" functions and the uses of power in the firm more widely construed and in the larger orbit of the economy? If a firm is performing its larger economic tasks in society—what may be called its coordinate economic function [16]—what priority would one give to the "constitutional" and "democratic-participative" types of management in the narrower orbit, as compared with the assignment of heavier responsibilities, and therefore *power*, to corporate governments so that these coordinate functions would be carried out?

Power to Carry Out Coordinate Economic Functions

IT IS POSSIBLE—even probable—that the heavier "social responsibilities" of business corporations, or what can more properly be called their coordinate functions in the economic process of society as a whole, will necessitate a reconsideration of the more "democratic-participative" types of management of the firm. These coordinate functions may even require a turn toward more authoritative executive direction *within* the administrative orbit of the firm, in the interest of wider representation of other-than-employee interests, and especially the representation in corporate governments of the public interest. This representation need not be direct, as in the form of public representatives on the board. Such a development seems unlikely. But in the decision processes of a firm there is certain to be increased emphasis on interests that reach beyond those of its employees at whatever level of command, and even beyond those of stockholders and creditors.

The burden on our economy is bound to become far heavier as the years advance. We shall have to produce very much more to fulfill our national purposes at home and abroad. There will be great pressure for a centrally planned economy to achieve that purpose. The only alternative will be an energetic program on the part of corporate managers voluntarily and legally to co-ordinate effort in industry to get out the goods, the right kind of goods, on time, and delivered to the right places, at acceptable prices. It is not at all certain that the job can be done in this voluntary way. But if it is to be achieved at all, corporate governors' hands cannot be tied in the management of their internal administrative orbits.

In terms of corporate polity this means far more than the nice balancing of the interests of customers, stockholders, employees, suppliers, and so on in the familiar formulas of enlightened and "socially responsible" managements. Nor is it a question of tinkering with the structure of boards, of cumulative voting, of "stockholder democracy," of a "people's capitalism," or of better management-labor relations to give the workforce a larger voice in corporate affairs. The question is one of a changing structure of values in American society and the gearing of the whole economic process, in both private and public enterprise, to the value system.

One cannot predict what the new scale of values will be, or to what aspects of it the public will give priorities. A catastrophe in the international arena might throw us quickly into a garrison-state economy. But, even in the absence of that, the indices point unmistakably to great sacrifices of personal pleasure and private luxury in response to inexorable demands of community, country, and humanity. The more far-sighted leaders today realize that our survival as a nation depends on more than the pursuit of self-interest in military alliances and something better than a tight-fisted policy of "foreign aid if paid" for. Probably nothing less than unadulterated altruism will get us any real "pay-off," if that is the way we want to measure the price of survival.

To meet the high requirements of the new scale of values, American business firms will not be expected either to socialize themselves or to become philanthropic institutions. The demands that society will make on business firms will be just the opposite: that they stick to the business of producing more of what society must have, and that they produce it more efficiently, and at competitive prices.

Emergent Types of Corporate Polity

THE IMPACT OF SUCH DEVELOPMENTS on the polity of firms is bound to be heavy. As pressures mount for production processes more nearly in line with the new scale of values, business firms will have to restructure their organizations for more efficient performance (in terms of input-output ratios) of their basic economic tasks. Pressures of this kind will squeeze the water out of the operation and leave little room for costly or irrelevant functions now being pressed upon managers for one reason or another, sometimes as "good business" or "good public relations."

Narrowly conceived theories of corporate self-government (like the ideas of "shareholder democracy" or "democracy at the workplace" as panaceas for the endocratic and oligarchical tendencies in large business organizations) may fall before a disciplined theory of a larger corporate constitutionalism that takes into account the coordinate economic and social functions of the firm. Extremist dogmas about the relation between "government" and "business"—complete autonomy for the firm, on the one hand, and complete regulation by public governmental agencies, on the other—may be expected to recede before pragmatic designs for the governance of industry. Pluralistic theory will play no small part in these designs as men of affairs become aware of the fact that the art of government must be cultivated in all sectors of society.

New types of corporate polity could emerge in response to pressures of this kind. These new types of corporate governance might arise not merely as new devices and designs of public regulation for *controlling* the power to govern in the business firm. They could be designed as dependable *instruments* of government in the private sector, coordinated for national and transnational purposes with the instruments of public government, but separable from the latter so as to permit the maximum corporate autonomy. As instruments of government, the newer forms of corporate polity would certainly contain workable restraints on the powers of private governments, but they might also, necessarily, offer broader ranges of power with respect to some internal corporate functions as well as limitations or eliminations with respect to others.

The real problem, in fact, is to define the functions that a business firm must perform and then to see to it that there is adequate managerial power to secure business performance on these functional premises. Doctrinaire approaches to this subject are worse than useless. There is no single pattern of corporate power that would be applicable to the enormous variety of business operations we now have, or will need, to match the new corporate, national, and transnational purposes. There will be no single "best form" of corporate polity; instead there may be a far greater variety of polities than we find in the area of public government.

Consider, to illustrate the point, the following types of business and ask whether a single pattern of power in the corporate polity would suffice for all:

1) High-risk and venturesome enterprise as distinguished from low-risk and conservative business
2) Profit-maximizers as distinguished from businesses with other objectives such as steady return on investment and "solid growth"
3) Fast-growing firms as distinguished from static firms
4) Single-plant as distinguished from multiplant firms
5) Single-product as distinguished from multiproduct firms
6) Firms supplying a single market as distinguished from those supplying a multiplicity of markets
7) Firms requiring integrated and coordinated control of productive activities as distinguished from those which are so highly decentralized as to require no central administration
8) Firms highly dependent on the creation and transmission of new knowledge (integrating research, industrial techniques, and operations under a working team) as contrasted with those in which such an integration of forces has little relevance
9) Firms whose products are high on the priority list of national purpose, as contrasted with those which are "expendable"

10) Firms whose capital resources must be recruited from widely dispersed points of origin as distinguished from those which have no such requirements
11) Firms that become instruments of development in countries now at the earlier stages of economic growth, as contrasted with firms operating only in economies at the stage of "high mass consumption" or "beyond mass consumption" [17]

These are only some examples of the ways in which business operations can be classified for the purpose of distinguishing the systems of governing power required in their respective polities. It may make the principle clearer to take a particular case—that of the airline industry—and examine it from the standpoints of power-structure requirements in the polity of the industry as a whole and the polities of individual companies in the industry.

An Example: The Airline Industry

IN THE AIRLINE INDUSTRY the extremely rapid developments in technology, especially the advent of the jet age, confront executives with the need for new policies in financing, procurement of productive capital goods, and marketing of services. The new facts of jet life, according to Sir William P. Hildreth, director general of the International Air Transport Association, exercise an inexorable logic of their own in the airline. "More than one company has already made drastic changes in its internal organization and many more must follow," and "the same logic, in the international field, is dictating new kinds of cooperation and rationalization as between airlines, in the pooling of services, facilities, and equipment." [18] The jet age thus has had an impact not only on the organization of single airline companies but also on a new form of private government (not so designated by Sir William)—the IATA—which transcends national frontiers and reaches into all parts of the globe as a power-and-authority-wielding entity.

For the consumer in this industry—the traveling public—the new speeds are wonderful. No place in the world now need be more than forty hours away from any other, or inaccessible to the two-week vacationer. No manufacturer need be more than forty-eight hours away from the consumer of his products, however remote from the factory; and no expensive intermediate inventories need stand between them. These time schedules will shrink in the years to come.

For the executives who govern this industry it is not easy to gear systems of corporate and intercorporate governance to the new tempo. The increased speed of the jets has brought a chain reaction for management: the need for flying to greater precision than ever before; the necessity for speed-ups in passenger handling, international clearances, and air-ground and long-line communications; capital financing in the amount of more than $5 million per jet plane plus heavy outlays for retraining of crews and mechanics; the recreation of whole new areas of maintenance and overhaul establishments; new concepts and practices in scheduling and maintenance; and, above all, new concepts and practices in marketing of transportation services. The marketing problem is especially acute in the jet age of transportation. An airline must sell as it has never sold before simply because it is producing services at an unprecedented rate.

The decision-making process in this industry taxes executive capabilities nearly to the limit; and—more important from our point of view—in analyzing corporate polity the scope of discretion becomes correspondingly large. The power and authority vested in managers of airlines and in such functional organs of private government as IATA is extensive. This latter instrument of government supersedes not only the authority of individual airlines but the authority, in practice, of public governments as well. *Whose* instrument of governing power is the polity of an airline company or the polity of IATA? What powers must such private governments have in order to serve those whose instruments these polities are? Power to keep the jets up to the highest consumer demand for the cheapest and speediest transport—or the power to do so only if other interests are first served, the interests of the owners of stock in these lines, the suppliers of equipment (who are often among the largest creditors), or perhaps the national entities whose prestigious instruments the airlines frequently are? Eventually the interests to be served will be transnational in scope.

The complexities of the interrelationships among suppliers, the government, and the public airlines should be noted. Frequently designs for commercial transport aircraft are subsidized by the government, are related to designs for military aircraft, and are integrally related to designs of communication or searching or firepower equipment, for example. The resultant compromises in design activity reflect significant aspects of organizational interplay and authority and value judgments. And related to decisions as to equipment are decisions as to replacement parts and servicing. Again, the government places certain demands upon aircraft-equipment suppliers for maintenance and parts supply which affect the patterns of maintenance and parts available to commercial airlines. Personnel-training policies and procedures are likewise affected. In the end, a sorting out of the special interests which the airline executive must take into account may serve little purpose other than to suggest the burdens he must bear. But, toward the easing of those burdens, the course suggested here—the development of the concept of corporate constitutionalism as a recognition of what is involved in corporate governance—may have vital importance in making it possible to cope with the strains placed upon executives.

The airline industry is perhaps exceptional in that it is a public utility; but it serves to illustrate one extreme type of the several types indicated above. One can see, in this example, the relative unimportance of the usual issues about democracy at the workplace or in a stockholders' meeting. The problem of corporate governance is far more embracing. In an industry such as this, one sees how far we have moved toward the "paraproprietal society" in which, as Father Harbrecht has put it, "present-day corporate managers are like the vassals of great domains." "They have control, but not ownership, of great wealth, yet their tenure of power is in fact limited by their continuing ability to perform a service" and there is "a certain standard of performance below which they cannot fall without incurring the wrath of the public and the displeasure of consumers." The power of these managers follows the control of property, and this control "gravitates to those who can, by the use of property, perform a function valuable to society." [19]

One might add that not only does this control over *property* gravitate to those who can use the property for socially approved functions, but also control over persons in the large organizations where such property is necessarily concentrated. Not only this, but the nature and extent of these controls (power) is determined by the functions to be performed. How large this power should be and the purpose for which it should be used are questions not to be decided in the abstract or drawn from the traditional canons of democratic or nondemocratic philosophy. They have to be decided with reference to concrete cases, specific industries, identifiable firms.

The power to govern in any firm is a pragmatic issue. One deals to an extent with questions of formal authority, since authority (as legitimized power) in any form is an indispensable ingredient of the power to govern. With the formal organization of governing power, one is also concerned, but not to the exclusion of informal organizations or sources of power arising from nonformal sources. The real issues touch on corporate power in relation to (A) corporate purpose, (B) national purpose, and (C) transnational purpose, with varying emphases upon one or the other depending upon the nature of the business.

As we have seen, the traditional classification of governmental functions (legislative, executive, and judicial) is of little use to the designer of corporate polity when he attacks the problem of adequate power to accomplish specific things for a particular business operation. Nor is it very useful to insist upon distinctions between democratic-participative and other forms of corporate governance. These distinctions are entirely appropriate in considering the question of *limiting* power in a corporate government, but not very helpful in the discovery of the necessary powers that should reside there; and, moreover, the problem of participation in the decision process cannot practically be confined to the narrower administrative orbit of the firm or even to the corporation as a "community of share-owners." The firm is more than that. And the firm, in turn, is an integral part of a whole industry. No industry, finally, stands alone and aloof, either from its peers or from society.

Power, if adequate in kind and degree, should be defined in functional terms that relate to a specific business operation. But a business operation is seldom to be circumscribed by the traditional boundaries of an autonomous enterpriser or an autonomous firm. The changing value systems of our society portend encroachments on the traditional autonomy and necessitates more commodious definition of the "firm." And as the area of coordination widens, the functions have to be redefined, with consequent impact upon the authority structure in the corporate polity.

We may therefore expect to see in future decades the emergence of a wide range of corporate polities as measured in terms of the power to govern the internal and external affairs of a company. In some, the powers of boards and managers over the internal affairs of a company will undoubtedly be greatly increased. The pattern of governance at the "administrative orbit" may become markedly bureaucratic and even authoritarian precisely because the responsibilities of executive managers as to external affairs will assume such heavy proportions. The constitutionalism of the corporation of the future, in other words, will develop into a pattern of power-and-restraints-on-power in a field far wider than that which is now ordinarily defined as the field of "the organization."

Part IV

RESTRAINTS ON THE POWER TO GOVERN

CHAPTER *10*

American Patterns of Constitutional Restraint

THE CONCENTRATION OF GOVERNMENTAL POWER in too few hands is, in the constitutionalist tradition, a threat to liberty and an invitation to despotism. But the techniques of distributing power vary considerably from country to country. Power distribution takes three main forms: territorial, functional, and chronological.

Territorial Distribution of Power

DISTRIBUTION OF POWER *territorially* in the fundamental order involves some form of federal structure. This is not the same as delegation of power from central to regional or provincial administrative centers as, for example, in metropolitan France. "A federal system distributes power between a common and constituent government under an arrangement that cannot be changed by the ordinary process of central legislation." [1] The basic charter establishes this distribution, which may be alterable only by formal amendment, as in the case of the United States Constitution, or through judicial interpretation. The constituent units of a federal system are entrusted with substantial powers of their own. In our system these units are the "sovereign states"; and while this designation is inaccurate, since their autonomy is to some extent limited by the basic charter, they do claim extensive and important residual powers that are nowhere defined in that charter.

Federations, on the other hand, are to be distinguished from looser forms of union. Federations have central organs that exercise authority directly over individuals within the constituent units. The central government represents these individuals, is elected by them, and can tax and regulate them directly. The constituency of the central government in a federation is popular and national. A federation is not a superstructure erected on the base of sovereign states. But the units of a federal system do draw their own authority to govern from their own peoples, and may—within certain limits—devise and change their forms of government as they will. In a true federation there is equality of the constituent states as to legal status, but not an unqualified right of secession.

Federalism is not an essential attribute of constitutional government, for many modern constitutional systems are unitary in form. But the case for federalism is impressive, given certain conditions. The advantages of a federal system have been well summarized by Arthur W. Macmahon as follows, though he observes that, except for the first point, these advantages are to some extent available in a unitary system:

> First, when diversities are pronounced and located with reasonable compactness, the geographical concentration of important powers secures greater correspondence between public policies and local majority sentiment on matters entrusted to the constituent governments. Second, by multiplying the independent legislative arenas, the system gives scope for experimentation, followed by unilation. Third, the multiplication of the bodies of elected officials who bear considerable responsibility in their own right broadens the opportunity for political participation. Fourth, the system is suitable for government over large or

> scattered areas. . . . Fifth, federalism lessens the risk of monopoly of political power by providing a number of independent points where the party that is nationally in the minority at the time can maintain itself while it formulates and partly demonstrates its policies and capabilities and develops new leadership.[2]

A federal, as distinguished from a unitary system, serves to guarantee and stabilize the institutions of local self-government while preserving adequate power at the center to meet the requirements and responsibilities of national union and the conduct of external relations.

Functional Distribution of Power

THE DISTRIBUTION OF POWER *functionally* appears in the characteristic American system of "separation of powers."[3] Traditionally we have a tripartite division into legislative, executive, and judicial powers, on the assumption that the nature of these powers requires that they be allocated to separate groups of officials in order to protect the liberties of citizens. The fusion of these powers, however, though suspect in our constitutional theory, is characteristic of other equally constitutional regimes.

Cabinet-parliamentary systems, as found in many English-speaking countries outside the United States, where the members of the executive are members of parliament and the government is in fact integrated in parliament, either reject the American theory and practice entirely or adopt a very different conception of separated powers. Some students of comparative government question the basic value of the theory. They urge the importance of distinguishing the kinds of *policies*[4] that governments must determine rather than the classically defined kinds of power of officialdom. They question the validity of the old definitions of "powers" and the idea that there should be three, no more and no less. They ask for a more realistic analysis of the key *problems* and *functions* of government.[5]

Reassessed in this way, the technique known traditionally as "separation of powers" becomes essentially a technique of responsible government "in which the exercise of political power is reciprocally shared and mutually controlled" [6]; and the control techniques as a whole are institutionalized in the constitution. The old tripartite pattern may have become obsolescent, even in the public governments of the American system, and it has never taken hold in our private governments, particularly in corporate governments. Lip service is paid to it regularly in ritualistic pronouncements. But the practice is different.

The "checks and balances" still operate, but not necessarily as contemplated in eighteenth-century theory and in the received dogmas of political oratory. Concentration of absolute power in the hands of a single power-holder would be anathema and is avoided by built-in structures that prevent it. But in seeking the truth about functional power distribution in our public governments as some guide to the nature of corporate constitutionalism one must be on guard against the familiar homilies, or too parochial an estimate of the meaning of power separation as a constitutional device. The true picture is more likely to appear from penetrating comparative analysis of modern constitutional systems—a science that is still in its primary stage of growth.

One of the most useful approaches is provided by Professor Loewenstein's discussion of "interorgan controls": the reciprocal relations among the several and independent power-holders in a whole system of constitutional government. These interorgan controls, as he sees them, are of two kinds:

> First, the power holders are constitutionally enjoined to perform a specific function in conjunction; . . . [they] share in the exercise of the function and mutually control themselves. Or, second, the individual power holder is constitutionally authorized to intervene, at his exclusive discretion, with the operation of another power holder and, thereby, counteracts it. . . ." [7]

In the first case, for example, there is joint action by president and senate as to treaties; in the second, a president may veto a congressional bill.

The four main power-holders in this analysis are, speaking generally for any constitutional system: the government (with us, the Administration), the assembly (Congress), the courts, and the electorate. Thus four patterns of interorgan controls are derived: "(*1*) the controls of the assembly over the government; (*2*) the controls of the government over the assembly; (*3*) the controls of the judiciary over the assembly and government; and (*4*) the controls of the electorate over the other power holders." [8]

Chronological Distribution of Power

THE ALLOCATION OF POWER in time is the third form of power distribution in constitutional regimes. A corollary principle is limited tenure of office, with periodic elections and regularized procedures for removal of public officers.[9] The principle applies not only to representatives in the "political" legislative and executive branches of government, but also to the judiciary and the administrative bureaucracy, though in different ways.

The accountability of representative officials is in part secured, at least in constitutional theory, by requiring them to return to "the people"—more accurately, the electorate—of their constituencies at stated intervals for a popular decision on their tenure of office. The periodicity of tenure is a debatable subject among constitutionalists, and the debates in constitutional conventions are illuminating on this point. The American system assumes, in general, the necessity of clocklike periods of two, four, six years, for example; while in the cabinet-parliamentary system the periods may vary with political circumstance and unpredictable government "crises."

Indefinite tenure "during good behavior" (as in the case of federal judges) or for the life of a professional career (in civil and military service) would not meet the requirements of constitutional theories of representative government as applied to the controlling political branches. While nonpolitical officers and other appointees are presumably held accountable to the political branches, the members of the latter cannot be held accountable to any other body than the political electorate. And while their accountability as representatives of the people is reinforced in other ways, such as public proceedings, freedom of speech, press, and assembly, and the party system, an essential element is the distribution through time of their power to act as officials.

It is significant that periodic elections have required, in every democratic system, an elaborate electoral machinery that does not run automatically. It is expensive to operate and necessitates the co-action of both public and private agencies. The problem of financing,[10] while not unsolvable, has not been solved to the satisfaction of critics of the American system of nominations and elections. But an electoral system is obviously indispensable to representative government and the question is not whether the system should be abolished but how it can be improved. The system necessarily involves, moreover, a mature party system with permanently organized opposition groups having legitimate status in the continuous process of government. These points need to be borne in mind in assessing the growth of corporate constitutionalism.

Accountability: Responsible Government

REPRESENTATIVE GOVERNMENT is sometimes equated with responsible government as a major device of modern constitutionalism for ensuring accountability of governors to the governed. But formal systems of representation and public electoral processes are only a part of the complex mechanism by which enforcement of accountability in the governmental process as a whole is sought.

Accountability in corporate governments raises several questions: *Who* is responsible to *whom* for *what*, and *how* is the claim on responsible parties to be made enforceable? The residue of historical experience in modern constitutional governments is highly instructive on these points. Those to whom public governments are responsible are defined today in democratic terms, or at least in far less undemocratic terms than formerly. Rulers by Divine Right believed that they were responsible to God alone. But even more mundane concepts of responsible government have limited the electorate more or less restrictively. And the methods of enforcing responsibility to the governed have varied widely. John Stuart Mill, writing a century ago on *Representative Government*, declared that only the most elementary steps had yet been taken to solve the problem. We have progressed somewhat farther along the way since then, but, clearly, not the whole way.

The problem of responsibility is central to all theories of constitutional democracy. A perfect "situation of responsibility,"[11] as Professor Spiro has said, is unattainable; but, he added, all could agree that

> the individual should, within the limits of the possible, seek to become responsible for his own fate. As a member of vast human organizations, he can assume this responsibility only by *contributing to those central decisions whose consequences will in turn affect him.* The norm of individual responsibility thus demands that citizens be given such opportunities for policy contributions, and, further, that these contributions be proportionate to the extent to which the contributors will be affected by or exposed to the consequences of the policies.[12]

The key questions, he goes on to say, in any constitutional system then become questions of choices available to citizens, of the resources available to them to implement their choices, and of their foreknowledge of the likely consequences of their choices.

In a tightly organized, totalitarian, and authoritarian society a citizen's choices are stringently limited. In a constitutional democracy there are opportunities to contribute to the centralized processes of making policies in the prevailing public and private organizations. The resources available to a citizen in making such contributions include all the important institutions of representative government: electoral systems, freedom of association and especially of partisan associations such as political parties, a sufficient dispersion of organizations —public and private—to permit representative government to work. Foreknowledge of citizens' choices can never be complete; but the bars to a greater sampling of the potential of choice can be lifted through institutionalized freedom of inquiry and communication, and the advancement of science in all fields of human relations can greatly contribute to it.

The nexus of accountability, by which those who make the most important decisions do so in response to the values and interests of those affected, is a complex of arrangements that can be subsumed under a modern theory of political responsibility. Power-holders, in the modern theory of constitutionalism, are held accountable to each other, through institutionalized arrangements, for performing the functions assigned to them. The electorate—itself a power-holder as of right—holds representative assemblies and elected executives accountable, and the assemblies and executives are held accountable to each other. "Responsible government," in Professor Loewenstein's phrase, "is one in which the exercise of power is reciprocally shared and mutually controlled." [13]

The institutions of constitutional government through which this reciprocal sharing and mutual controlling of power are affected are not infrequently criticized as time-consuming, expensive, and inefficient. But democracy, by its very nature, is inevitably turbulent and disorderly to the perfectionist observer who prizes above all else the neatness of a simple organizational chart and the reassurance of conformity.

The Protection of Private Rights

THE FOURTH BROAD CATEGORY of constitutional restraints refers to an arsenal of substantial guaranties of individual liberties against the powers of public government. These guaranties protect a zone of individual self-determination. Unlike the power-distribution technique, this one is a complete denial of the legitimacy of any public power exercise within the reserved zone.

The difficulties that arise in modern constitutional systems in the application of this technique present a challenge to man's ingenuity in constitution building. How define the reserved zone? And how can the arsenal be stocked without invoking the very power of public government that must be restrained if liberty is to have any meaning? A grave dilemma faces every constitutional democratic state today, moreover, in the struggle with transnational totalitarian movements. As these movements infiltrate the democratic societies, civil liberties are used to undermine all liberty; yet to fight fire with fire by denying freedom to the sworn enemies of liberty can lead to repressive measures that are destructive of the theory and practice of our bills of rights.

The Declaration of Independence and the bills of rights in state and federal constitutions in the United States formalized ideas about the anterior rights of men and the right of resistance against unlawful political authority that had been germinating ever since the end of the Middle Ages. American institutionalization of these basic restraints on public government has been influential both abroad [14] and at home. The underlying theory of our bills of rights were best expressed by John Locke in his *Second Treatise of Civil Government* (1690). The rights of men existed in the law of nature independently of states and their laws; and while some of them were alienable and entrustable to public government or might be surrendered with due compensation, others were inalienable in that no man could divest himself or his posterity of them, even by his own consent.

Where the rights so recognized are translated into effective and continuing restraints on public governmental power (legislative and executive), there are regularized procedures (in the American system, essentially judicial) that a man can avail himself of to ensure that they will be respected. The right, for example, not to be deprived by public governments of life, liberty, or property without due process of law is judicially enforceable under the Fifth and Fourteenth Amendments of the federal Constitution and in most state constitutions. So are the rights to "equal protection of the laws" and those liberties enumerated in the first ten amendments of the federal Bill of Rights. These are rights that are not respected in autocratic regimes, or even in some that lay claim to the constitutional imprint. That they are not respected is due to the fact that no adequate institutions of restraint have been developed there.

In our own constitutional system institutionalized restraint is not infallible. Fundamental rights have been abridged by legislation and administrative action that is judicially sustained.[15] The judiciary, though it is a special guardian of constitutional liberties, is also a coordinate branch of public government and therefore an instrument of public power. Its function in the exercise of judicial review of legislative and administrative acts is not exclusively the guardianship of the constitutional rights of citizens against government; it must at the same time construe constitutional clauses that grant (or reserve) governmental powers. Constitutionalism, as we have seen, embraces adequacy of powers to govern, as well as restraints on that power. Courts must construe constitutional clauses of both kinds.

The requirements of governmental power tend to increase rather than diminish for many reasons, not least the necessity for mobilized strength to combat enemies both foreign and domestic—the latter including impersonal evils of an economic or other character. Nor is this all. The mobilization of *public* governmental power is frequently regarded as necessary as a counterweight to large *private* organizations which, as private governments, are capable of encroachment on fundamental rights of citizens. The positive exercise of public governmental power, in other words, is itself a technique of constitutional restraint directed at despotic private governments.

The state, on the other hand, is called upon increasingly to buttress the right of association as a means of establishing a so-called social balance of power as a system of counterpoises in the "private sector." Collective bargaining is an example of this. Antitrust policy, too, does not go so far as to atomize business organization and reduce the competitive arena to Hobbes's war of each against all. One result of these trends toward private collectivities, legitimized by positive state action, is to rear new potential enemies of those fundamental and classical rights of the individual that bills of rights were designed to protect against *public* governmental action. And thus the age of organizations presents the old problem of an arsenal of constitutional guaranties of individual liberty in a new form.

In orthodox American constitutional law this problem is relegated to ordinary legislation. Theoretically, it is up to the national and state legislatures, acting under constitutional powers, to protect individual liberty against dangers that loom in the great private collectivities. In some of the more recent constitutions abroad the problem is met explicitly at the constitutional level. In the Bonn Basic Law for West Germany, for example, political parties which "in view of their aims or the conduct of their adherents are aiming at the impairment or elimination of the constitutional-democratic order" can be declared unconstitutional by the Federal Constitutional Court.[16] But under our constitutional system the banning of subversive political parties or other organizations is a matter for legislative action, and the protection of individuals' rights against the collective action of such bodies is a legislative, not a constitutional, issue.

Under our system of constitutional law, as it has developed by precedent, incorporated bodies themselves enjoy the protection of bills of rights as "persons" not to be deprived of their liberty and their property without due process of law.[17] These collective artificial persons are private governmental bodies [18] in their own right, thus raising the question of protecting the rights of natural persons against encroachments by such private governments. This question, under prevailing conceptions, is not, however, a question of constitutional law since the rights enumerated in federal and state constitutions can be invoked only against public governments.

Should there now be an extension of the orthodox rules of our public law so as to bring within the ambit of constitutional limitations these *private* corporate governments as well as the *public* governments at national and state levels? Or would it be preferable to leave the matter entirely to the development of internalized corporate constitutional restraints, whether or not advanced by the intervention of statutory action? In other words, are the fundamental liberties of the citizen, insofar as they are encroachable by corporate action, to be protected by intracorporate constitutional bills of rights or by applying the apposite constitutional clauses in federal and state constitutions? The apposite clauses include not only the due-process clauses in the Fifth and Fourteenth Amendments but perhaps all of the protections enumerated in the entire federal Bill of Rights (Amendments I–X).

This question is obviously but one aspect of the broader issue of corporate constitutionalism as a whole. If we start from the premise that constitutionalism embraces an aggregate of control techniques of which the protection of private rights is but one, extending as well to the nature of the constitution itself, the distribution of powers, and accountability procedures, then the general question is whether corporate constitutionalism requires *public* intervention in the corporate governmental process or can be left to the corporations themselves. And if public intervention is the answer, shall it be in the form of *statutory* regulation of the internal corporate constitutional structure or the application of certain *constitutional* clauses (federal and state) to the corporation?

CHAPTER *11*

Restraints by Public Government

THE DEMAND for a constitutional restructuring of the large corporation is pitched at two levels. There are those who insist that it can and must be done only by the intervention of public government. Others see it only as a problem of self-imposed reform. Some combination of these methods, it is true, is at times proposed. But these two basic approaches need to be distinguished. One means the imposition of extrinsic restraints on corporate governments; the other means reliance on internally generated restraints.

External and Internal Constitutional Limitations

IF THE CORPORATION is to be "constitutionalized" exclusively through the intervention of public government, it will be done through federal or state action or both. In either case, a distinction must be drawn between ordinary legislative and administrative rule making as to the governance of corporations, on the one hand, and, on the other, judicial intervention armed with certain restrictive clauses in federal and state constitutions that now apply only to federal and state governments.

The use of statutory and administrative means to change systems of corporate governance would not be new. The application of constitutional limitations in federal and state constitutions would be the innovation, although there is some evidence that courts have already begun to move in this direction. Through statutory and administrative rule making—notably in state blue-sky laws and in the series of acts in the 1930's governing securities offerings and securities exchanges—public government has already intervened to some extent in the reconstruction of corporate constitutions. The judicial cases, on the other hand, which extend parts of the Bill of Rights and the Fourteenth Amendment to corporate (as distinguished from public) governments, add up to no clear and indisputable rules of public law for corporate constitutional reform. And when both types of externally applied limitations on the corporate constitutional system are taken together, it still remains true that there is relatively little public intervention in the internal affairs of the large corporation.

Limitations on Corporate Power

PREREQUISITE TO ESTABLISHING the doctrine that constitutional limitations on public governments apply also to the private governments of business corporations is the demonstration that the latter kinds of government are really public in character or are now so intimately related to public government that constitutional limitations do apply.

The argument that there is such a nexus is interesting. In the crudest form it is simply that all corporations, as creatures of the state, are thereby invested with a public purpose. When this argument is urged as a simple corollary of legal positivism, it means that a corporation is *only* a creature of sovereign will. In the more historical form of the argument it is urged that the earliest business corporations were made "bodies corporate and politic" for reasons that included governmental as well as private business purposes. The early companies, in other words, were supposed to be, to some extent, arms of the sovereign and could not escape a certain public character. It is urged, moreover, that today this public character inheres in the business corporation as a collective organ with powers granted to it by public agencies.

The distinction between public and private corporations, however, is now so well established in our constitutional law that these arguments are less than persuasive. The distinction is ordinarily traced to *Dartmouth College* v. *Woodward* (1819),[1] but it had already been made four years earlier by Justice Story in *Terrett* v. *Taylor* (1815).[2] He declared that, while a legislature might alter the property rights of "public corporations which exist only for public purposes, such as counties, towns, cities," it was contrary to the "principles of natural justice," "the fundamental laws of every free government," "the spirit and letter of the constitution of the United States," and the decisions of "the most respectable tribunals" to hold that "the legislature can repeal statutes creating private corporations or confirming to them property already acquired under the faith of previous laws, and by repeal can vest the property of such corporations exclusively in the state, or dispose of the same to such purposes as they may please without the consent or default of the corporators."[3]

In the Dartmouth College case Mr. Justice Story confirmed this public-private classification in these words:

> Public corporations are generally esteemed such as exist for public political purposes only, such as towns, cities, parishes and counties; and in many respects they are so, although they involve some private interests; but strictly speaking, public corporations are such only as are founded by the government, for public purposes, where the whole interest belongs to the government. If therefore the foundation be private, though under the charter of the government, the corporation is private however extensive the use may be to which it is devoted, either by the bounty of the founder, or the nature and objects of the institution.[4]

The purpose of the classification of corporations into "public" and "private" in that case was to preserve against legislative encroachment the vested rights of a private eleemosynary corporation. The rule soon was applied to business corporations and has never been altered. Beveridge's biography of Chief Justice Marshall declares that "it is undeniable and undenied that America could not have developed so rapidly and solidly without the power which the law as announced by Marshall gave to industrial organization." [5] Marshall, of course, wrote the major, and usually quoted, opinion in the Dartmouth College case, but it was Webster, in his brief for the college, and Story, in his concurrent opinion, who brought out the precedents and made the clear distinction between public and private corporations.

Justice Washington, in a separate opinion, was even more emphatic:

> A private corporation . . . is the creature of private benefaction, for a charity or private purpose. It is endowed and founded by private persons, and subject to their control, laws and visitation, and not to the general control of the government; and all these powers, rights and privileges flow from the property of the founder in the funds assigned for the support of the charity.[6]

When the definition of private corporations as established in 1819 was later made to include business corporations, the doctrine of corporate autonomy still rested mainly on the vested rights of property in the incorporators, as it had rested in that case on the private property of the founders of a college. The upshot of this is that Americans have not regarded the private corporation—whether business or eleemosynary—primarily as a creature of the state but rather as a convenient device for collective action by property-owners. The emphasis on vested rights in private property was clear in invoking of the contract clause of the United States Constitution and, later on, the due-process clause of the Fifth and Fourteenth Amendments as a bar to legislative encroachment on corporate property rights. It would, in fact, be hard to find in the development of our constitutional law any strong precedents that assert the concession theory of corporateness to the extent of insisting that business or other private corporations are "bodies politic" or arms of public government.[7]

On the contrary, what Berle has termed the theory of enterprise entity [8] comes much closer to describing the relatively modest role that the sovereign actually plays in the so-called creation of corporations, and the insignificance of any supposed use the state makes of the corporate entity as an arm of government. "Courts have long recognized," wrote Berle, "that . . . a corporation is at bottom but an association of individuals united for a common purpose and permitted by law to use a common name," [9] and not essentially a legal person owing its life to sovereign act. He showed how, in case after case, the "corporate entity" has been regarded in law as taking "its being from the reality of the underlying enterprise, formed or in formation"; and that, while the sovereign grant of corporate form "sets up a prima facie case that the assets, liabilities and operations of the corporations are those of the enterprise" as a separate entity, "where the corporate entity is defective, or otherwise challenged, its existence, extent and consequences may be determined by the actual existence and operations of the underlying enterprise, which by these very qualities acquires an entity of its own, recognized by law." [10]

The objective of Berle's paper was not, of course, to prove the nonpublic character of a business corporation, but only to provide a unifying theory that would take into account the voluminous literature and case law that seem quite inconsistent with the classical concept of the corporation as merely an artificial person coming into existence only through creation by a sovereign power. One recalls Mr. Justice Holmes' observation that "commerce among the several States is not a technical legal conception, but a practical one, drawn from the course of business," so that "the mechanical application of legal formulas [had become] no longer feasible" [11] in the interpretation of the commerce clause. In much the same way the courts have had to take cognizance of the relevance of economic effects in applying the theory of legal personality to problems of the corporate entity. In practice, the courts have had to follow substantially the approach of John R. Commons in looking at the "going concern," [12] an economic reality of collective action, when they deal with corporate cases.

One must conclude, then, that the argument which relies so heavily upon positivistic legal theory and the historic cases of business corporations as "bodies politic" to show a nexus between corporate governments and public government is an unreliable argument. This path of reasoning, in other words, leads nowhere in establishing that corporate governments should be made accountable through the application of national constitutional limitations.

But there are other lines of argument that are not so readily disposed of.[13] One of these lays stress on the undeniable fact that large aggregates of persons and property in corporate form have depended upon public governmental power. They have done so not merely in order to acquire legal personality in the corporate entity; more importantly, they have done so in order to define authority relationships *within* the corporate aggregate as a species of private government, and to support authoritative action by these private governments in their relations with third parties. These authority relationships depend, in the last analysis, upon public governmental power exercised legislatively, administratively, and judicially. For, while it is arguable that collective action in corporate form for the purpose of business enterprise is different only in degree from collective action in noncorporate form (as in partnerships), the difference is so substantial that most large industrial enterprises elect the corporate form.

The argument then goes on to say that, having elected the corporate form with its greater advantages to a business enterprise, the corporation acquires special powers that directly affect the rights of citizens in a way that the unincorporated enterprise would not do. Thus some vital freedoms of the individual may be seriously encroached upon unless constitutional restraints are made applicable to the modern corporation.

The applicable constitutional restraints are said to include not only the First, Fifth, and Fourteenth Amendments to the United States Constitution, but also the commerce clause. While the commerce clause is a grant of power to Congress, and not a protection of private rights, it has been construed as a limitation on anyone who burdens unreasonably or restricts arbitrarily the interstate commerce which Congress alone may regulate.

Racial segregation of interstate passengers, for example, by carriers may be violative of the Interstate Commerce Act as a prohibited burden on the commerce that Congress is empowered to regulate and has regulated in declaring that it is unlawful for a carrier to subject "any particular person . . . to any undue or unreasonable prejudice or disadvantage."[14] If the flow of commerce is to remain unobstructed, the courts may eventually widen the rule to include many kinds of corporate action that place an undue burden on many kinds of interstate transportation and traffic.

As to the direct constitutional restraints—in the Bill of Rights and the Fourteenth Amendment—it is elementary that these limitations inhibit public agencies and not private persons or private governments. Yet private corporations may be regarded at times and under certain conditions as acting in such a way as to bring into operation these constitutional restraints as applied to them. Insofar as a private corporation becomes an agent of a state or the federal government in actions that transgress constitutional rights of individuals, it could be brought within the constitutional prohibitions. The provisions of the Fourteenth Amendment, for example, "are addressed to every person, whether natural or juridical, who is the repository of state power."[15] When a manufacturing corporation tried to exclude from the streets of its company town a distributor of religious tracts, who was then convicted under the law of the state for refusing to leave the company's property when requested, the Supreme Court found a violation of the Fourteenth Amendment. The state had attempted to impose criminal punishment on the distributor of the tracts in the exercise of a fundamental liberty; the company could not so govern the community located on its property with the use of state enforcement agencies.[16]

Acts by private corporations that invade the fundamental liberties of a person, committed under powers granted to the corporation by a state and enforced by the state's courts, could thus come under judicial scrutiny as violative of constitutional limitations. Labor unions that use in a discriminatory manner powers which have been conferred upon them by an act of Congress have been barred from such practices [17]—not, it is true, on the ground that they thus violated the Fifth Amendment, but on the ground that the statute (the Railway Labor Act, in the case cited) prohibited the discriminatory practice; but the Court made it clear that the statute, had it not been so construed, would have been unconstitutional under the relevant clause. The representative of the labor union had been "clothed [under the Act] with power not unlike that of a legislature which is subject to constitutional limitations on its power to deny, restrict, destroy or discriminate against the rights of those for whom it legislates and which is also under an affirmative constitutional duty equally to protect those rights." [18]

Similarly, it may eventually be held by the Supreme Court that business corporations can, under certain conditions, be treated as public governmental organs bound by constitutional limitations to observe due process and equal protection of the laws. The "crucial factor is the interplay of governmental and private action." [19] The interplay of governmental and private action need not be in the form simply of a grant of state power to the corporation and state intervention to uphold corporate action thus authorized; it may be in the form of a more complex relationship developing from the impact on corporate governments of the demands and restrictions of government defense orders.

It is a basic principle of our constitutional law today that the Fifth and Fourteenth Amendments provide no shield against merely private conduct. But is the conduct of corporate governments merely private conduct? Is not the governance of a large corporation at least quasi-public business in that it affects the lives and property of a multitude of people, as a result of powers that are inextricably linked, in the general law of corporations and the economics of collective action, with community power and authority? The difficulty with such an argument is that no bounds for its application can be stated. It might reach any large aggregate, such as labor unions, universities, churches, professional associations, and so on.

It might be argued that a business corporation, simply as a *corporate body*, is inextricably tied in with public governmental power and thus is brought within constitutional limitations. But nonprofit corporations would by the same token be subject to constitutional restraints. Something beyond corporateness *per se* must enter into the brief. And it is obvious that in the absence of corporateness a large aggregate of persons may act collectively to disrupt commerce, interfere with public purpose as declared by Congress, and encroach upon private rights in ways that could theoretically be attacked as "unconstitutional."

Such types of action, however, can all be restrained by statutory as distinguished from constitutional bars. The question then becomes one of strengthening the police powers of the states as well as existent or added powers of Congress to correct abuses of power in private governments. The conclusion must be that, while the cases and the literature do show a strong trend toward broader construction of federal constitutional restraints on private governments, we are left far short of the decisive steps envisaged by the advocates of judicial review of corporate action. The *external* restraints on corporate governance are and will probably continue to be mainly outside the field of constitutional law as interpreted by the courts.

This does not mean that the constitutional theory of American society will undergo no profound changes with respect to the role of the modern corporation in the whole social structure. It means only that the emergent constitutional theory could develop otherwise than *via* the judicial application of federal constitutional limitations to the private governments of corporate enterprises. Without denying that there are significant inchoate rules of constitutional law in the judicial declarations above cited, one may invite attention to other, and perhaps far more significant, trends in our governmental system.

There is increasing attention to the pluralistic character of the American economy and of American culture generally. It has long been recognized that a new kind of federalism is implicit in this broadly conceived structure,[20] and that a certain balance of power [21] is necessary not only in the public governmental mechanism but also in the whole structure. The modern corporation will assume an important status in this balance of power, once the theory is crystallized. The germs of a theory of social federalism were clearly present in the *Federalist* papers; and today, with the rich resources available to scholars [22] for the study of both public and private governments, we are on the verge of a more mature statement of federal principles on a nonparochial basis.

From such a mature theory of balanced power in society as a whole there will emerge practicable types of restraint on corporations as well as all other associations, in the interest of protecting individual rights while simultaneously preserving the necessary social aggregate powers assignable to various groups. The techniques or devices of constitutional restraint that will emerge as statable rules for external control of corporate governance will transcend the rules of American constitutional law. Some of these devices will doubtless be incorporated in the formal rules of our constitutional law. But the entire corpus of corporate external constitutional restraints will certainly be of much broader scope.

The beginnings of this trend are to be seen in such areas as industrial jurisprudence (primarily as developed in collective bargaining), the codification of law and practice regarding "pressure groups" and lobbying, the relations between influential private entities and public governmental agencies, the growth of transnational entities (including multinational business corporations) and their interrelationships as well as their relations with public governments, and the development domestically of such organs as the UAW Public Review Board.[23]

The strongest argument for the applicability of United States constitutional limitations on corporate governments is that in the nature of things "the corporate organizations of business and labor have long ceased to be private phenomena . . . that they have a direct and decisive impact on the social, economic, and political life of the nation," and that "the challenge to the contemporary lawyer is to translate the social transformation of these organizations from private associations to public organisms in legal terms."[24] This thesis has been developed by Professor Arthur S. Miller[25] in a recent study urging the following propositions:

1) The Constitution was framed on the theory that limitations should exist on the formal exercise of power in government but not on control exercised unofficially.
2) The essential problem of individual liberty, however, is one of freedom from arbitrary restraints and restrictions, wherever and however imposed.
3) The Constitution should be so construed as to apply to arbitrary applications of power against individuals by centers of private government.
4) The main flow of group decisions in the factory community would not be thrown into litigation or controversy by such a constitutional construction, but only those which directly and substantially affect an individual.
5) It would take only a slight modification of present constitutional doctrine to effect such a constitutional construction.[26]

By the "factory community" Miller refers to those "large semi-autonomous economic organizations, called by Peter Drucker the 'industrial enterprise' and by Adolf Berle the 'corporate concentrate,' which are the basic units of economic federalism."[27] The factory community, says Miller, exercises two types of power: one in making decisions about the direction and intensity of investment, the nature of economic development, and so on; the other in decisions "that directly affect the value position of individuals."[28] He thinks that certain clauses of the federal Constitution could be invoked in restraining the latter type of power, but not the first type. For the restraint of power in the former category he sees the necessity for a general reorientation of our constitutional theory so as to embrace private governments.

The problem as to the former category of power exercise by private governments is not—as Miller properly observes—simply a question of resolving conflicts of group interests in the domestic arena. It has important implications for our foreign policy. Our constitutional law and theory as they stand today make no adequate provision for a national consensus as we face outward as a people to weather the storms of transnational trade and international conflict.

The Broader Pattern of Constitutional Restraints

THE ARGUMENT THUS MOVES into the more general area of constitutionalism as a broader range of restraints on governmental power—public and private—than those available to courts under the doctrine of judicial review. Miller raises the question of a revision of our public constitutional law and theory to make room for the "factory community" and other concentrates as power-wielders. But there is also another question: to what extent is it possible or wise to adapt to these private governments some, or all, of the patterns of regularized restraint historically developed for public governments?

The catalogue of devices for ensuring regularized restraint on the power of public governments is a long one, and no attempt will be made here to exhaust the list. But some of the more important types of restraint must be noticed, for some of these are being urged today as necessary for the constitutionalizing of the business corporation. They should be examined with this question always at the forefront: do the formulas of modern constitutionalism apply to private as well as public polities, and to business polities in particular?

The principles of constitutionalism are ancient. But it is not necessarily true that all of the techniques of modern constitutionalism, as these have been developed in public polities, are directly applicable to the business polity. It may be questioned, in particular, whether the techniques of American constitutionalism are appropriate. As any student of comparative government knows, the American solutions of the problem of restraints on government are not uniform even among the states of our federal system,[29] nor are the American solutions as a group identical with those found in other countries such as parliamentary governments of the British Commonwealth and democratic governments on the continent of Europe.

Among the more important types of constitutionalist devices to be found among free societies, these [30] are outstanding:

1) A constitution that prescribes the fundamental order
2) Distribution of power
3) Accountability of the governors to the governed
4) Protection of private rights

Although it is sometimes said that mechanical devices for ensuring justice in the commonwealth can never outrank in priority the basic consensus among the citizens of a free people that liberty must be preserved, it is nevertheless true that in all constitutionalist systems of government it has been found necessary to descend from this general proposition to the particulars of workable and regularized restraints. Some observations on the nature of these practical limitations on power should therefore be added here.

Constitutions and the Fundamental Order

IN EVERY CONSTITUTIONAL REGIME today except that of the United Kingdom an attempt is made to establish a fundamental order through a written constitution. But, whether written or unwritten (the distinction is relatively unimportant since the English constitution is in fact made up partly of basic statutes, while in other countries custom and convention both supplement the written charter), the constitution ranks above ordinary legislation and is accorded a certain fundamentality. The source of its authority lies deeper than the source of authority for the daily and current acts of officials.

The constitution is a fundamental decision about the scope of official decision making. It reflects the continuing consensus in a community that certain allocations of power and the restraints on official power must be generally adhered to and not changed abruptly or without "constituent" consent. Such consent may be inferred or explicit. Explicit consent appears in the formal process of constitutional amendment; but changes in the fundamental order—even under so-called rigid constitutions of the American type—may be made by unchallenged practice. And in England, whose constitution is said to be "flexible," no alteration in a fundamental statute would be made, even by the "sovereign" king-in-parliament, without an intervening general election between a formal proposal to alter it and binding action in the newly elected representative body.

The documentarian conception of a constitution prevails in most countries, primarily as a result of the American experiment with written constitutions dating from the eighteenth century. We "reposed our trust in the power of words engrossed on parchment to keep a government in order." [31] The interpretation of those words may be entrusted to a supreme censorial body—as in the American institution of judicial review—or, alternatively or additionally, to those who are empowered by the words to make great decisions. Even in the United States, the classic example of judicial interpretation of the constitution, there is limited scope for judicial review, and strong presidents as well as forceful legislators have at times interpreted their constitutional powers as they saw fit, free of judicial caveat.

At bottom there is the abiding idea that for all officialdom a constitution is a greater law, a charter of the people granting only limited powers to their governors, and a source of original and unalienable rights of men against government. In this sense a constitution is "a symbol of distrust of the political process—a symbol of democracy's fear of democracy." [32]

But, in addition, there is the wider and deeper implication of "community" that asserts increasingly the "primacy of the political"—that is, the community organized as a nation-state —and brings under scrutiny the internal affairs of all private groups. For the power generated by men acting in bodies under the banner of freedom of association is power that has increasingly to be harnessed to the general welfare and to the traditional requirements of constitutional justice for the individual person. The dilemma of liberty and authority thus resolves itself today into a search for justice that will end in neither the total politicization of free associations nor their complete liberty to organize their own internal polities in disregard of community purpose.

CHAPTER *12*

Restraints in the Corporate Constitution

WE TURN NOW TO THE QUESTION of the *corporate* constitution as a "symbol" of restraint (rather than an "instrument" of positive government). We shall examine those techniques of restraint on corporate governments which might find a place in the corporate constitution itself, as distinguished from restraints imposed directly by public law.

As in public governments, the essentials of constitutional restraints on power in corporate governments can be examined under four major headings:

1) The corporate constitution as a "rule of law"
2) Distributions of power within the corporation
3) Accountability through responsible government
4) Protection of private rights

These types of restraint might be imposed upon companies entirely by public action in that the corporate governmental structure would be required to meet certain normative standards set by law. Such a radical and procrustean solution of the problem of corporate constitutionalism is less likely to commend itself than a more discriminating approach. Business enterprises vary so widely that blanket requirements would be unacceptable. Intrinsic systems of restraints on corporate governments can be worked out in a wide variety of ways, with widely divergent patterns of governance developed voluntarily, and not by fiat of law. Many of the emergent corporate constitutional systems will be, to a large extent, self-generated, though the impetus may well come from the outside.

Already there is a remarkable growth of company-generated "management science," with far-reaching effects upon the corporate constitutional system at its administrative core. It is true that reform of the system beyond this core—for example, in the stockholder-management relationship—has been in the main the work of public law, and not of self-generated changes. But there are also areas, such as corporate-community relations and corporate-customer relations, in which the outer reaches of corporate constitutionalism have been effected by voluntary efforts on the part of companies themselves.

The discussion that follows, with respect to each of the four major topics listed above, does not assume either an exclusively public-law approach to the problem or a purely company-generated revision of the corporate constitution. Both approaches may be involved. In either case, however, the restraints on corporate governments to be discussed are *intrinsic* in that their primary source is not either in federal or state constitutions or in federal or state statutory and administrative law. The problem, in other words, is whether it is possible to erect *within* a large corporate enterprise a system of restraints on its governing authorities along the general lines observable in constitutionally governed public entities.

The Corporate Constitution as "Rule of Law"

AS WE HAVE POINTED OUT, there are two major fields [1] in which the intrinsic codification of corporate constitutional principles may be expected eventually to emerge: (1) the core area of administrative coordination, and (2) the larger area at and beyond the periphery of this administrative core, in which there is a constellation of corporate-related interests. As we have seen, the business corporation of today has no written constitution worthy of the name that covers either field. But it is not necessarily true that constitutional government is absent. It is only that one must seek corporate constitutional principles less in explicit charters of government than in a generally uncodified form, in scattered documents, and even in the unwritten usages, customs, and conventions that in practice determine the basic authority relationships.

Constitutionalism in the state has emerged from man's quest for practicable restraints on absolute power and the substitution "for the blind acceptance of factual social control [of] the moral or ethical legitimation of authority." [2] The result is a theory of government based on consent and its implementation by active participation in the governmental process by those over whom social control is exercised. The constitution, in this way, has "an intrinsic *telos* [in] institutionalizing the shared exercise of political power." [3] It embodies norms that in fact govern the political process. It is not merely nominal and unapplied, or "semantic" and paraded for show in the absence of any real participation in the governing process by the several power-holders—including the electorate—or any other workable and operating restraints on power.[4]

Corporate constitutions may be said to be normative in this sense only if we assume the identifiability of their basic principles in some statable and stated form; and if, moreover, the identifiable basic document or documents to which one thus refers are operational. Here the searcher is confronted with almost insurmountable difficulties. As to the core administrative area of corporate governance there are articles of incorporation, bylaws, and basic written policies. But even these are not definitive; much of the relevant material may be elusive to the casual observer: written and unwritten communications among the principal officers, collective-bargaining agreements and work rules, usages that have never been formalized, and behavior patterns at the workplace that can only be described by assiduous research.[5]

If one were to designate as the corporate constitution merely the charter and bylaws, it would seem in many instances more "nominal" than "normative." The business corporation has a formal polity that is somewhat like a parliamentary-cabinet form of constitutional government in the English style. In nineteenth-century England corporations were sometimes referred to as "little republics"[6] with a form of representative democracy, though there were critics[7] who foreshadowed the contemporary debate about managerial and trust-fund control separated from ownership. But this formal-legal view of corporate polity is effective for other reasons.

It is erroneous to designate as the corporate constitution the articles of corporation and the bylaws, and especially the charter alone. This assumption is often made, however, with misleading conclusions about the real constitutional principles that prevail in business corporations. There can be no doubt that a basic and authoritative allocation of functions of corporate governance is made in the charter, and that the ultimate authority from which this basic allocation springs is a "constituent power" in public government—specifically, the state of incorporation. It may be argued that this constituent power has in practice been "pre-empted from the state"[8] as a result of general incorporation laws and the freedom of incorporators to fashion their own "little republics." But it can also be argued that, while the corporate charter and bylaws are authorized by this public constituent power, the real democratic base of this private government is the stockholder constituency.[9] This base is rooted in private property rights of the stockholders. Their actions in voting such property interests (not by the one-man-one-vote rule, but *pro rata* by shares) and in balloting on corporate policies are important indices of the basic constitutional principles of any corporate regime. The apathy of this owner constituency is well known. The managers of a company with a half-million stockholders may call the tune on elections of directors and on policies. But the owner constituency is a fact not to be ignored in assessing the source of authority for some basic "constitutional" legislation in corporate polities.

Such basic legislation, amounting in fact to significant changes in the authority structure of a corporation, is exemplified in referrals to the stockholders of stock-option plans and plans for the reorganization of financial structure. Here, again, it is arguable that such plans are management-generated and that stockholder voting is in practice management-controlled through the proxy system. But this raises questions of representation and responsible government,[10] and does not vitiate the significance of stockholder actions as an integral part of the corporate constitution.

On purely formal grounds it might be objected that stockholder actions of this sort are analogous to ordinary legislation in public government and should therefore be considered outside the boundaries of corporate constitutional law. But, given the importance of the bylaws in a corporate government and the significance of the corporation's financial structure in the basic allocations of authority in the corporate polity, the analogy fails. Stockholder action of this sort is more nearly comparable with a public referendum on constitutional amendments to state constitutions.

The comparative rarity of any decisive action by the stockholder constituency when such action is opposed by management is nevertheless a consideration. Because of the prevailing standards of business propriety, excluding as they seem to do the propriety of "corporate raiding,"[11] any nonmanagement-generated move by stockholders to control the affairs of a corporation is likely to be a spectacular case that will go down in the constitutional history of that particular corporation as a notable precedent and by no means an ordinary action of stockholder legislation or litigation. Similarly, judicial decisions arising out of stockholders' suits become important corporate constitutional precedents, particularly in view of the fact that *ultra vires* cases are so rare nowadays.[12]

The important precedents, in other words, in the form of landmark cases precipitated by stockholders' actions, will rank in any particular business corporation as a part of its constitutional development and must be considered, along with the charter and bylaws, as indicative of the basic structure of the corporate government. That the mores of the business community inhibit such actions and that courts and legislatures frown on them would seem to indicate a certain rigidity in the constitutional structure of the "endocratic" corporation. Corporate "endocracy," in Eugene V. Rostow's usage, refers to a corporate system of government where stockholding is widely scattered and "the directors normally control, or come close to controlling, the electoral process from which their powers normally derive." [13] Because of the difficulty of, and resistance to, bringing the endocratic corporation's internal governmental structure under the control of the stockholder constituency, either acting alone or with the support of courts, administrative agencies, and legislatures, the constitutional structure of these large companies is not easily changed by any conceivable "constituent power."

In the American constitutional system it is a fundamental principle of our public law that the Constitution is no mere collection of hortatory phrases. It is a part of "the supreme *law* of the land" and, as such, is enforceable by the courts and binding on all public officers. It is law that can be amended by the constituent power as defined in the amending article. While that power is invoked infrequently, the procedures for invoking it are clearly spelled out and have been used on twenty-odd occasions. The fundamental law is also the *operational* norm for public governmental action, as the institution of judicial review clearly demonstrates. Should there not be, in the case of corporate governance, a comparably clear-cut method of invoking the constituent power of the corporation? And should there not also be a comparable method of testing the constitutionality of corporate legislative and administrative actions?

The hazards in such a comparison between public and

corporate constitutional law are evident. There is no agreed understanding as to the *identity* of the corporate constitution. And the *enforceability of its provisions*, even if generally understood to exist in statable propositions, could not easily be assigned to any corporate prototype of public courts exercising the power of judicial review. No such corporate courts exist, and if they were created it would be necessary to alter the whole extant theory of corporate governance, which is based on the English idea of a cabinet-parliamentary-electorate chain of accountability and not at all on the American theory of separation of powers with implied judicial supremacy.[14]

The present constitutional crisis in the corporation is in large part traceable to confusion of thought on these basic matters. As the opinion grows that corporations are governments, the search for a constitutional basis for these private governments is an inevitable consequence. The facile generalizations about corporate charters and bylaws as corporate constitutions do not hold up on close inspection, and even if they did we could find no workable institutional device—comparable to judicial review of legislative action—for internal enforcement of the corporate constitution so narrowly defined. *Ultra vires* actions in public courts do not fill the bill, and not only because this device of restraint on corporate governments is so rarely used. The public courts are no real substitute for a corporation's own judiciary at work on the interpretation of the corporation's own constitution if we are to have a sound development of intrinsic restraints on corporate governmental power.

Proposals for intracorporate monitors to keep corporate governments within legitimate bounds have never gained much acceptance. One of the more interesting is Professor Bayless Manning's idea [15] of a kind of "second chamber" with powers of review over certain board and managerial decisions. But this is not, nor was it apparently intended to be, any proposal for a radical transformation of the corporate governmental system as, indeed, any system of internal judicial review would be. Proposals to add public and full-time professional "outside" directors to the board are likewise irrelevant here, for such directors would not have specialized powers of a constitutional character.

The "rule of law"—the corporation's own fundamental law, based on its own conceptions of justice—can be made to prevail by intracorporate constitutional devices only if these conceptions are sufficiently formalized (not necessarily in one definitive document) to permit normative applications of it, and only if the applications of the fundamental law of the corporate constitution can regularly be made by specific organs of corporate governance. Today neither the fundamental law nor the specialized organs are there to see. Yet the demand for both is constantly growing.[16]

The design for a true corporate constitutional system, however, awaits the imaginative skills of constitution-makers in this specialized realm. The jurists might have been expected to contribute to this task more than they have done, but where they are not still held in thrall by the old dogmas of corporation theory they tend to invoke public regulatory power as the key to a solution.[17] The sociologists and the political scientists might turn to the task of corporate constitution making if they could escape the thralldom of governance in the public sector and relax their polemics against Big Business. Managers and directors are only beginning to see the problem in its quasi-political context; they tend to stop with generalized and ambiguous formulas about the arbitral functions of the managerial corps in balancing a constellation of interests.

None has yet shown how that most basic of all principles of constitutionalism—the restraining influence of the constitution itself—can be applied to the corporate constitutional system. As the debate sharpens, we may expect to see a polarization of the arguments around the following issues:

1) What is the *constituent power* of the corporation? From what definitive group in society does the basic authority structure of business corporations now derive its con-

tours? Is this source acceptable as we move into the last half of the twentieth century?

2) *How shall this basic allocation of powers in the corporate polity be determined and codified*—in corporate charters as prescribed by the state, in charters and bylaws as drafted by the incorporators and directors themselves, or, perhaps, in a combination of these methods plus co-action by many groups such as labor unions and other "outside" bargaining interest groups?
3) *Is a mature system of corporate constitutional law possible or desirable*—one in which the corporate constitution is operationally normative and enforceable as a kind of supreme law of the corporation? And, if enforceable, by what means—an intracorporate system of judicial review, or some other institutional device?

Corporate endocracy means that the authority structure of large public-issue enterprises is in practice left pretty much in the hands of boards of directors, and they, in turn, are largely controlled by "insiders" at the executive management level in many instances. As Professor Eugene Rostow has pointed out, the discretionary authority of these boards is very wide indeed, although the qualifications he notes are not insignificant. These qualifications—arising from public law and the rules of security exchanges, as well as other sources extrinsic to the corporate polity itself—impose upon corporate governments certain requirements as to the constitutional structure of the polity. But it is still true that when all of these extrinsic limitations are added together there remains a wide range of fundamental issues of corporate governance in regard to which the board of directors can institute substantial changes.

It is not too much to say that the board is precisely the point at which corporate constitutional reform must begin if extrinsic restraints imposed by public law are to be forestalled in future years. That this proposition will be regarded with hostility by many—including executive managements and directors themselves—is patent. Not only is the job ahead a formidable one, calling upon the application of principles of political science with which managers and directors are seldom familiar, but, more importantly, there is the factor of inertia. "Let well enough alone" will be the cry. The cure for corporate endocracy, some will maintain, is more endocracy: what the business corporation needs is more, not less, centralized direction, particularly in view of the recent antitrust cases that point up the heavy responsibility of business leaders to keep subordinates in line.

The fact is, however, that the parallel demand in public government for greater power at the center—the national government, and especially in the executive department—has not yet, fortunately, relaxed the counterdemand for constitutional restraints on inevitably augmented centralized authority. The problem is not to be solved, either in public or private government, by dispersing the necessary power to govern, but rather by seeking those devices of restraint that channel indispensable powers to legitimate ends.

We turn now to one of the classic methods of power distribution as the first of these devices.

Distribution of Corporate Powers

AS A DEVICE OF RESTRAINT on corporate governments, the several forms of power distribution—territorial, functional, and chronological—are all exemplified to some degree in contemporary corporations. To what extent do they achieve the constitutional purpose of regularized and workable channeling and balancing of power to the various organs of corporate governance?

CORPORATE FEDERALISM

Most of the discussion about federal technique, as a constitutional device for curbing the abuse of power by dispersing it territorially and as applied to modern corporations, concerns the corporation as a part of a larger federal structure. The problem of federal structure *within* a corporation, as a part of its own internal distribution of powers, is not adequately dealt with.

There is a good reason for this. The legal structure of the business corporation is such that any multiplication of decision centers in the intracorporate governmental system would ordinarily occur only as a result of a central policy formally adopted by the board of directors or on its authority. "Decentralized" and "deconcentrated" companies are not federally governed. The devolution of powers to component units in a corporate structure is a central legislative act and does not bind the corporate legislator. A decentralized company can be recentralized at any time that it suits the board to do so. This is not true federalism, and it is doubtful that a truly federal corporate government exists in any large industrial company.

If it did exist, it would be a case of *constitutionally* established distribution of powers between central and component governing components in the company, with no possibility of the central board acting alone to alter that power distribution. The central and local units in a federal system are competing power units; they are held in equipoise by a fundamental rule of law which embraces both and which no one unit—central or local—is authorized to disturb. It would require something different from the usual corporate charter to effect such a power distribution in the structure of corporate authority.

The purpose of federalism in democratic constitutionalism is not only to secure a high degree of autonomy for the component federal-unit governments but also to protect individual liberty.[18] Neither objective is a value of the highest priority in a business corporation. Profitability and efficiency in operations are more likely to be the guiding purposes, and for these purposes some kind of decentralization may prove to be useful, but hardly along federal lines.

The experience at Du Pont and General Motors seems to have shown that "decentralization of operations and coordination of control—organizing different activities to operate as separate groups with a minimum of conflict toward common ends . . . may provide a means of utilizing the advantages of both large-scale and small-scale enterprise." [19] This technique, of course, falls far short of the federal technique, not only because of the centrally coordinated control but also because the decentralization of operations is a reversible reaction always controllable at the corporate center of command.

Decentralization and devolution of authority upon components and persons away from the center of command may or may not be accompanied by decentralization of responsibility. It is often said that, while a corporate board of directors may delegate authority, it cannot delegate responsibility. But this has been challenged, at least within the administrative structure of an industrial company, by Harold F. Smiddy. Decentralization in organizing, applied earlier to secure geographic, functional, and product decentralization, is now, he believes, focused on genuine decentralization of responsibility.[20]

Decentralization of responsibility along with authority, however, has never been carried to the point of real federalization in any company, nor is it likely to be. Federalism as "the juxtaposition and counterbalance of two territorially differentiated sets of state sovereignties" so as "to restrain the state Leviathan" [21] can have no parallel in corporate constitutions short of a radical revision of corporation theory and the more general political and economic theory that prevails in the United States. The point can be made more clearly, perhaps, by contrasting with all these the syndicalist and guild socialist assumptions of a different order, where society is envisaged as a free and flexible association of autonomous production and distributive associations based on collective ownership and carrying out their functions as community-oriented organizations.[22] Industrial self-government by the producers was a romantic idea, anarchistic at base, which was turned upside down in fascist corporativism to become an extreme form of statism. The American assumptions are radically different in positing the corporate unit as a unitary private organization, founded on private property rights and managed integrally on behalf of the owners.

When the "new" managerial philosophy of decentralization

of authority and responsibility proposes something less than complete centralization of management, one has to understand this as nothing more than a qualified unitary system of corporate governance. The board and executive managers at the top do not and cannot relinquish ultimacy of authority nor final responsibility to the private owners of the enterprise. The arbitral function that they perform in "balancing the interests" of various groups that contribute to the enterprise as a whole is nothing more than a prudent sensing of the economic, social, and political forces that have to be taken into account when corporate business decisions are made.[23] There is no real federalism, geographic or functional, in the structure of authority within the business corporation.

"Management by objectives" as contrasted with "management by control," [24] and "authority of knowledge" rather than the authority of command, are concepts that are increasingly applied in unitary corporate governments with a considerable degree of decentralization both of authority and responsibility, and, perhaps, with good results in morale, productivity, and profitability. But one must not confuse these concepts with the federal technique as a corporate constitutionalist device aimed at restraint on power.

It is possible that the use of cybernetic theory for self-regulating systems [25] may open up new ways of introducing into a corporation's organization structure more far-reaching principles of component autonomy than those now envisaged in the decentralization of authority, and that an approach to federal structure may thereby emerge. It is also possible that as organization theory matures, the rationale [26] and practice of decentralization will lead to reorganization at the *administrative core* of business corporations and that the reorganized administration will bear at least some of the earmarks of a federal structure.

But these trends leave one short of the mark. The real problem is not at the administrative core, but further toward the periphery where the interests of stockholders and other creditors, managers, employees and their unions, and customers have to be reconciled. Corporate "power" as it affects all these interests is in essence managerial power—taking management now to include the board and top executives—and no constitutional restraints on that power through a federal device seem likely. Not, at least, until there is a basic revision of the prevailing principle that the constituent power of corporate governments lies in the stockholders, or in the "sovereign state," or both.

FUNCTIONAL DISTRIBUTION OF CORPORATE POWERS

A doctrinaire application of the separation-of-powers theory of constitutionalism to the internal structure of corporate authority relationships would be ridiculed by most businessmen. Yet it is by no means an idle question whether the underlying rationale of power separation does not apply equally well to any governmental system, public or private.

It has become fashionable in some quarters to deride separation of powers, even in public government, as an indefensible doctrine, and it is often pointed out that the functional counterpoises inherent in the American system either become an intolerable barrier to expeditious governmental action or are disregarded in practice because the idea is really unworkable. But the doctrine continues to have stanch defenders[27]; and, despite the obvious necessity of some fusion of powers in national and state governments in the United States, there is little likelihood that the system will be abandoned here in favor of a cabinet-parliamentary system or the French application of the doctrine.[28]

The reasons are not entirely historical or inertial. As Loewenstein's[29] and Friedrich's[30] analyses suggest, there are logical and psychological, as well as historical, grounds for dividing powers constitutionally, and history confirms that this division is necessary for a free people. The inherited forms of "interorgan controls" may be subject to revision to meet the needs of an industrialized society; but the substratum of rationale is of enduring validity.

The rise of the "endocratic" corporation, with its widely

dispersed shareholding and the separation of control from ownership, likewise introduces new considerations that make it necessary to examine the relevance of this basic rationale in corporate governments. In smaller corporations, or in those in which owners of shares exert effective control over management by means of immediate control of the board, the problem does not arise. But it is a different matter in the endocratic corporation.

In all but endocratic corporations the internal system of corporate governance is roughly comparable with the English cabinet-parliamentary system; the administrative and executive corps of the corporation are analogues of the ministries and the cabinet, which are in turn responsible to the supreme legislative body—the board of directors, who in turn are elected by the whole body of stockholders. There is no separation of powers, in either the American or French acceptance of the term, in such corporate governments. But there is probably adequate control of management by the shareholders of non-endocratic corporations, leaving aside the question of adequate protection of minority security-holder rights.

There is also, in such corporations, a species of judicial restraint, though it is of course a restraint available through the public judiciary and not a system of internal corporate courts. The possibilities of protecting minority rights through derivative stockholder suits and *ultra vires* action may be unduly limited, but these limitations are removable by statute. It is true that "the governed" in the case of all corporations include more than the security-holders, and that the classical remedies via judicial restraint are not an adequate safeguard of the rights of employees, customers, suppliers, and other traditionally nonowner interests in corporate affairs. But it is assumed—perhaps without good grounds—that these other interests are defensible through extracorporate mechanisms such as the market, collective bargaining, "countervailing powers," public consensus, and the like.

In the large endocratic corporation, however, one may properly raise the question of separation of powers in the light of historical experience in public governments. This is not to say that the question is irrelevant in nonendocratic corporations, but only that it is least relevant in those in which stockholders' interests are not clearly represented by board action and in which the cabinet-parliamentary model does not in fact work.

Corporate Interorgan Controls In the endocratic corporation the four basic patterns of interorgan controls suggested by Loewenstein as elementary principles in public constitutional systems may well be applicable. It is evident that in this respect corporate governance is defective in these particulars: First, the controls of the board over the executive management are of doubtful effectiveness in many instances. Second, the controls of the executive management over the board are said to be excessive.[31] Third, there are no controls by a corporate judiciary over the board and the executive management. And, fourth, the controls of the corporate electorate—the stockholders—over board and management are severely limited in the large public-issue corporation.

Interorgan Controls: Board and Executive Group The interrelations of board and executive group vary greatly from company to company. Board independence of managerial authority is excluded in principle when the board is made up entirely of "insiders"—that is, full-time company officers. But even with "outside" directors it is doubtful [32] that most boards function as the decisive body with respect to the strategic policies of corporations. The selection of corporate officers and the setting of dividend policy [33]—certainly two of the most important types of strategic decision—will not be determined by a board of insiders through independent judgment.

The debate about "insiders" and "outsiders" on the board involves other issues besides that of interorgan controls in the corporate government. But the significance of this issue will receive more attention as the science of intracorporate politics develops. Nor will the problem be solved merely by a wooden application of the separation-of-powers doctrine. Sidney Weinberg, an investment banker with long experience as director in more than thirty corporate boards, has said that outsiders are "in a special position to review disinterestedly the work of the executive group as a whole as well as to advise them," [34] but he has also emphasized that they need to be fully informed with respect to the decisions they make in a directors' meeting. Unless they are willing and able to devote considerable time to the study of materials relevant to the issues presented at board meetings, they cannot in fact perform the interorgan-control function.

It is not possible, in view of the paucity of evidence, to generalize accurately about the present status of this control function in the modern corporation. The available studies,[35] although somewhat extensive, are inadequate for the purpose at hand, primarily because they fail to present comparable data for systematic analysis. For any given corporation one must know something about the history of its own internal constitutional development in order to present a true picture of the board in the total corporate structure. For comparative analysis, both historical and typological, of board control over the executive group and vice versa, the data-collector must have before him a theoretic construct of interorgan-control systems if scientific conclusions are to be drawn. This is a task that no one has yet undertaken, and there is a real need for it.

A primary consideration in such a construct is clarity in distinguishing between the functions of the board and those of the executive group. On this functional distinction there will be a wide range of opinions among those with director experience. The available studies, however, would suffice as a basis for a heuristic model. A point of departure is R. A. Gordon's assumption that "business leadership belongs where it now is—with the executive group," [36] but that the board has at least the functions of naming the chief executive and his compensation, acting as competent advisers to management, and acting as "management auditors." Elaboration of the board's functions beyond this point, in the heuristic model, would depend upon consensus among competent observers of the board as an institution.

Once the definitive list of board functions was determined, in the model, the functions could then be specified more precisely *in terms of interorgan corporate controls*. The next step would be systematic elicitation of comparable data from a sufficiently wide range of actual company experiences in order to test the hypotheses implicit in the model. Have the boards of companies A . . . *n*, for example, over a given period of years, acted as management auditors with respect to points P . . . *n*, and with what results? And so on with other board functions posited in the model. Systematic and comparative analysis of the board as an effective instrument of interorgan control in the corporate constitutional system might then be possible in a way that is precluded by the available narrative accounts.

Interorgan Stockholder-Management Controls Gordon's opinion, in 1945, was that a new type of board, independent of management and owing its allegiance to no single group within or outside the company, was needed.[37] This is a normative judgment based upon his own empirical studies; it is probable that many would disagree with the prescription, but disagreement would be more persuasive if one had an up-to-date presentation of the facts.

Most of the disagreement with the prescription springs from the idea that the fourth type of interorgan control mentioned above—that of the stockholders over board and management—is the most significant and is in fact operative. Here, also, the relevant data are hard to come by on a systematic, comparative, and historical basis, company by company. There is no adequate working model of the board-stockholder relationship, nor are there empirical studies that could test the validity of interorgan-control hypotheses in this relationship in a sufficient number of comparable situations. The board-stockholder relationship raises issues with respect to responsible government in the corporation.

Insofar as the board is the chief *policy-determining* organ of corporate governance, with *policy execution* left to management, the separation-of-powers principle focuses upon the board-management relationship. In traditional corporation theory the board acts on behalf of the corporate electorate, speaks for it, represents it, and is thus in a position to exercise the same kind of control over management that a parliament would—acting on behalf of a democratic electorate—in controlling the cabinet and the ministries of a parliamentary system. Direct control [38] by the electorate over the executive group is thus ruled out, as it would not be in a presidential-congressional system of public government where the chief executive can and must go directly to the electorate. It is ruled out because in the classic corporate model the line of responsibility runs from management to board to stockholders. But if we find that in fact there is no such line of responsibility, that in fact much of the policy in corporations is made by executive groups independently of board-stockholder control, some basic problems of corporate political theory arise.

Must there not be some newly contrived system of checks and balances, in this case, to meet the requirements of an adequate interorgan-control system? The problem is one that has received little attention in this context. It seems to point to some yet-to-be-developed organ of corporate governance to supplement the control functions of the board. A proposal made recently by Professor Bayless Manning [39] suggests one way to fill this missing link in the corporate interorgan-control system.

Manning dismisses as unrealistic and romantic the Corporate Democrats' remedy of strengthened control of stockholders over boards and managers. In his hypothetical model of a non-owning, nonvoting shareholder corporation—introduced for exploratory purposes—there is no attempt to reestablish the lost linkage between "control" and "ownership." Let us assume, he says, that we have a corporation where shareholders simply own their shares and nothing more, and have, furthermore, no right to vote at all. The shareholder's position "would be quite similar to that of a voting trust certificate-holder with all economic rights in the deposited stock but no power to elect or replace the trustees by vote."[40] How ensure managerial responsibility in such a corporation and at the same time permit the necessary discretionary authority for corporate officers?

Many of the present principles of law would still apply in the protection of shareholder interests, such as full and periodic disclosure of managers' business conduct to security-holders and perhaps also to a responsible judicial or other public agency. But some further organs of supervision over corporate affairs would be required "in a shareholder world without voting rights,"[41] and for Manning it was conceivable that such new institutional safeguards would be far more effective than the obsolescent voting-stock system. Some mechanism would need to be developed, he thought, to supervise management dealings in corporate funds for nonbusiness purposes. This mechanism would be "extrinsic" to management, and not necessarily a part of the structure of corporate government itself; it might be supplied judicially, legislatively, or administratively by public government. But it might also be in the nature of "new nongovernmental machinery" for the supervision of managerial behavior in corporate matters affecting the personal interests of managers, such as personal compensation.[42]

To what extent the new organ—if a part of the internal structure of the corporation—would constitute an effective interorgan-control system within the corporation itself Manning did not clarify. He did observe that, as to the entrepreneurial functions (as distinguished from "nonbusiness" decision making) of this model corporation, management would need to have "the broadest latitude for decision in business matters and that the present business-judgment rule be continued or even extended"; and in this respect "the law for the model corporation would depart radically from the restrictive operational rules which govern ordinary trusts designed for other economic objectives."[43]

The substitution, then, of some new corporate constitutional device for the traditional stockholder voting as a restraint on managerial power does not necessarily preclude widened managerial discretion. Whether one likes it or not, the larger public-issue corporations cannot be effectively controlled through an internal electoral system based on the stockholder constituency. With heavier responsibilities reaching in many directions—not excluding responsibilities to the general public—boards and executive groups will naturally demand and get larger authority.[44] How this larger authority can be constitutionally checked by internal arrangements and without resort to external controls imposed by public authorities is one of the most urgent problems of corporate governance today.

DISTRIBUTION OF CORPORATE POWERS IN TIME

Finally, there is the distribution of corporate powers *in time*—a constitutional device whose significance is often overlooked in both public and private governments. The chronological distribution of governing power, not only to separate persons and groups at different time periods but also to the same persons and groups in specified time-segmented sequences, is a basic technique of control. Its function is not well understood, even by experts in the science and art of government. They tend to confuse the chronological distribution of power with other devices of constitutionalism. Because limited tenure of office is associated with parties and elections, for example, the timed sequence of office holding is ordinarily treated in the textbooks as a subordinate aspect of the electoral process. It is, of course, a separate and distinct—and, indeed, a major—subject in the whole area of constitutionalism. Similarly, the timed sequence of supply authorized by representative assemblies to fuel the engines of administration is often confused with—or subordinated to—the legislative and administrative processes of government.

But it is a more systematic and also a more useful procedure in analyzing constitutional systems to treat under one heading all devices for restraining power through chronological periodicity. Budgets have to be submitted annually or biennially; appropriations and authorizations do not run on indefinitely; there are one-, two-, five-, and ten-year plans; a congressman may acquire powerful seniority status but only after surviving the biennial return to his constituency for a renewal of his mandate a good many times consecutively; a Republican Administration is tolerable to the Democrats partly because they can have another go at it in not more than four years; the loyalty of the Loyal Opposition in the United Kingdom is not unduly strained since the electoral sequences are flexible and the game of politics is far less rigidly calendared than it is with us. So one could go on throughout the political system and identify all of the devices of chronological periodicity in power control.

It is the same in corporate governments. There are annual stockholders' meetings; annual reports and annual budgets; appointments and elections on a one-, two-, or three-year basis or for indefinite tenure; long-range planning may cover ten- or twenty-five-year periods in the more farsighted companies; dividend policy is similarly determined in such companies to avoid disturbing annual fluctuations in the dividend rate; financing is time-oriented with care; there is periodic collective bargaining with careful attention to the periodicity of all arrangements made at the bargaining table, affecting as they do a whole range of commitments to the suppliers of wage labor; and the whole complex of corporate policy, calculated along the axis of time, has to be meshed in with the chronological periodicity of public governments.

If little systematic attention has been given to chronological periodicity as a device of public constitutionalism, even less is evident in the study of corporate constitutionalism. Yet in corporate governments there is urgent need for a critique of certain aspects of the problem. Everyone knows that the annual stockholders' meeting is a farce as a device for periodic *control* of boards and managers by holders of voting shares, and that it more nearly approximates an annual ritual for the security of those already in power. There have been studies of the tenure of directors, but little coordination of such studies with the tenure of executive groups and the tenure of those further down the line, where the initiation of policy usually occurs. The relationship between time-oriented collective agreements on labor supply and other aspects of long- and short-range corporate planning has not been systematically analyzed. Nor is the meshing of corporate with national planning, in reasonable time sequences, the subject of penetrating study for a range of the most influential corporations.

There is a wide, unexplored field of inquiry here for the corporate constitutionalist. What would be the effect, for example, of a different periodicity in the electoral process involving shareholders if the English system of cabinet-parliamentary government were adapted to corporate governments? Instead of metronomic regularity of mandate seeking by directors vis-à-vis the corporate electorate, imagine the possibility of votes of no confidence when crises arise in the affairs of a corporation. Or assume the widening of the electorate conception to include all those interests which now are presumably "balanced" by managerial judgment, and then assume further a periodic (not necessarily in fixed time sequences) referral of strategic managerial decisions to this larger electorate for a clear mandate. The effect upon the present so-called self-perpetuating oligarchy in management would be considerable—disastrous, perhaps, but also possibly salubrious.

Or assume that there is a parallel to be drawn between the professionalized managerial corps in corporations and public governments. The civil service has bureaucratic characteristics in Weber's sense, and tenure of office in public bureaucracy is governed by criteria entirely different from those which apply to tenure in the political branches—legislatures and elected executives with their political appointees in immediately subordinate positions. How should one systematize and institutionalize the chronological periodicity of personnel selection and removal in these separate and distinguishable corps of corporate governments? There is a trend of thought that insists upon professionalization of corporate management at the very top—in boards of directors. Is this consistent with the basic principles of corporate constitutionalism?

These and other questions related to the distribution of power over time in corporate governance cannot safely be answered on speculative grounds or by simple comparison with public governments in democratic-constitutional regimes. They require extensive case studies of particular corporate governments, in time depth and on a comparative basis.

Responsible Government in Corporations

RESPONSIBLE GOVERNMENT in the public sector is a constitutionalist technique that centers on electoral systems, party government and the principles of representation. None of these seems easily applicable to the modern public-issue corporation.

There is no agreement among corporation theorists as to the definition of terms in the chain of responsibility in corporate governance. *Who* is responsible to *whom* for *what*, and *how* is his responsibility to be enforced? Each of the italicized terms is highly debatable today. As to the first term, the "who" in this formula may refer to board or executive group, or to both. As to the second term, responsibility to "whom" raises arguable issues about the relative positions of various groups of claimants on the corporation: the stockholders, the consuming public, the employees, the suppliers. As to the third term, responsibility for "what," one gets answers ranging all the way from the simple requirement that corporations be run for maximum profit to stockholders, to the more recent multiple demands of numerous contributor-claimant groups, including the claims of the "general public." As to the fourth term, the "how" of enforcement of responsibility, it is fair to say that only the most elementary steps to identify ways and means have yet been taken.

In the absence of agreement about the precise referents for these terms in the formula of corporate accountability, it is very difficult to construct a viable theory of responsible government in the corporate polity. The first term is the least debatable; one must assume the locus of considerable power in the board-management complex, and therefore the locus of corporate responsibility at this point. The *particular persons* who bear responsibility for decisions made on behalf of the corporation are not thereby identified, however.

It is customary, in the legalistic conceptions of corporate responsibility, to point specifically to the directors, individually and collectively. But legal liability and quasi-political responsibility are different conceptions; here we are concerned primarily with the latter. The responsibility which those who make the important decisions in a corporation owe to others who bear the brunt of those decisions may be to some extent enforceable by law in suits against directors. But who would contend that this remedy is adequate for holding the real decision-makers to full accountability for their actions as influential policy-determiners? The formulation of policy in corporate governments is not sufficiently exposed to public scrutiny for the purpose of identifying the real determiners of policy. And even if that process were clearly a matter of record, open to all those who have an interest in policy decisions, there is now little or no opportunity for the persons affected to bring their points of view to bear at every step in the policy process in such a way that the decisions will be "integrative" in Mary Parker Follett's sense of that term.

To say, then, that the responsibility for corporate decisions can be fixed at the board level alone is to deal in fictions remote from realities. In public government it is possible to bring out by congressional investigation, public hearings, a free press, and open debate those points at which specific persons at various stages of the policy process influence the final decision. The exposure to public scrutiny is not by any means as full as some would have it, to be sure, but the contrast between the governmental process in the public and private sectors is still sharp. In both cases there are areas of policy making which cannot, for security and other reasons, be subjected to public scrutiny. But in public government nondisclosure is presumed to be the exception and not the rule. It is otherwise in corporate governance.

Because of this essential privity of the decision process in business organizations—a characteristic of private government that is to some extent inseparable from the competitive system—it will always be difficult to pin the responsibility for the exercise of power where it belongs in order then to enforce responsibility on specific persons.

The notion that a corporate regime is directly comparable with a cabinet-parliamentary system, where the cabinet (read "board") can be held responsible to parliament (read "stockholders"), is often presented uncritically as the answer to the problem of responsible government in the corporation. But there is no "question" or "interpellation" in corporate governments. Directors do not resign, nor do boards fall, in response to any procedure comparable with those developed in English constitutionalism. The annual meeting of stockholders is no substitute for parliament in continuous session.

If there were a corporate parliament in continuous session, moreover, who would be the rightful corporate MP's? Certainly not the shareholders alone unless one accepts the most thoroughly traditional conception of the corporation. Members of parliament are representatives of democratic constituencies. There is as yet no general agreement on the question of constituencies of corporate governments. Who should be represented in these governments? The answer depends on the function a business corporation is expected to carry out.

That answer is, again, a highly debatable one. According to Berle, the large industrial corporation has to "supply a market, develop the art, gather savings . . . make jobs and maintain stability" and, more and more, "to submit itself to and become an active and assisting member of some planning mechanism of some kind." [45] Others would provide answers ranging all the way from profit maximization for shareholders to the general welfare of the community. At the latter end of the spectrum there arises the demand for some kind of "social accounting" [46] that must inevitably lead to radically different corporate institutions of government to ensure accountability of this sweeping kind.

The Protection of Private Rights

INTRINSIC CORPORATE constitutional restraints for the protection of private rights against those who exercise power on behalf of the corporate aggregrate are to be distinguished from methods currently proposed to enforce "due process" in public courts. Are there not ways and means available—aside from the techniques of representative government—to institute internal constitutional restraints that will protect private rights directly and without resort to public government?

Nearly fifty years ago Louis D. Brandeis testified to the Commission on Industrial Relations [47] that his main objection to the very large corporation was that it made possible, "and in many cases inevitable, the exercise of industrial absolutism." The worker had no vote; in the political state he did have a vote. "There develops within the State," he said, "a state so powerful that the ordinary social and industrial forces existing are insufficient to cope with it." The contrast between political liberty and "industrial absolutism" seemed to Brandeis a dangerous anomaly.

Since that time we have seen the elaboration of the theme in the critique of the "Organization Man" and the widespread concern about "human relations in industry." In many companies there has been an earnest attempt to replace authoritarian management with permissive systems that tend to give employees a more lively sense of participation in the productive process and thus to dispel some of the dysphoria at the workplace of which the humanists complain so bitterly. But these moves, however laudable from an ethical point of view, sometimes run counter to other demands, such as discipline, order, and business performance as required by law and the competitive realities. Nor do they satisfy the needs of employees for regularized procedures to secure their rights in important respects.

The rights of free speech, freedom of inquiry, freedom to publish,[48] freedom to associate cannot be secured for employees in a large organization without some institutionalized remedies *within the corporation itself*. An intracorporate judicial system might be established to protect such rights, and both the substantive rights and remedies to enforce them might be defined with particularity in a written company policy, or a series of policies. These written policies would become a part of the "fundamental law" of the corporate government and therefore binding upon any supervisor with respect to the rights of his subordinates.

The enforcement of such rights would be the province of a specialized company component created by the board for this purpose. Many of the procedural standards of "due process" in public bodies would be applicable to the operations of this intracorporate component. And just as the requirements of due process vary among public agencies, so may they be adjusted to the particular needs of the business organization. A new corpus of corporate constitutional law would be developed to meet these needs.

Only the most modest first steps have yet been taken in this direction in the large corporations, and it is not clear that any have gone so far as to establish quasi-judicial remedies within the company organization to secure the rights of employees. The rights of others in the corporate community are, in general, protected—if they are protected at all—by law or through collective-bargaining agreements. Least protected, at the administrative core of corporate governments, are the rights of persons in middle management. Their rights are not and will not be, predictably, the subject of collective-bargaining agreements. Sooner or later something comparable with the "GI Bill of Rights"—an act of Congress setting up a court of military appeals—may be needed to protect such rights. The source of such a "bill of rights" would be a written policy enacted by the corporation board of directors and binding upon all managers from the executive level on down.

The rule of law in corporate governance, insofar as private rights are protected against arbitrary action, involves much larger issues than those touched on briefly in this chapter. The subject is indeed so important, involving as it does the range of policy as it affects human values, that we shall devote the remainder of the book to it.

Part V

CORPORATE POLICIES AND HUMAN VALUES

CHAPTER *13*

The Span of Corporate Policy

UP TO THIS POINT we have dealt primarily with the structural and procedural aspects of corporate government. In the present and following chapters we turn to substantive issues of a different order. The structure of private government within the large corporation, and the processes by which governance in this comparatively autonomous sphere are carried on are matters of vital importance to a free society. The human values that should dominate in a free society cannot be maximized if government in its private sectors is despotic and the public sector alone attempts to live up to our best constitutionalist traditions. A major thesis of this book has been that a larger measure of constitutionalism is possible and necessary in large corporate enterprises.

Corporate Dynamics

WE NOW TURN to issues of a different kind. The focus will be less on corporate polity, corporate constitutional structure, and constitutional process, and more on corporate policy, strategic decisions, and the current problems of running a business. In general, the emphasis is thus on corporate dynamics rather than corporate statics. The dynamics of corporate enterprise embrace the study of the forces operating in the "field" within which executive decisions activate the environment and are also conditioned by that environment.

The decisions that corporate executives make fall into two broadly distinguishable categories when one wants to know the ethical implications. On the one hand, there are the day-to-day, year-to-year decisions about running the business as a profitable enterprise. Problems of finance, engineering, production, marketing, and so on fall into this category. On the other hand, there are decisions as to the role of a corporation in society. Into this category fall problems of adjusting to the environment, fitting corporate purpose to the prevailing ethical norms, and reform both within corporations and in the social structure itself for the better achievement of the ideal goals of all.

The line between these two kinds of executive decision is not always clear in practice. Problems of marketing, for example, may very well raise fundamental issues about antitrust policy, and antitrust is an issue that goes to the heart of social ethics in a highly organized economy such as ours. Yet the line can be drawn for analytical purposes. In the contemporary—and often confused—debate about the social responsibilities of businessmen and the duties of corporate citizenship, it may be useful to distinguish between the pursuit of profit by just means and the pursuit of justice *per se* by a corporate enterprise as a major power center in a pluralistic society.

For most businessmen, the more meaningful approach, to their "social responsibilities" is likely to be one that begins at the grass roots and deals primarily with the kinds of decisions they have to make regularly in the course of ordinary business operations. They tend to resist, as practical men of affairs, the higher levels of abstraction at which much of the contemporary debate about their rights and duties is carried on. They do not readily accept the idea that, as businessmen, it is one of their primary tasks to attain the good, the true, and the beautiful as ideal goals. And in this assumption they are undoubtedly correct, the division of labor in our society being what it is today. The precise meaning of "business" may not be clear to all; but there are, after all, other institutions in society whose task it is to pursue through specialized means those ideal goals.

Nor does this more prosaic acceptance of the business aim preclude a prudent regard for just means of achieving it. And in the present chapter it will be shown that justice and regard for human values do enter into decision-making at the most prosaic grass-roots levels of operating a business. This is shown in a somewhat detailed examination of the functional types of work done in any large corporate industrial enterprise, pointing at the same time to the policy areas in each function which raise ethical questions. Having done this, we can then turn in later chapters to the questions of corporate citizenship and corporate justice in a larger sense. Here we begin with the less expansive issues arising in the course of running a profitable and productive enterprise.

A Schematic View of Business Functions

BUSINESS OPERATIONS in such an enterprise can be classified into eight functional kinds of work:

1) *Research and Engineering*, including basic and applied research with respect to the product lines of the company; advanced and developed engineering; design engineering; production engineering; setting up of engineering standards; the development of research and engineering administrative practices; and research and engineering personnel development
2) *Manufacturing*, including facilities engineering; manufacturing engineering; supply and use of materials; shop administration; quality control; manufacturing administrative practices; and manufacturing personnel development

3) *Marketing*, including marketing research; product planning; advertising and sales promotion; sales and customer relations; product services; marketing administrative practices; and marketing personnel development
4) *Finance*, including corporate financing; banking; accounting in all aspects (general accounting, tax accounting, personnel accounting, manufacturing cost accounting, and distribution cost accounting); credit and collection; auditing; investor relations; insurance; financial administrative practices; and financial personnel development
5) *Legal and "Corporate"* functions as to contracts, taxation, patents, trade regulation, and labor relations; administrative practices in the law department; and legal personnel development
6) *Employee Relations*, including recruitment; employee education, training, and development; wage and salary administration; employee benefits; employee health and safety; personnel practices; employee communications; employee relations administrative practices and personnel development; and union relations
7) *Public Relations*, including plant community relations; relations with public governmental bodies; specialized relations with certain publics such as educational, scientific, and charitable institutions; institutional advertising and other forms of relations with the general public; public relations administrative practices; and public relations personnel development
8) *Corporate Governance and Administration*, including corporate constitutional development; internal legislative and administrative organization and procedures; managing (planning, organizing, integrating, and measuring, or, alternatively, some other scheme for subdividing the work of managing in all the functional fields of work carried on in the enterprise as indicated in points 1–7 above); and administrative practices and personnel development in the field of corporate governance and administration

Here we have a panorama of practically all of the established and recognized functions that have to be performed in any large corporate industrial enterprise. The emphasis given to one or more of these functional areas will vary from company to company. In some companies, for example, the marketing function may require far more personnel than manufacturing. Also there are great variations from company to company—and in a single company over a period of decades—as to the degree of centralization in operations. The schema above contemplates a highly diversified company as to product lines and a considerably decentralized one as to structure, as well as one that organizes its total work both by function and by product. Thus, each function requires, in this schema, its own administrative apparatus (at both operating and staff levels) and therefore a separate provision in each case for administrative and personnel practices. In less complex organizations many of these subfunctions would not appear discretely.

It will be observed that the eighth and last functional area is not so designated in any contemporary industrial corporation. In its place one sometimes (though rarely) finds a provision for the special function of "managing" or "administration" as a separate kind of work. The struggle to get this function recognized has been a long one, and even now it is frequently ignored organizationally or subsumed under the remaining functions. One reason for this is the failure to see that managerial expertise is as indispensable to industrial production as other capital resources, and that this special kind of human resource demands professional training quite as rigorous as that required in the financial, legal, engineering, manufacturing, marketing, public relations, and employee relations functions of an enterprise.

But there is a more significant reason, still not understood even by many specialists on management. It is the *raison d'être* of the present book. Corporations have to be managed, yes; but this is only one aspect of the larger problem of corporate governance. The several functionally defined departments of a corporation will be managed or administered largely by functionally specialized personnel. There is, of course, a place at staff or service levels for managerial specialists. But the comprehensive oversight of governance as a corporate functional problem requires expertise of other dimensions as well. The subfunctions in this field, as indicated under point 8 above, are still either inadequately manned in every large corporation or not manned at all. We shall return to this subject in a moment.

The Uncodified Areas of Policy

LET US NOW LOOK BACK over the panorama of functional types of work to be done in a large industrial corporation and indicate some of the basic issues that arise in each area—issues which present to business leaders the need for fairly clear policies by which a company should be guided in order to measure up to prevailing ethical norms. No attempt will be made here either to state the norms or to formulate specific policies. That is a job for each company. If freedom of enterprise means anything, and if corporate autonomy in a pluralistic society is in itself a value worth preserving, then the task should be left to every private organization to work out for itself. Our present aim is only to suggest illustratively some of the more important subjects on which well-considered company policies would greatly strengthen the companies that chose to adopt them and be guided by them.

The term "policy" is used here in a special sense.[1] Corporate policy is a projected plan of action designed to achieve certain major objectives of the corporate enterprise as a whole. When reduced to written form and set forth in an official company instrument, a corporate policy will state the common purposes to be served by the plan of action as described in the document, careful attention being given to the method of formulating the objectives so that all of the interests involved will have participated in the draft of a policy at every stage of its development.

The plan of action may be either mandatory or permissive. A policy may be directive in the form of instructions, with little scope for variation in administrative application; or it may leave the way open for discretionary action within stated bounds and in accord with stated norms. The advantage of written policies, drawn up according to basic procedures and set down in standard forms which can be widely communicated throughout the company, is that the scope of discretion can in this way be more clearly defined. The purposes can also be more accurately formulated and widely understood. As a general rule, every policy document should combine both the purposes and the plan of action in one place, together with designation of the persons (or classes of persons) to whom it applies. Those who are responsible for implementing a policy as well as those who are authorized to enforce it, and how it will be enforced, should also be indicated in the text of a written policy.

Company policies, in this sense of the term, are a species of basic company legislation. Every company has its rules and regulations, usually codified in some way and printed for distribution. Less attention is given, paradoxically enough, to legislation of a higher order which lies somewhere between the rules and regulations of everyday shop practice and the resolutions of boards of trustees. Yet it is in just this area that the warp and woof of corporate justice are woven. Policy as it affects the lives and property of its employees, its stockholders, its customers, its competitors, and that "general public" in whose name so much lip service is paid to the abstraction of "social responsibility"—here the span of policy is still largely uncodified.

Managers move into this area with the most cautious reserve; they do not undertake with alacrity the responsibility of drafting policies on large issues. Indeed, they tend to resist it. This is an area full of political land mines. Intracompany politics as well as outside pressures warn that conflicts of major interests are involved. Written policies on such issues require the disclosure and candid statement of the nature of these interests in a way that exposes the vacuity of glittering generalities about company objectives. Getting down to cases is painful intellectually and endangering to status for some managers and company organizational components. Like purely objective job analyses, policies based on the realities of the situation point all too clearly to hitherto undisclosed and unattended responsibilities and to redundant operations which people do not like to have disturbed.

Some Needed Policies

CONSIDER, FOR EXAMPLE, some of the issues on which company policies could well be formulated not only for ethical reasons but simply for the purpose of strengthening the enterprise as a profitable productive operation. The examples below are illustrative only and do not purport to cover exhaustively each functional type of work in a company.

RESEARCH AND ENGINEERING POLICIES

Patents The acquisition and protection of patents, their use, release, sale, and transfer, are all matters of vital interest to a company, to its various components, and to the public. The reconciliation of the competing interests of a company as a whole, its component operating departments, individual employees who develop new processes or invent new products, vendors, licensees, and the nation involves legal, economic, and moral claims and conflicts. Abstract "justice" is undiscoverable as a guide to action here. Free-wheeling, on the other hand, without any attempt to standardize company policy or to make company practices conform to legal norms, can damage the company's prestige and its profitability performance.

MANUFACTURING POLICIES

Procurement The purchase of materials for production, the letting of contracts, and the shipping of goods are all matters in which production departments must have considerable discretion as to prices, payments, and delivery schedules. But a company code of ethics, taking into account the interests of suppliers, can be incorporated into a policy which will at the same time meet productivity requirements and serve other intracompany interests.

Productivity The efficient utilization of certain physical, financial, and human resources to create goods and services that are useful and salable is productivity in a broad sense; and the productivity of a company as a whole must be measured by standards that will differ from those used to measure productivity in manufacturing operations separately considered. Production policies for manufacturing, however, cannot safely be drafted only with an eye to input-output ratios in manufacturing departments themselves. A good many intracompany interests are involved, and so are external interests. It may be costly to avoid stream pollution and to institute smoke control, for example; productivity in a narrow manufacturing sense will suffer. Productivity policies that will protect the interests to the same degree are unattainable; but ill-considered policies can be quite as damaging in the long run to, say, the stockholders as they may be to the public at large.

MARKETING POLICIES

Quality of Products In setting the standards for product quality there are many claimant interests for whom common ground for concerted company action needs to be spelled out in policy. Manufacturing costs; quality control in production; predetermination of product performance under conditions of customer use; postdetermination of actual performance and provision for information feedback to research and engineering, manufacturing, and other departments; pricing procedures; the impact of a poor product on the company "image"—these considerations, which should enter into a policy on product quality and performance, will not actually be given weight unless several departments (functionally defined) are represented in preparing the policy and required to assume specific responsibilities in carrying it out.

Pricing Policy Terms of sale of company products properly involve most functional departments, none of which can safely be ignored and some of which will be important reflectors of external interests that need to be taken into consideration in pricing policy. "Fair" prices are prices that deal fairly with customers but not less fairly with stockholders, competitors, and others. Marketing practices that are the exclusive preserve of a few secretive company officials can lead to damaging consequences for many innocent bystanders within and without a company. Collusive price fixing, with subsequent criminal prosecutions and civil damage suits under antitrust laws, results in loss of company prestige, a drop in the value of its equities, and displacement of employees not involved in the conspiracy in restraint of trade. The legal and public relations departments must be prepared to channel to those who make and carry out price policy the specific claims of "public interest" (as expressed in antitrust and so-called "fair trade" laws, in public opinion trends, in the professional literature of economists, political scientists, jurists, sociologists, and so on), while other company departments at the same time present their special claims and interests. Especially significant are the finance and corporate-governance-and-administration departments. Financial considerations in price policy include cost accounting, measures of profitability, and relations with stockholders, financial institutions, securities dealers, and so on. Pricing policy affects the department of corporate governance and administration because of the intimate relation between antitrust policies of public government and the preservation of corporate autonomy in a freely competitive economy.

FINANCIAL POLICIES

Investor Relations In this field there is need for a number of policies dealing with the operative meaning of shareholder "ownership" in today's large, publicly-held industrial corporations. The attachment of a company to a political economy based on private property rights is testable by its own policies as they affect ownership rights. Superficial "stockholder relations" of the conventional kind designed to keep share-owners selectively informed and safely in line can be distinguished from the more basic concern about striking a balance between stockholders' and others' claims on company assets. Policy on the distribution of earnings is rarely encountered. The protection of and accounting for assets is governable by stated procedures and in accordance with accounting concepts and standards that can withstand the scrutiny of diverse functional specialists in a company as well as outside professional groups.

Capital Investment Policies governing the investment of fixed assets should be formulated and subject to periodic review by representatives of all functional departments in a company. There are considerations of both business and public policy. As to the latter, the rate and method of saving for a nation will necessarily affect a company's investment policy; the policies of private corporations in this field also affect national savings trends and practices. Within a company there are many diverse claims and counterclaims as to accumulation of earnings, reinvestment of profits, and so on. Written policies covering such subjects are usually avoided (as in the case of distribution of earnings) because fixed policies necessarily encroach upon director and managerial discretion, or, more plainly, upon their freedom of arbitrary action. In public law we have the concept of due process, which in principle precludes arbitrary action by public officials, as, for example, the prosecution and punishment of persons for violating a law which sets forth no clear and ascertainable standards of conduct. In corporate governments this idea of due process has no counterpart in the control of discretionary action by boards and managers to whom individual owners of property transfer the right to govern its use.

LEGAL AND CORPORATE POLICIES

Compliance with Law It is elementary doctrine in most companies that employees should abide by the law; not so clearly evident are written policies on the subject of compliance and responsibility for noncompliance, especially as to laws on taxation, trade regulation, patents, governmental security requirements, and labor relations. Compliance, as such, is a primary concern of legal departments of companies; but obviously these departments do not master the substantive and specialized knowledge in each of the fields of law just listed. Company policies of compliance in each field can be drawn properly only after careful consultation of relevant specialists both within and outside a company. Solemn and sanctimonious protestations usually seen in company public pronouncements that all "good corporate citizens" obey the laws have no place in these policies. If a rule of law as it stands is oppressive of company interests in certain respects, policy would better face the conflict and require compliance but provide for relief through legitimate procedures prescribed in the policy itself (such as company action to urge the amendment of certain statutes; provision for intracompany procedures to prevent employees from being caught between the upper and nether millstones of public policy and "business-is-business" demands; and intracompany procedures for adjudicating conflicting intracompany claims in questions of compliance or noncompliance with state and federal laws).

EMPLOYEE RELATIONS POLICIES

Compensation "Fair compensation," like "fair prices," is a question-begging epithet. In collective bargaining on wages as well as in salary adjustments, the terms of compensation are to some extent regulable by policy even though determined in part by impersonal market forces. The factors entering into the regulable area of compensation are thus a subject for intracorporate legislative standards. Measurement-of-service-rendered as a basis for pay scales; community wage and salary levels; special compensation for special services, high-risk assignments, and so on; wage and salary differentials based on hierarchy, seniority, race, sex, and other considerations; benefits in lieu of or in addition to monetary compensation: these are all elements in setting up company standards for compensation. "Fairness" and equity in setting these standards is not likely to be discoverable in theological treatises. Rather it will be whatever approximation of justice is possible when good policy-making procedures are followed. All the relevant interest groups have to be heard—and this includes more than the employee relations specialists; the financial, legal, and intra-corporate-governance functional departments are necessarily involved. We speak here only of the company's written policy governing compensation and not the collective and individual bargaining procedures in connection with employment of personnel.

Employee Rights, Privileges, and Immunities As industrial polities evolve away from the more or less benevolent despotisms of the past to what may be the constitutional corporate governments of the future, more and more emphasis will be put on the so-called "rights" of employees in all grades. Company policies, insofar as they exist at all in this area, now touch the subject only peripherally. Working conditions, health and safety rules, the right to bargain collectively, grievance procedures are some of the peripheral aspects now dealt with in many companies, though not in most on the basis of policies drawn in accordance with procedures indicated above. The "rights" of employees usually derive from unilaterally imposed rules and regulations or bilateral management-union agreements; and in both cases there tends to be *ad hoc* treatment of special problems as they arise. While sound and useful as a way of building up what might be called the common law of employee relations, this approach will eventually be complemented by more comprehensive corporate "bills of rights" based on comprehensive consideration of all contributor-claimant interests, including those of the stockholders, customers, and the general public.

Among the most important policies needed are on these subjects:

Freedom of public utterance, including the right to speak, write, and publish

Freedom of association, including, but not restricted to, the right of association for purposes of collective bargaining; the development and maintenance of noncompany interests through external associations

Freedom of information and education, including access rights to all sources for these purposes

Procedural safeguards to secure these and other rights as against arbitrary managerial action

PUBLIC RELATIONS POLICIES

Plant Community Relations Company policies assigned to protect "neighbors" and local natural resources and to coordinate company plans for expansion, contraction, and removal of facilities have to be drawn in terms of diversified interests, not excluding those of the ultimate owners of the local plant, the company's creditors, its customers, and "community" in a wider—perhaps national—sense of the term. Compensatory arrangements in contraction and removal operations may properly involve nonlocal external interests; procedures for hearing and adjudicating such claims are necessary elements of a written policy.

Communication Policy The rights and responsibilities of the several functional organizations in a company with respect to the use of communication media vis-à-vis external persons and groups can be spelled out in a written policy. Certain media (such as telecommunications systems) have become important instruments of company operations and influence. They also suggest new and perhaps revolutionary techniques for better articulation of intracorporate constituencies in the internal system of corporate governance as well as external corporate affairs, such as quick consultation of stockholder, customer, and other interests preparatory to strategic planning at the level of executive management. The general flow of communications through all media between company and public is becoming a specialized field with significant policy implications.[2] It can no longer be left to haphazard and completely decentralized controls. The top communication specialist has to be a close associate and counselor to executive management.

POLICIES ON CORPORATE GOVERNANCE AND ADMINISTRATION

Government Relations Company relations with public governmental agencies have moved from the earlier stages of general disengagement and occasional, often furtive engagement of public support or immunity against public regulation, through the more recent stages of "political participation" (a form of pressure) and co-action (as in government defense contracts). Still to be attained is a clear policy of systematic co-action and sharing of the burdens as well as the powers of governance in society by public and private agencies. Company policies must move into this area.

Intracorporate Constitutional Forms and Procedures As pointed out generally in this book, this subject is little cultivated as a discipline, but it is now time for continuous attention to it by special personnel in each company and by specialized components in the largest companies. Company policy should specify the appropriate plans of action to make this possible.

Administrative Procedures and Practices Specialized components in this area are more generally encountered. Policies for standardizing procedures and practices at the administrative level (from the executive managers down, and not including the interactions of boards and stockholder groups) are also not rare. They may frequently be found, however, to have been drawn by methods which do not sufficiently bring in all the interested parties as participants in the process. The result is often an unintendedly severe hierarchical administrative organization which may not contribute to a company's profitability or to the purposes of a free society.

Conclusions

IN THIS CHAPTER we have reviewed the span of corporate policy with respect to the ordinary business functions of a productive and profitable enterprise. We have seen that within each of the eight major functional areas, covering specialized types of work to be done in accordance with fairly well established principles of division of labor, there are numerous problems which have general ethical significance as well as significance for the business as such.

In pointing up the ethical import of these problems, we have shown that the need for written policies frequently arises where that need is frequently overlooked. The need arises not only from the sheer size and expansiveness of large corporate operations. The cohesive properties of written policies, especially necessary in large decentralized corporations in order to marry the advantages of widespread delegation of authority and those of collective resources, are obvious; and the failure to reduce general norms to documentary forms undoubtedly accounts for some cases of mismanagement. But our primary concern here is not more efficient management. The analysis has a different objective: to set forth in a comprehensive way the emergent ethical issues inherent in operations that are essentially "business" operations, in the more restricted sense of that term.

In the chapters that follow we can now turn to the larger issues of corporate citizenship. The meaning of "corporate citizenship" and "corporate justice" emerges clearly only after exploration of the grass-roots issues just surveyed. On the other hand, as we shall see, these larger issues do deserve separate consideration, for they can too easily be lost in preoccupation with the day-to-day business problems.

CHAPTER 14

Corporation and Community

The Good Corporate Citizen

WHAT ARE THE QUALITIES of a good corporate citizen? The answer lies not so much in abstract analysis of the social responsibilities of the corporation as in the executive response, in particular corporations, to the problems indicated in the preceding chapter. There we looked at a schematic span of corporate policy covering all the major functional kinds of work done in large industrial enterprises. The essence of corporate citizenship is to be found in the way a company handles its workaday problems in these functional fields. It is to be found, more explicitly, in the kinds of decision a company's board and executive managers make with respect to finance, production, marketing, internal governance, external relations, and other business problems.

The solution of these problems in accordance with prevailing norms of business ethics is the first requisite of good corporate citizenship. But, as we have seen, a company is more likely to meet this standard if attention is given in a systematic way to the entire span of policy. This means more than *ad hoc* disposition of issues as they arise in the ordinary course of business. It means that in each functional field studied effort must be given to the selection of salient and persistent issues in the field, and to the general resolution of these issues in the form of written policy documents. The purpose of this procedure is to clarify the common purposes to be served in recurrent conflicts of diverse claims, to specify courses of action —usually discretionary within stated bounds—and to provide ways and means for enforcing the policy as drawn. Adequate authority must be specified and responsibilities defined.

The norms of good corporate conduct thus arise from the grass roots of a company, since policies of this sort cannot be drawn *in vacuo*. Policies have to be threshed out in successive meetings in which all the competing interests are represented. They must be based on experience, and the fruits of experience come mainly from people who have been on the firing line in their respective functional and subfunctional fields of work. In a highly decentralized company organization, the drafting of policies requires close collaboration among representatives from a number of functional fields, and among those at both operating and staff levels of company personnel. The clash of minds at work over a policy document is usually productive of a draft that can stand up when it is finally put to use.

But, it may well be asked, how can the *norms* of conduct be derived solely from the pooling of experience and the resolution of internal conflicting interests? Is there not an independent source of the norms of good corporate citizenship? How can one be sure that the claims of "society" will be stated, recognized, and met fairly? The answer lies partly in the fact that every specialist—whether he be in marketing, manufacturing, legal work, or public relations—will have encountered many of the claims of public interest in the course of his specialized work. External claims leave their impact at many points in the ordinary course of business operations. Legal and marketing departments, for example, are acutely aware of community norms relative to antitrust. Public relations work requires one to study the "corporate image." Labor relations specialists must be informed about the public philosophy in their field.

This, however, is only a partial answer to the question of tuning in on the wave lengths of "public interest." The norms of corporate conduct are not necessarily discoverable through the collected antennae of the specialists. Corporate survival, as a general goal of good management, may elude the specialist intent upon his own field of interest. The long-range goals of a company may or may not be consistent with those of the community. Opportunities for growth and service may be missed if one fails to assess long-range trends in the social, economic, and political environment. What is worse, the viability of the enterprise may at length be jeopardized unless one thinks of it as an organic part of society.

Corporation and community, in other words, can be thought of in ecological terms. It is possible that no Kantian categorical imperative can be discovered as the ultimate source of corporate ethics. The qualities of corporate citizenship are nowhere defined in holy writ. But some, at least, of the rules of right corporate conduct are surely derivable from careful study of those environmental conditions which can determine the success or failure of an enterprise. Corporate ecology is a necessary, if not a sufficient, tool of the corporate policy-maker.

An Ecological Approach to Corporate Ethics

A CORPORATION IS AN ORGANIZATION with more than a few organismic characteristics. It flourishes—or declines and dies—in an ecosystem [1] which is still little understood. Some of the most significant determinants of corporate action are to be found in the living social, economic, and political environment of a company. Most of the decisions which corporate governors have to make are in the realm of discretionary action, but the range of discretion is often far more limited than is usually assumed. The protection of defensive barriers against environmental controls and the constriction of corporate autonomy requires unremitting attention to the environment in all of its aspects.

To put the matter in another way, corporate decision-makers have to pursue a path of enlightened self-interest by illuminating for their own guidance an extensive terrain lying far beyond the immediate boundaries of the corporate self. This is one of the conditions of corporate survival. Some one or a few at the helm of an enterprise must be in a position to survey that terrain with great care, and the survey cannot safely be left to the specialist in any one of the functional fields we have described in the preceding chapter.

The corporate environment can be classified in various ways. Distinctions can be drawn, for example, between the environment as an *economy* and as a complex of public and private *governmental systems*. On the other hand, *ideological* influences in the environment may be either favorable or inimical to a company's purposes; or, putting it the other way around, a company may be so out of step with ideological rhythms in the ecosystem that survival depends upon its getting in step.

Another way of dissecting the corporate environment for analytical purposes is to distinguish local and more distant community relationships. Legally, a corporation derives its "life" from a sovereign state; but in fact it lives by virtue of sustenance provided by a community more realistically defined. In fact, the interrelation between a company, as a going concern, and the ecosystem in which it flourishes cannot be understood except in terms of a variety of communities ranging all the way from those defined geographically to others defined functionally.

Besides the local communities where a company's productive installations are established, there are the larger political communities with geographically defined jurisdictional boundaries in which it "does business" under prevailing rules of law. These larger, politically defined communities are controlled by local, state, national, foreign, and international governing bodies—all of which may limit the range of corporate discretionary authority.

There are other types of community of a functional character. A company's stockholders and creditors are, for example, part of a more or less geographically dispersed financial community in which banks, security dealers, security analysts, and so on, figure significantly. Its customers may live and operate in far-flung parts of a state, a nation, or the world. Its suppliers are usually similarly dispersed.

The indirect—but often influential—relationships of a company with its environment may involve educational, professional, scientific, philanthropic, religious, and other communities. More and more it becomes a part of a company's "public relations" function to establish mutually beneficial relations with such communities.

The ecosystem of a corporation thus extends into many human relationships not easily subsumed under the functional headings we considered earlier as guides to the more important company policies. The character of a corporate citizen is largely determinable in terms of these other ecological relationships. Whether a company is a "good" or a "bad" citizen may thus be answerable in part by exploring such relationships, not with abstract norms of justice in view but rather with this question in mind: Is there an *ecological balance* in the company's way of living with its environment?

Ecological balance does not require a company to contribute more than it receives from its environment. The emphasis, therefore, is not on "social responsibilities" alone, but on rights as well as duties—if one must put it in legal-ethical terms—or, more realistically, on a healthy and self-sustaining organic interchange in the ecosystem as a whole. The biologists, speaking of balance in a biological ecosystem, do not make *ethical* distinctions between predators and nonparasitic animals and plants. But they do note the fact that disequilibrium in a biological ecosytem can be caused by the extraordinary success with which certain predators kill off their prey, thus exterminating themselves by exterminating their food supply. In this way an otherwise balanced biological ecosystem may simply disappear from the face of the earth, as in the case of a wilderness destroyed by the introduction of plants or animals that cannot be checked by natural countergrowths.

In the same way we can think of a social ecosystem, as Boulding has suggested, which may not be so complete in itself as a self-contained biological ecosystem, but is still subject to substantially the same laws of survival. A social ecosystem may decline and disappear because of the heedless exploitation and exhaustion of certain key natural resources. It may also suffer from imbalance among human groups, particularly as to their respective inputs and outputs affecting the system as a whole. Ecological succession, too, may leave redundant forms of human organization to die on the vine, as it were. Epochal changes in the needed stores of knowledge and in ideas, in the ecologically necessary ways of accumulating and using capital, and in the growth and distribution of human populations may all affect the equilibrium of a given ecosystem.

The modern corporation as an institution seems to have become a "natural" element in the contemporary ecosystems of the Western industrialized world. Particular companies, however, are born, grow, continue to survive, or die, in environments which may be benign or hostile. Measured in geologic time, corporations are no more secure against decay and death than animals and plants. Their place in the earth's local and global social ecosystems is assured only insofar as they continue to be natural elements therein. We may like to assume that man's will and his ideals can determine the outcome. Within limits this is so. The corporate form of organization is itself an artifice of man, and executive decisions can surely determine the corporate course in very stormy seas. Still, the corporation was in many respects a natural response to the needs of the times. The social ecosystem that brought it forth keeps it here, and may eventually dispose of it, is controlled by natural laws of which we know little.

The decision powers of the corporate executive are limited, ecologically speaking, by forces which may be largely beyond the control of policy-makers. Wise policy in running a large corporate enterprise is directed toward steering the ship rather than controlling the winds and the sea. The able business executive tries to capture in his imagination the nature of the environment in which the corporate struggle to survive is carried on. Perhaps one would speak more realistically of a capture of this environmental picture by the *corporate* imagination, since it does involve a collective effort by many specialized minds.

The environment to be envisaged is both physical and biological. In the nuclear age which we have so recently entered, the entire social ecosystem is subject to radical disequilibrium and disruption on a scale never before contemplated—this because of potential changes in the physical environment. The nonhuman biological environment, too, is subject to radical change in short periods of time from other causes. Depletion of living natural resources and the necessary exploitation of still unexploited resources (such as those in the seas) will profoundly affect many enterprises now dependent upon a passing phase in ecological succession. The dimensions of our social ecosystem, until now confined to space at or very near the earth's surface, are changing so rapidly that new opportunities—and new limitations—lie just around the corner. Corporate enterprise as a whole will be affected by these changes, and in some companies the consequences may appear very soon. They may be catastrophic; or they may be providential—from the standpoint of their owners. In the grand succession of ecological change the probable costs and rewards to individual persons and particular corporate entities will not affect the total outcome very much.

There are nevertheless certain areas of corporate policy in which degrees of wisdom can be decisive in adjusting to the environment, and even in effecting beneficial changes. It is in these matters that we can more profitably discuss the impact of corporate policy on human values and assess the character of corporate citizenship. Let us consider, as illustrative, one of the major policy areas in which corporate governors can reasonably be expected to exercise good ecological judgment as the path toward ethical judgment.

Intergroup Conflict and Antitrust Policy

THE PROBLEM WE SHALL EXPLORE lies in the general area of intergroup conflict and mutual aid, two aspects of survival in the social ecosystem in which a company lives. As in biological ecosystems of plants and animals, so in social ecosystems the twin principles of conflict and cooperation apply. An understanding of these principles as they affect the survival of a given company is a prerequisite for wise policy.

A company is unavoidably—and perhaps beneficially—in conflict with other human groups in the environment. Competition, in the classical economic meaning of the term, is presumably a beneficial form of conflict. But the classical doctrine did not posit beneficial consequences to the competitors as the major norm. Competition is rivalry in which the fittest survive on a higher level and progress "in the long run," regardless of short-run particular losses. But competition is rivalry in accordance with the rules of the game, and in a competitive system an economy is subjected to rules of the game in the form of antitrust laws.

When we considered, in the last chapter, the legal and marketing functions of a corporation, we indicated as an important policy area that of compliance with the antitrust laws. In fact, however, policy on antitrust is of general and fundamental importance to the enterprise as a whole, and is intimately related to all corporate survival in our social ecosystem. This seems not to have been generally recognized in the governments of certain of our largest and most respectable corporations, even though formal policies had introduced into their own governmental systems the requirement of compliance with antitrust policy.

Compliance, to be sure, has been variable. Thus we have had deliberate violations of the antitrust laws for years by some executives of large electrical companies. The written directive policies of these companies, which forebade contravention of either the spirit or the letter of those laws, were violated. These illegal activities were carefully hidden from company top commands and from public prosecutors. The condemned acts were criminal—conspiratorial price fixing—and they were also inimical to the interests of the companies themselves.

In some of these companies the condemned activities were discovered prior to public prosecution, and company disciplinary action was undertaken. Other companies took no disciplinary action, on the ground that public penalties were sufficient for the purpose. The companies pleaded guilty on certain charges and entered *nolo contendere* pleas as to others. Some of the executives involved served jail sentences and paid heavy fines. The companies themselves were subjected to civil suits brought by hundreds of their customers—mostly public-utility companies and municipalities—who sought treble damages under the terms of the federal antitrust laws.

These cases raised numerous issues of both public and corporate policy. On the one hand, there were renewed protests against the public antitrust policy in general or at least in its present form, thus raising more basic questions about the nature of a competitive system in the presence of huge industrial corporations. On the other hand, there were questions of corporate governance, especially as to the nature and scope of the authority to govern recalcitrant executives and as to the locus of responsibility in the corporate structure for illegal acts of executive employees.

As to the first matter—the public policy of antitrust—it is obvious that doubt prevails in the highest quarters of corporate governments about the wisdom of the policy. The practicability of antitrust in the long run, in a mixed economy so heavily dependent as ours on large corporate enterprises, is questioned. Yet the Sherman Act, together with similar statutes, has almost the status of fundamental law in the United States; and although its wisdom has always been challenged by a critical minority, the law still stands as an element in the competitive system.

The competitive system, assumed as fundamental in the Sherman Act, is a structured system despite its unplanned growth. Implicit in this structure are the institutions of private property, contract, profit making, and freedom of trade. In the institution of private property, law and usage determine who is to hold and control the resources of an economy. Contractual usages determine the ways in which persons and resources are combined for productive purposes. Profit making is a reward for producing marketable goods and services. So long as industry is open to all who want to venture into the competitive game, arbitrary prices at unreasonable levels can be avoided and monopolistic practices can be curbed. But the curbing is not automatic. It requires restraint by public government. This, at least, is the rationale of antitrust. The antitrust policy is an indispensable adjunct to a competitive system characterized by freedom of trade.

Now the attacks upon this rationale have been legion and are not new. They have never succeeded in reversing public antitrust policy *in principle*, but they do not recede in vigor. Nor do they fail consistently in practice. The legalized exemptions from exposure to the competitive system are numerous, and they cover increasingly large sectors of the economy. Subsidies, protective tariffs, licensing, "fair trade" or resale-price maintenance laws, collective-bargaining statutes, patent and copyright laws, the extension of the public-utility concept of business—all these are examples of limiting factors that constrict the field of free trade. The outright repeal of the Sherman and Clayton Acts would win little public support. But, as Justice Holmes once observed in skeptical comment on antitrust, combinations arise out of the nature of things, since the primitive state of war by each against all is not necessarily a desirable pattern for an economy. Today in the chambers of corporate governments there is increasing concern about the rationale on which these basic statutes rest. No company has rescinded its own policy of compliance with antitrust. Some responsible executives, however, would like to see more active efforts to revise or abolish the basic statutes.

Self-interest is by no means the only explanation for this concern, which is also shared by many students of the problem who have no ax to grind. The coexistence of huge private corporate enterprise and *free* enterprise in a competitive economy may be untenable. The demise of one or both may be predictable—and not on preferential grounds, but because of the inner forces and the environmental conditions slowly working in the ecosystem as a whole. Few can say with assurance what should be done about it. Certainly this is by no means an issue to be left to the lawyers and the economists alone. It is an issue that runs deeper into problems of international rivalry at political as well as economic levels, and into problems of population-resources ratios.

It runs also to basic problems of governance in a pluralistic society. It becomes a problem of governance because it raises questions of corporate authority dispersal and authority concentration. At the threshold there is the problem of managerial authority over marketing processes, and, beyond that, over the resources of a whole society. When corporate governors are willing to face that fact squarely, together with the implications for human values, they can then hope to deal constructively with antitrust policy in public government and in their own corporate households. The same can, of course, be said of public governors, and especially Congress. But we are concerned here with private governments, on whose shoulders rests a considerable share of the responsibility for the shaping of public policy itself. And, in any case, the private corporate governments of this country must face the problem of policy within their own bailiwicks.

It is significant that during the court proceedings in antitrust cases brought against twenty-nine electrical companies, one of the judges declared, on behalf of the Department of Justice, that the federal government had not charged and did not claim that any member of the board of directors of one of the companies had knowledge of the conspiracies pleaded in the indictment. Nor, according to the judge, did the government claim that any of the directors or the president of the company had personally authorized or ordered the commission of any of the acts charged in the indictment. The president and board of that company were not indicted, but the company was fined and several subordinate executives were fined and imprisoned.

In the press it was asked: "Who runs the store?" Was that company not governed by a responsible board and executive management? The federal judge who sat on these cases declared that, while the real blame lay at the doorsteps of the corporate defendants and those who guided and directed the policies of these corporations, there was insufficient evidence to convict persons in the highest echelons. It would be naïve, he said, to believe that the violations of law, so long persisted in and affecting so large a segment of the industry and involving so many millions, were facts unknown to those responsible for the conduct of the corporations involved. At stake, he added, was the survival of the kind of economy under which America had grown to greatness, the free-enterprise system. The conduct of the corporate and individual defendants alike had "flagrantly mocked that image" as "a free world alternative to state control or socialism and eventual dictatorship."

These were hard words, coming as they did from a member of the federal bench. Judge J. Cullen Ganey described the case as a "shocking indictment of a vast section of our economy." But it was also an indictment of corporate governance in these firms. While most of the public commentary on the case emphasized the failure of business ethics, little of it went to the question of managerial authority. On neither point was there much penetration beneath the surface of these issues. On the issue of business ethics it is not enough to deplore noncompliance with the law, to chide management for allegedly condoning this in subordinates, or to denounce the "organization man" who goes along with price-fixing and bid-rigging conspiracies which he knows are wrong but which cannot be avoided if he hopes to retain status and a big salary. These points are less interesting to the corporate ecologist than a really bedrock debate about antitrust policy itself would be. And less interesting, too, than an inquiry into the evident breakdown of the governmental process in the offending corporations.

The time has come for penetrating inquiry on both points; and one can reasonably expect business leaders to participate in such a debate, and even to initiate it. They need to do so not because they have some hazy notions of social responsibility in these matters, but because the very survival of corporate enterprise in its present form is at stake. It may well be that corporate enterprise can neither make its proper contribution to the social ecosystem nor draw sustenance from it with a structure of antitrust law as it stands. Nor does it seem likely, given the increasing demands of public policy on corporate governments, that the latter can avoid tighter authority structures in their own governmental systems.

It will require boldness of leadership on the part of corporate executives to tackle these problems openly, comprehensively, and with breadth of vision. The temper of the times is such that a bold approach may be far from popular. There is much talk today about more permissiveness in corporate governance, about the need for decentralization and delegation of authority, and for introduction of democratic processes in all private governmental sectors. The trend, moreover, is toward more, not less, public control in these sectors. These trends may or may not be morally attractive, depending on one's preferences. The real question is whether they are ecologically sound.

Social Change and the Norms of Corporate Policy

THE SOLUTIONS OF SUCH PROBLEMS as these cannot be reached by repetition of clichés about freedom of enterprise and other old saws drawn from the conventional wisdom of another day. The world moves on. We have a mixed economy, and one that must adjust to new trading relationships with strong common markets abroad. National defense makes enormous demands on the private sectors, converting them into quasi-public sectors in fact if not in theory. And the force of technological change which has revolutionized military strategy is bound to revolutionize social strategy in other fields. In the process, the social function of business enterprise will change, and with this change will come new conceptions of corporate enterprise.

The changing conceptions of the corporate role in society will have profound effects on business ethics, and therefore on the norms that will enter into the formulation of corporate policies in every functional field of work in the corporate enterprise. These new norms will have originated not so much in the internal restructuring of business organizations for the more efficient achievement of the traditional goals of profitability and productivity, though such restructuring will be far from insignificant. They will have originated rather in the external demands on business organizations as organic elements in a larger social structure struggling for survival in a global environment that sets its own independent demands.

We are not talking here about an economic interpretation of history in Marxian style. The environmental demands upon society, and therefore on the business corporation, are more than economic; nor are the immanent, indwelling forces of the whole social ecosystem statable in the Marxian-Hegelian terms of dialectical materialism. The poverty of this communistic analysis of social evolution is already becoming apparent even on the other side of the Iron Curtain, and on this side our own economic determinists are a waning influence. Many of the determinative forces at work are noneconomic, but even with respect to economic forces alone there is certain to be a revisionist trend that will leave its mark eventually on the thinking of corporate policy-makers. Some of the indications of this trend will be observed in contemporary events not to be underrated when one considers the changing relationships of corporation and community. We list some of them here as illustrative only and not as a systematic or exhaustive account.

The Impact of Science

PREOCCUPATION WITH ESTHETIC and ethical values is giving way—and on a global scale—to the search for truth about animate and inanimate nature, "the way things are," and the *possibilities* of achieving desired goals under scientifically observable conditions. The great conflicts of interests between peoples and cultures, and between traditional and developing societies, are more likely to arise when we debate the "good" life or a "good" society or what we think is beautiful or ugly. It is hard to transcend one's own cultural complex in such debate. The search for scientific truth about possibilities is debate of another order. One of the great things about the sciences is that they have in them the possibility of effective unambiguous communication on a completely world-wide scale. Decisive for the growth of science is a climate favorable for the unprejudiced study of things as they are, yet one in which the idea of progress in history prevails. A combination of belief in the possibility of progress and respect for the pursuit of scientific truth underlies our own culture in its most "successful" stages of development—successful, that is to say, in making the ecological adjustments required for survival.

We Americans are apt to attribute leadership in the free world to other causes. The businessman, in particular, may attribute it to the "free-enterprise system." But the economic system itself is part of a larger ecosystem shaped historically by political conceptions of freedom, and not least those of the Age of Enlightenment during which our constitutional foundations were laid. It was an age of gifted scientists who probed not only the nature of the physical universe but the nature of society as well.

The climate of free doubt and free inquiry is one of the essential conditions of political and economic freedom. Business ethics can best be understood in relation to the preservation of such a climate, a point well understood by those corporate executives who now see the necessity of helping to preserve it through corporate support of scientific and educational institutions. For the same reasons, however, there is need for corporate support of free inquiry in a larger sense: the firm stand of industrial leaders against obscurantist movements, against the suppression of freedom of utterance in private as well as public sectors, and against the diversion of social resources away from activities which contribute to the growth of new knowledge.

The Impact of Political Change

THE ETHICAL BASES of corporate-community relationships are now undergoing epochal change because of the passing of old and the emergence of new conceptions of "community." This change has both political and nonpolitical aspects, though the two are closely related. The political map of the world has been largely redrawn since World War II. Scores of new sovereign states have been born, especially in Africa and Asia, while the spheres of influence of imperial European nations have shrunk. While the Soviet empire has expanded at a rapid rate in the half-century since the Russian Revolution, the "West" has now begun to take on the contours of a counterpoised force of remarkable dimensions. These changes are due in part to industrial growth and commercial interdependence, but also to the technological revolution in communications.

We began, after the war, to form an Atlantic Community as a bar to communist imperialism. That community had its economic base in the Marshall Plan and its military foundations in NATO. For the first time in our history the United States became allied permanently with the Western European powers for both economic and military defense of the free world. And in less than two decades after the war our commitments on behalf of the free world have led to alliances in every part of it, extending far beyond the Atlantic Community. The "Fortress America" concept has given way to United States leadership of the free world, with vast implications for the American corporation.

When we talk now of corporate-community relationships it is utterly unrealistic to confine our attention to plant-community relationships or even to the wider relations of a company with state and national governments. The real community from which large corporate enterprises draw their sustenance and to which they have correlative responsibilities is one of intercontinental dimensions. The scope and character of the new "community" environment of corporate enterprise are only slowly being recognized by executives. They will fail or refuse to understand this environment at their peril. Already it is clear that an issue decisive of our survival as a free nation has to be faced: the forging of Western unity through appropriate trading relationships between the new Common Market in Europe and our own long-established common market—now a federation of fifty states.

The moral imperatives that will guide corporate policy in the future, in respect of corporate-community relations, will need to be drawn with such considerations as these in mind. The unity of the West, not only in its economic ties but also in its military and political solidarity, will be primary conditions of corporate survival. Many relatively small enterprises may be able to prosper regardless of the solution of these larger problems of public policy. It is hard to see how corporate executives in the big companies can avoid facing these problems, simply as a matter of business policy.

The Impact of Economic Growth

CORPORATE SURVIVAL depends upon economic growth, not only in the national community but in the entire free world and especially among the developing new nations, most of which lie in the southern hemisphere. There is thus a North-South problem of economic growth as well as the East-West confrontation of competing communist and noncommunist economic systems. The ethical imperatives shaping corporate policy will be determined in part by the position which corporate boards and executive managers take on issues of public policy concerning economic growth.

On the East-West issue, Abram Bergson's recent study [2] of the Russian growth rate is instructive. He finds that, while the Russian claims to a growth rate of 9 or 10 per cent are exaggerated, they are not so greatly exaggerated as some have thought. He estimates that during the early 1950's the Russian growth rate was 7.6 per cent. For the years 1955–1958 it was 7 per cent or less. In the future the rate is likely to slow down to about 6 per cent a year. The growth rate in the United States has been far less than this, while in some of the spectacularly expanding economies (Japan and Germany, for example) it has been far greater.

The principal reason for the faster rate of growth in the Soviet economy, according to Bergson, has been political control over the rate of investment. A very large part of the gross national product is invested by the Soviet government; in the United States, market forces mainly determine what share of GNP is to be invested and what part spent for other purposes. It is an open question whether, in our own economy, we can achieve and maintain the growth rate we want without more nonmarket investment controls. Careful analysis [3] seems to indicate that American consumers may be spending their country into economic stagnation. Economic growth in this country has probably been dangerously slowed down by the limited availability of savings.

Savings are needed to finance added plant and equipment as well as to replace worn-out or obsolescent capital stock. Without savings the nation's productive capacity tends to remain static, with implications not only for the health of corporate enterprise but also for the strength and security of the United States as leader of the Western world. Net capital formation in current prices declined from 13 per cent of the net national product in 1869 to 1888 to less than 10 per cent in recent decades, according to the most comprehensive studies. The patterns of American spending encourage higher and higher per-capita consumption, with little prospect of substantial increases in personal savings and therefore of a larger supply of savings available for capital investment.

The commonly held view that greater consumption and less saving are needed to expand the nation's economy stands at odds with such conclusions as these, however. Consumer caution and an increased propensity to save have been viewed with alarm in some quarters because of the feared effect on "recovery." If more dollars are channeled into savings, so the argument goes, fewer goods will be bought and then we shall be unable to consume the output of our present capacity, to say nothing of an expanded plant. Even now, with production and personal income at record levels, some 15 to 20 per cent of our manufacturing capacity lies idle.

This argument is not invulnerable. Others say that a higher rate of investment will stimulate economic activity and in itself expand demand and purchasing power. Economic growth, however, can certainly be combined with a high savings rate. In Japan, where the rate of growth has recently approached 9 per cent—as against less than 3 per cent for the United States—the rate of savings is three times ours. In 1960 the Japanese set aside 35 per cent of their GNP for investment.

We do not attempt to resolve the issue here. Obviously, it is one that requires more than rigorous economic analysis, however. The basic question is what economic growth means to public and corporate policy-makers, what we want to achieve through it, and what must be done at both public and private governmental levels to achieve the desired results. One purpose is a strengthened Western world in the East-West conflict; another is a successful attack on the North-South problem—that is to say, a strategic move toward converting the revolution of rising expectations in the southern hemisphere into a constructive rather than a destructive force.

Conclusions

THE TRUE NATURE of good corporate citizenship is to be found in corporate-community relationships. But today those relationships are more and more difficult to define, mainly because the nature of "community" is difficult to grasp.

The community of which a given corporate enterprise is a part can be conceived in ecological terms. There are organic relationships between the corporation and the social ecosystem of which it is a part. Whether the corporate enterprise constitutes a healthy part of the system and contributes to balance in the system is always a basic issue for corporate policymakers. They have to be concerned as much with balance in the system as a whole as they are with the internal, ordinary, run-of-the-mill business problems which must be solved in order to keep the corporate organism healthy.

The scope and characteristics of the larger community, or social ecosystem, in which an enterprise survives and flourishes, or decays and dies, cannot be understood today unless one takes a global view. Certainly a nationalistic position alone will not suffice, for the national community—the United States—is irreversibly involved with much larger aggregates. The United States, as the leader of the free world, has at the same time had to face the facts of interdependence among very large groups of nations. The fact of interdependence—political, economic, and military—is probably too little recognized and acted upon at the level of corporate government. If it were to be recognized, then the problem of corporate citizenship would be less difficult to solve.

Finding the path of "right conduct" in corporate policy is not so much a matter of discovering a Corporate Decalogue. One must not, of course, discount the teleological elements of corporate policy-making. There are ideal goals for the free society in which we live that cannot be alien to the thinking of a "hardheaded" business executive. But hardheadedness has its place. Our point here is that orientation to the realities of running a business includes a realistic picture in men's minds of what that world outside actually is, and that the epochal changes occurring there will inevitably be reflected in the policies of a company which survives.

CHAPTER *15*

Corporate Justice

THE NORMS OF CORPORATE POLICY are not drawn from natural law, as some "brooding omnipresence in the sky," nor from the great books of theological and ethical literature. Corporate justice cannot be found in a neatly codified form in some Corporate Decalogue. The standards of right conduct for corporate governors are in practice set by rather more mundane processes. The goals to be pursued by executive action are determined mainly by resolving clashes of interests so that common courses of action can be pursued on the basis of compromise.

Corporate Justice as Compromise

ONE SEES THE DYNAMICS of corporate governance in this constant process of resolving the competing claims of various contributors to the work of establishing and maintaining a large corporate enterprise. The observer of this process focuses attention primarily upon the major functional kinds of work ordinarily done in such an enterprise. These functional areas appear clearly in what we have called the span of corporate policy. In each functional field there are crucial policy issues that require executive attention at the highest levels of corporate governments. In resolving these issues, directors and executive managers must be guided, in the first instance, by a judicious weighing of contributor-claimant interests. Such interests range all the way from those which are internal to the organization to those which are active outside of it. Internally, there are highly specialized groupings of the organization's personnel: the executive groups in various functional departments, the subordinate employees in more or less complex chains of command, and, at the top, the stockholders' representatives who sit on the board. External to the administrative organization are the stockholders themselves, the corporation's creditors, the customers, the suppliers, the competitors, and the general public. The stockholders are, of course, not external to the *enterprise*, though they are clearly external to the organization which sustains the enterprise as a going concern. In one way or another, all of these contributor-claimant groups make demands upon the top command of the organization; and at that critical point most of the competing claims are resolved by decisions on corporate policy.

The guiding principles which determine the direction of policy at this critical point are derived largely by empirical methods. Corporate governors, like public governing bodies, try to "balance the interests" of the competing groups, and in doing so they engage in a complicated system of bargaining. Corporate policy, like public policy, is thus mainly the outcome of bargained compromises. But at best it is far more than this. Ideally, there is a general interest that has to be grasped by the minds and hearts of the so-called interest-balancers. There is such a thing as public interest as a basis for public policy, and the public interest is not identical with the compromise of special interests. Similarly, in corporate governance there is a general interest for the corporate community that is not identical with the complex of bargains struck at the level of top corporate command.

The Public Interest and Corporate Community Interest

THE EXISTENCE OF SUCH a public interest, or corporate community interest, is often denied. Yet in the search for Justice—whether in the large letters of the state or in the smaller letters of the corporate community—one can hardly be satisfied with an answer that identifies politics with "deals" or corporate governance with compromise. Categorical imperatives stated in grand abstractions do not meet the need for other elements in the justice of public and corporate policy. But there are important sources for the norms of equity and fair dealing beyond the limited arena of interest conflict.

In the preceding chapter we examined some of these sources with respect to corporate relations with the more inclusive social environment. In the present chapter we shall examine some of these sources with respect to intracorporate relations—that is to say, within the corporate community itself. By the corporate community we mean then the administrative organization of an enterprise. It comprehends not only the directors, the executive managers, and other personnel who give their full time to running a business, but also the basic stockholder interests. In this chapter we shall inquire into the possibilities of finding certain ethical norms for corporate policy governing relationships among these groups in the corporate community elsewhere than in the bargaining process or balancing of interests. As to corporate relations with the larger community, we have seen that ecological considerations play an important role.

In these external relationships, it is true that ecological considerations can be interpreted simply as a case of enlightened self-interest. Prudent regard for the environmental conditions of corporate growth and survival is not necessarily the same as pursuit of the Good, the True, and the Beautiful by corporate policy-makers. But perhaps it is as near as one can reasonably expect them to come to a pursuit of justice in the abstract. Corporate intelligence work in clarifying the environmental conditions for business success is becoming more demanding as markets extend beyond continental to hemispheric and global dimensions. Perhaps the most substantial contributors to corporate justice in the abstract today are precisely those who strive to understand the political, social, and economic characteristics of the great society so rapidly emerging. National survival and, indeed, the defense of the West will depend heavily upon the gearing in of private enterprise with the larger purposes of free societies in our epochal struggle against tyranny.

The search beyond bargaining for norms of policy in corporate internal relationships may be illustrated by considering the two most fundamental types of relationship: those between stockholders and the corporate governing group, and those between employees and the managerial elite. In both cases, no doubt, a rough kind of justice is done in the normal course of business operations, simply by the bargaining process. But in the politics of compromise the long view is too often obscured. In the two kinds of relationship to be considered here, corporate policy-makers need the vision to see their decision making as institution building. Social institutions which preserve human values fundamental to a free society can be buttressed—or undermined—by the kinds of corporate policy adopted in the relationships we are to consider.

Stockholding and the Institution of Private Property

THE RIGHTS AND DUTIES of stockholders have been widely debated in recent decades. The status of stockholders in a particular enterprise can ordinarily be determined by prevailing legal norms and the bargaining position of various share-owner groups. With the wide dispersion of corporate share ownership, however, larger issues arise. They touch at length the question of private property as a social institution.

Shareholders, in the opinion of some critics, are a group that enjoys indefensible privileges. James F. Lincoln, who heads the Lincoln Electric Company of Cleveland, thinks that

American business is in trouble because it overcharges the consumer, overpays the stockholder, and treats the wage-earner unfairly.[1] The usual absentee stockholder, he insists, is treated with far too much consideration. This stockholder contributes nothing to the efficiency of the operation. He buys stock today and sells it tomorrow, takes little interest in the company, and may not even know what it makes. Why, asks Lincoln, should he be rewarded with big dividends?

At the other extreme stands the argument that management's major responsibility is precisely that of maximizing profits for stockholders, since the corporation is nothing but the instrument of those who own it. It is said to be an instrument of private property and completely responsible to private property, and not at all responsible to "society" at large or to the great variety of claimants who beat a path to its doors—frequently much faster and more effectively than the stockholders do—demanding a "fair share" of the corporate usufruct. Thus, Kelso and Adler, urging a "Capitalist Revolution" to convert our presently "mixed capitalism" into a "completely capitalist society," would restore to shareholders "their full powers and rights as the owners of capital and the employers of management."[2] Capital, not labor, they say, is the major producer of wealth.

Few business executives would find either of these arguments attractive. Both arguments, however, are made by stanch defenders of a capitalist as against a socialistic and collectivist economic system. There are obviously a good many different opinions among "conservative" businessmen and economists about the role of stockholders in a corporate enterprise. It is one thing to pay lip service to the owners of the stock in a corporate enterprise, and another thing to determine—in particular cases—what they deserve to get out of it because they hold pieces of paper that represent property rights. The more basic question is really what kind of property right those pieces of paper stand for. The argument, at its roots, gets into the institution of private property and the effect of the corporate system on that institution.

PRIVATE PROPERTY AND THE CORPORATE SYSTEM

The role of stockholders—quite specifically, the relationship between management and holders of share certificates—thus becomes at bottom a deeply ethical issue. The institution of private property certainly lies at the foundation of our whole social system. If it be true, as is now increasingly urged, that the institution of private property is undergoing fundamental change as a result of the corporate system, then one must ask what the norms of corporate policy should be when the management-stockholder relationship is involved.

There can be no doubt about the premises of corporate policy when direct attack on the institution of private property is involved. Public policy, for example, that seems to be headed in the direction of socialization of the economy will be opposed by corporate executives. Collectivism in the form of public ownership and control of enterprise would amount to an attack on the institution of private property in such vast sectors of the economy as to raise the gravest problems about maintaining a free society. Yet the large, publicly held business corporation is a kind of private collectivism; the wide dispersion of stock ownership has preserved the form but perhaps not the substance of private ownership in these great private collectivities. Private property, originally in the hands of millions of persons who owned it, passes into the collective treasury of great companies, where the property rights of the original owners become remarkably attenuated. Personal control over the property is exchanged for collective control at a managerial center over which the stock-owner has very little control.

This separation of ownership and control was, of course, the necessary condition for the emergence of corporate enterprise, was understood in the beginning by investors as a necessary condition, and has never been disputed as a basic condition for the phenomenal industrial development of all economically advanced countries. In capitalist (or, if one pleases, "mixed capitalist") economies the merging of private capital into the great private collectivities—the corporations—never in principle extinguished the private-property character of the capital so merged. Private property in the form of savings was thus exchanged for certificates of share ownership and not, as in communistic regimes, expropriated by public governmental agencies and merged without trace into nationalized operations. The share-owner has a negotiable instrument that is his, and the merged property, though transferred to a pool under corporate ownership and control, is still private property in the sense that it is not lost in Leviathan's maw. The share-owner, moreover, still has some power over its use—though the nature and extent of this power are not easily defined, and their definition is one of the basic problems of our political economy.

Most stockholders are far less concerned, however, about the nature of this power—a question of corporate governance—than about the value of their equity in terms of earnings, appreciation, and salability. The greater concern about this latter aspect of private property in corporate shares is shown in the emphasis during the past few decades on securities markets, the regulation of brokers and exchanges, and the disclosure of information about corporate financing. On these matters, legislators have been active. But as to the internal governance of corporations they have been relatively inactive. There has been little concern, that is to say, about preserving the nexus of power (and corresponding responsibility) between stockholders and corporate managements.

Perhaps there is little that can be done by legislative and administrative action in public governments to tighten up that nexus and to reinvigorate the institution of private property in our corporate system. A shareholder's confidence that his place within the system is secure, a confidence based squarely on the feeling of undiluted ownership in enterprises through ownership of stock, can perhaps be restored only by appropriate action in the private governments of these enterprises. It is fair to say that in the functional area of corporation finance there is no more urgent problem than this. Corporate policy on stockholder relations has to date skated along on the surface of this problem. Elaborate plans for huge annual stockholder meetings; beautiful brochures for transmitting annual reports to share-owners; intensive campaigns to extend shareholding to millions more of the population and thus establish a so-called "people's capitalism"; executive oratory on these and related themes—all of these techniques merely bypass the central issue.

Individual property ownership simply is no longer what it was when a man was the master of a domain that he could see, the boss of a field or a shop that was indisputably his, the owner of tools that he possessed physically. He now looks to a complex of contracts, equities, and expectancies over which he has very little control.[3] He may enjoy many material advantages unknown to his forbears; but, though his security may be greater than theirs was, he is poorer than they were in the tangible wealth he controls directly. Property meant real assets to them; to him it means promises: security, mortgages, bonds, bankbooks, and paper money—symbols of ownership but not actual possession of things symbolized.[4] These symbols are "law-born entities," whose ability to command control over the things behind the symbols depends on the survival of the highly complex system of public and private government which sustains them.[5] In neither public nor corporate policy are the conditions for sustaining these symbols clearly stated, spelled out, and made the subject of continuous review.

If these conditions were to be so stated and subjected to constant, penetrating study with an eye to preserving the institution of private property intact, there might be less concern than there is today for the graver implications of separating ownership from control and use of private property in large corporate enterprises.

"Private" property has never, of course, been completely private in the sense of total exclusion of external claims on what one possesses. The separation of ownership from control was not a novelty introduced by the corporate system. The feudal system was an outstanding historical example of this separation; intricate systems of subinfeudation left in the hands of subtenants the real possession and use of lands which tenants-in-chief and kings "owned." In modern times the claims of public governments greatly qualify the private character of property to which title is held by nonpublic persons. If taxes are not paid on property, the sovereign may seize it and may otherwise claim it for public purposes under the power of eminent domain. Public governments may impose many restrictions on the use of private property, as in zoning, building codes, nondiscrimination laws, conservation laws, laws on national agricultural policy, and restrictions on transfers of property across political boundaries.

With the rise of industrialism the need for large aggregations of capital led to the pooling of private owners' funds in corporate enterprises which took on many of the characteristics of public governments in their controls over the pooled properties. Common ownership and management of capital aggregations in the corporation, because of the governmental structure of corporate enterprise, led to wider separation of ownership and control than in such other forms of pooling as partnerships and limited partnerships. Indeed, the advantage of the corporate form over these other forms of business organization lay in the greater power of corporate managements over the pooled capital. The important traditional right of a property-owner to manage and control his private property was thus lost, even though what he got in return—certain claims on returns from the enterprise—was more advantageous to him. As students of the modern corporation have pointed out, the result has been a system of corporate *power* which has largely replaced, at least in the large corporations with widely dispersed shareholding, a system of pooled private property. The holders of the power are corporate managers. They are thus the governors of private polities.

While it is true that these private corporate polities are theoretically reared on the foundations of private property rights, the ownership at the base has become highly fragmented. "The common stockholder today is, by and large, a claim holder, with legal rights to some of the fruits of the enterprise when, as, and if the directors agree that the tree is ripe for shaking."[6] Upon liquidation he has rights in the assets after senior claims have been paid off. Creditor groups, holding secured and unsecured loans to a corporation, through such techniques as bankruptcy proceedings, mortgage foreclosures, and enforcement of contractual obligations giving them a voice in control of the enterprise, may in fact exercise powers over corporate property that were traditionally regarded as qualities of the "real" owners.

Separation of ownership of private property from the physical control of it, however, has gone much further today than this. A large part of the savings of individual persons, originally held by them as private property in the traditional sense, is now merged in pooling arrangements that attenuate the nexus between a man and his property to extraordinary degrees. An owner of property in shares may hold a piece of paper that is not a claim against an aggregate of capital in a specific corporate enterprise, but merely a claim against a financial institution which holds other pieces of paper that are claims on capital aggregations in numerous corporate enterprises. The working capital in these enterprises is thus several removes distant from the holder of shares in, say, a pension or profit-sharing trust, an investment company, or a mutual fund.

MIGRANT MANAGERIAL POWER AND BENEFICIAL OWNERSHIP

The divorcement of management from beneficial ownership in these types of investment raises questions about the changing conception of the institution of private property under conditions of such fragmentation of property originally invested. The "passive recipient" shareholders grow in numbers every year while the power and prestige of managerial groups continue to wax. Attempts, on the one hand, to render the recipient shareholder less passive and, on the other hand, the managers more "responsible" are not very impressive. In this book we have been concerned mainly with the latter half of this problem—responsible government in a constitutionalized corporation. Some critics of the general trend we have just described will say that this solution of the problem is but a partial one at best, insisting rather on more stringent public regulation.

But if there is to be more stringent public regulation, what will be the ends sought, and what means will be appropriate to those ends? The present analysis suggests that one of the desirable ends to be pursued—whether in public or in corporate policy—is a revitalization of the idea of private property in its traditional sense. As people invest more and more of their savings in corporate enterprise, either directly in the form of common stock in aggregrates of working capital or indirectly in the form of investment in mutual and pension funds and the like, how can they be made to feel that the basic institution of private property is not being undermined?

The danger is not only in the "separated" power of the managerial class over property; share-owners themselves tend to lose that traditional sense of responsibility for the use of their property which was more than incidental to the institution of private property. Delegation of the rights of ownership has gone very far indeed; in return the share-owner expects income and security. But power follows the control of property, and control tends to pass into the hands of managers in the larger financial institutions.[7] These managers, and not the original investors, become the responsible parties simply because the power lies there and not in the shareholders. Yet their power, concentrated as it is, tends to be limited to specified service functions. Society focuses its attention on the real power centers for the purpose of seeing to it that these service functions are both limited and performed. The point is that attention is not focused at all on the original shareholders, who have neither much power nor much responsibility for the use of the great pools of private property to which they have contributed their savings. This alone is a loss to the vitality of a free society.

But, more particularly, the "migration of power"[8] that characterizes our corporate system as it evolves into a new kind of capitalism is a migration of controls into large financial institutions where the true capitalists—those who actually risk their own money in their own enterprises—are quite remote from the scene. Economic power, and with it responsibility for the use of property, thus tend to be drawn away from the generality of individual property-owners and into these institutions. That is why Father Harbrecht sees the transition away from "a society organized by individual property ownership and diffused power" toward one in which power, and not property ownership, is the organizing principle.[9] He calls the emerging social structure "the paraproprietal society," beyond property in the sense of ownership of tangible things. It is paraproprietal "because in it the connection between man and things, which is another way of saying property, is so attenuated that the fundamental function of property is not dominant, though it still serves a purpose. . . . Where once the concepts of property served the function of attaching things to men, they now serve the function of assigning powers over things [as in transferring control over property to others]."[10] The thing itself is not transferred, but power over it is. Things are not exchanged so much as power over things. Thus we pass from a property system to a power system.

In this transition there is no abandonment of the laws of property, nor is there a complete surrender of the power over property by people who are the original grantors of power. The latent resources of people rest partly in the basic laws of property inherent in our juridical system, and more importantly in the political institutions of democratic public government. There are reserved powers in the people which can be brought to bear both as public and private governmental mechanisms fail. It seems fairly certain that the public governmental mechanism will be used far more extensively than it has been in the past.

The latter alternative is not one that can be contemplated without considerable apprehension. People who become the beneficiaries of a paraproprietal society without any sense of operating its productive enterprises—because of their remoteness from the controls—are likely to make demands upon the fruits of enterprise which far exceed the supply. That is one great danger of excluding the great majority from any substantial participation in the control of pooled productive property, and of reducing to near zero their comprehension of the financial complexities of the system as a whole.

PROBLEMS OF CORPORATE FINANCIAL POLICY

All of this poses enormous problems in the area of corporate financial policy, with particular reference to stockholder relations. One group of problems concerns stockholder enlightenment: the presentation by management of a clear picture of the attenuated nature of share-owners' property rights with the transfer of controls to financial institutions. An accurate picture must, of course, first be drawn in the minds of managers themselves before it can be projected. A second and more basic set of problems concerns the changing character of managerial responsibilities to share-owners in productive enterprises, on the one hand, and, on the other, of mutual managerial responsibilities in the financial institutions and the productive enterprises whose equities are held in pension funds, mutual funds, investment trusts, banks, and insurance companies.

Clarification of the major issues in this latter category of problems is somewhat slow in coming. Robert Tilove [11] has suggested some of them. He has shown that financial institutions account for a major part of the total net purchases of common stock, and he believes that the significance of their aggregate holdings of common stock in the prime corporations can be expected to increase. He advocates disclosure by law of any effort by particular pension funds to acquire the stock of other companies of moderate size for the purpose of exercising control or influence, an effort that the trust companies resist. Because financial institutions generally own so much of the common stock in corporations, he thinks that there is a disquieting potential for control by such institutions, even though the trust companies that control the investment programs of most self-insured pension funds are anxious not to utilize that potential for various reasons.

But Tilove says that the trustees of pension funds, like other institutional investors, cast their proxies consistently on the side of company managements. Would it not be a more assiduous discharge of their duties as trustees if they were to abstain from voting on run-of-the-mill issues, he asks, leaving these to be decided by the individual stockholders? And should they not publicly disclose their votes on the more important issues? The interests of stockholders and management are not always the same. Self-insured pension funds, as he points out, are not the only potential source of concentrated economic control over corporate affairs; the problem is by no means new and is not limited to pension funds. The dramatic rate of their growth has highlighted the problem, since pension funds can conceivably accumulate enough assets to buy up significant parts of ownership in corporations. Interestingly enough, this practice has already begun.

The more general problem has excited less public attention. But, clearly, it presents to corporate managements everywhere issues of corporate financial policy that bear a direct relationship to the institution of private property as one of the foundations of economic freedom. The dynamics of corporate government in this area thus involves basic ethical issues for corporate directors and executive managers. The ethical issues tend to be overlaid by highly technical problems of corporation finance; that complicates the matter of bringing such issues into the arena of public discussion.

Employee Freedoms

THE SEARCH FOR NORMS of corporate policy in the field of employee relations, as in the case of stockholder relations, leads beyond bargaining processes. Collective bargaining has been one of the most important methods of arriving at principles of equity and fair dealing, at least with respect to blue-collar employees and some other unionized sectors of labor. But collective bargaining does not of itself meet the requirements of public interest, even where it is well established.[12] And with respect to nonunionized employees it cannot even be expected to do so. They must seek justice in other ways—by individual bargaining and through reliance on corporate policies over which they exercise little or no control.

Let it be emphasized at the start that when we speak here of employee freedoms we refer to the freedoms of all corporate employees, including those at managerial as well as nonmanagerial levels. Nor is the issue simply that of the Organization Man *versus* the Free Spirit untrammeled in any degree by structured work patterns. Nobody enjoys such complete freedom in a society so highly organized as ours. Yet there are fundamental freedoms, recognized in any free society, which must somehow be preserved regardless of where a man works. Freedom of inquiry, freedom of utterance, freedom to associate for lawful purposes, and freedom of religious and political beliefs must somehow be protected against arbitrary encroachment if the society which underwrites these values is to deserve the name of a free society.

Constitutionalism is alive in societies that provide procedural safeguards for these freedoms. It is moribund where the practical safeguards are neglected. And the safeguards, in a society based on constitutionalist principles, are to be found not only in the structure and processes of public government; they are substantial as well in the governance of private sectors. That, at least, has been the burden of much of our argument in this book, where we have been concerned with one of the most important private sectors: incorporated business enterprise.

We shall consider here, for illustrative purposes, but one of the employee freedoms: freedom of utterance. The guarding of this fundamental freedom has seldom been the subject of explicit and detailed corporate policy, and is still only peripherally touched by public policy so far as corporate governance is concerned. The law of collective bargaining does to some extent touch the issue in attempting to prevent coercive utterances that affect the bargaining process. But the subject reaches larger issues.

FREEDOM OF UTTERANCE

Liberty is not merely the absence of restraint by public governments. The definition of liberty as the absence of restraint, as the Handlins [13] have shown, is the product of historical conditions peculiar to political and social structures of the eighteenth and nineteenth centuries. We have become accustomed to think of our freedoms as constitutional guaranties protected mainly by restraints on federal and state governments. The literature on the subject is, thus, biased in its major emphasis upon these negative aspects. "To define liberties as unconnected negatives upon compulsion rules out of consideration the problem many men consider most pertinent of all, that of describing the attributes that make a society free." [14]

To the man or woman who joins a corporate enterprise as an employee—of whatever grade or rank—the meaning of liberty appears in the way one's life can be lived despite the necessary restrictions on one's action arising out of this vocational association. Certainly the bills of rights in state and federal constitutions are not the key to one's freedom of personal development on the job. Nor does one ordinarily expect to invoke restraints judicially on corporate governments in order to remove the bars to freedom of speech, of assembly, or of association. In fact, a man does not worry so much about what others are doing to check him as he does about opportunities to do the things that he wants to do.

Liberty for corporate employees is in this constructive sense positively encouraged by many enlightened managements. Opportunities for on-the-job training, educational pursuits on the outside, and recreational activities of all kinds—all at company expense—are increasingly the rule in large corporations. On the other hand, these are opportunities which usually are offered on relatively narrow grounds of corporate self-interest. "Employee satisfaction" is the measure of the success of such programs; or they are held to be justifiable as means of "personnel development" for better job performance, preparation for promotion to slots that have to be filled, the making of managerial material, and so on. This is not universally true, of course. But it is exceptional to find a company where "personnel development" is an end in itself and supported as such by company policy.

COMPANY POLICY ON EMPLOYEE FREEDOMS

A company policy on employee freedoms—a company bill of rights, as it were—is a rarity. Instead, one frequently encounters rules and regulations restricting liberty as a condition of employment. The assumption is, of course, that what is not prohibited can be done at an employee's discretion; but this is only a formalistic way of putting the matter for logical purposes. It is not the average employee's way of thinking about the scope of his own liberty. For many, liberty ends at nine and begins at five—that is, for the wage-earner without supervisory responsibilities. For others, and especially at higher managerial levels, liberty ends when the job begins. The absorption of one's life by the job, twenty-four hours a day and seven days a week, is not unusual, and in some organizations is the normal expectation. The compulsion is not necessarily company-centered; it may be employee-centered, too, as a fulfillment of some personal need.

Whatever the source of this compulsion, in the very nature of our highly organized society we need more than ever before to carve out areas of personal autonomy to ensure against undue encroachment on personal liberty by organizations. But that can best be done by a dual approach to the problem. On the one hand, it is certainly necessary to carry into private organizations the principles of public law concerning liberty *against* government: due process, bills of rights, and so on. On the other hand, a more positive approach is required: the conception of personal liberty as the development of personal attributes and powers in a man who is regarded as a being touched with some spark of divinity and capable of achievements that the Organization knows not of.

If this be considered a flight of fancy, let us note with some care the primitive stages of development in which we now stand with respect to employee freedoms. Only within recent decades have we overcome the dire effects of Anglo-American juridical notions of conspiracy as applied to organizing for collective-bargaining purposes. Freedom of association in this realm is even now strongly resisted in many companies, especially for the white-collar employees. But even if the battle were to be won there, this special kind of employee freedom would be an elementary step. It would be but a first step, at the bread-and-butter level, toward the liberal development of human virtues. Nor is freedom of association for collective bargaining the necessary and sufficient road to such a development.

The opportunity to stretch one's mind and to achieve one's creative capacities to the full depends upon unlimited freedom of inquiry, untrammeled association with colleagues anywhere who are engaged in creative work, freedom to write, and freedom to publish. Deliberate and systematic encouragement of such conditions through company policy is the positive approach to employee freedoms. But the obstacles that lie in the way are many. These obstacles are partly legal and partly a matter of the philosophical limitations of business leaders.

THE NECESSITY FOR INTELLECTUAL FREEDOM

To take the latter point first, it is evident that corporate enterprise in the future will depend more and more on the services of theoreticians: scholars and scientists in practically every field of learning. The "hardware" aspects of running a big business tend to become a good deal easier to man than the "software" side of research, planning, and controls. Business philosophy has heretofore been shaped largely by the production of things; the shift to service makes new demands on intellectual and creative capacities. The competition for people with these capacities is now becoming acute. One of the major problems of managing is the managing of scientific personnel. The old axioms of management do not seem to be applicable. New ways of recruiting, developing, and holding manpower have to be devised.

One of the difficulties in doing this arises from failure to conceive of employee freedoms in a positive way: the active and systematic encouragement of intellectual growth in the corps of corporate employees, not merely so as to serve a company better but also to develop Man Thinking, as Emerson defined the American scholar. For it is no longer true—if it ever was—that the only place for the scholar is the university; he is needed, and needed badly, in the business corporation, too. He is also needed in public governmental agencies, which now begin to complain that businesses entice him away with bigger salaries. In all three sectors—business, government, and university—the problem arises of setting up the conditions under which theoreticians can work.

LEGAL BARS TO INTELLECTUAL FREEDOM

In business corporations there are special legal problems that beset managements when they try to set up these conditions. Theoreticians want to write articles or books, give lectures, teach courses, and otherwise communicate with the intellectual world outside corporate walls. They must do so if they are to avoid intellectual stagnation, and they will in any case rebel against restrictions on communicational activities that are second nature to them. From a company's point of view, however, there are real problems here.

A company, in the first place, has certain very real responsibilities for statements made by its employees in certain sensitive areas. It may be liable for libel when such statements involve third parties. It may have tort responsibility when such statements can be construed as representing facts on which others might reasonably be expected to rely. When knowledge of the content of such statements can be imputed to the company, they may be used to prove the intent of the company. Where lobbying acts are applicable, employee statements may be construed as company statements regarding legislative proposals. A company, in other words, cannot avoid concern about its own responsibilities arising from freely circulated utterances of its employees when such utterances are made by employees on matters within the scope of their jobs.

It is true that a company could not reasonably be held responsible for what an employee does or says beyond the scope of his employment; but how much freedom does that leave him? Things done at the direction of a company, in its name, or during working hours are within the scope of employment. But for the intellectual worker it is hard to define the time during which ideas develop, and to distinguish between the contributions to his thinking which come from company association and those which come from elsewhere. Identification with a company in the public utterances of an employee may be necessary simply in order to ensure the direction of responses and to establish professional status. Yet such identification can entail company responsibilities. It may also fix company rights in his intellectual product, of which an employee may not be aware, thus raising the question of proprietary information.

THE PROBLEM OF ECONOMIC REWARDS

So, in the second place, there are problems for a company with respect to the economic rewards of an employee's intellectual product. Can he publish books and give lectures in the field of competence for which the company employs him, and receive remuneration on his own account? An extreme position would be that all fees and royalties must go into the company treasury, and that a substantial salary must suffice for compensation. This position means that the company owns the Man Thinking and not merely the time he gives to it under the contract of employment. Perhaps the rule would not apply to extracurricular activities, such as novels produced by a computer specialist or the paintings of an executive manager. But these exceptional cases leave unanswered the harder questions about scientific writing in one's own specialized field. In an economy based on respect for profitable enterprise, must a scientist choose between selling his mind for a fixed salary and free-lancing? Perhaps this is the inevitable dilemma of the organizational age, but it is not one that promises the best returns for intellectual work.

These economic aspects of employee freedom of utterance are not, however, the decisive ones. More important are the problems of clearance. An employee who does not have the urge to publish will seldom be disturbed by company rules for clearance of statements he may want to make publicly in the field of his special competence. In many of the functional kinds of work done in corporate enterprises, publication is neither a necessity nor a thing that occurs to an employee as desirable or even possible. But with the rapid growth of specialized functions of a highly intellectual character, communication with one's intellectual fraternity is a necessity—for reasons both of personal fulfillment and of company advantage. This is probably more clearly recognized in those functional areas where the disciplines are established—in law, in engineering, in accounting, for example. It is beginning to be recognized also in newer disciplines such as the science of management. But even in these fields company clearance can impose serious obstacles to employee freedom of utterance. A company lawyer, for example, or a specialist on marketing would be inhibited in publishing his views about antitrust policy.

The general tendency is toward caution on the part of company managements when freedom of speech and press is involved. The cautionary posture is well advised on legal grounds, for in public policy—reflected in legislation—there are still no guidelines for *corporate* freedom of utterance, and in fact the law of labor relations presents very real obstacles to statements that may be construed by courts as coercive of employees' rights to associate for the purpose of collective bargaining. The whole problem of freedom of utterance by employees of corporations needs to be attacked at the level of the public philosophy and public law as well as at the level of corporate policy. We are dealing here not just with the problem of wage-earners who may or may not want to join unions, but with the whole range of corporate employees up to executive echelons, and including those who do intellectual as well as manual work.

POLITICAL ACTIVITY

The problem of employee freedoms extends as well into political activities of employees. Good corporate citizenship seems to be inseparable from recognition of employees' citizenship obligations. And these individual obligations to the general community cannot be discharged unless all employees are free to speak their minds on civic issues. Their freedom to do this, however, is more likely to come from positive company action than from the negative method of restraints on executive supervision. Company policy that comes out squarely and affirmatively for employee participation in politics at all levels of public government, supports such participation by encouraging party membership in any lawful party, encourages public service by revision of rules governing leaves of absence and pension rights is one thing. Company policy that merely imposes penalties on supervisors for encroaching on employees' rights as citizens is quite another. The first approach is constructive; the second is negative or at least noncommittal on the fundamental principle involved.

The fundamental principle in this civic matter, as in the question of freedom to publish, is one of corporate citizenship in larger dimensions than are ordinarily assumed. The corporation is a new kind of community within the greater community, national and international in scope. The stature of a man as a true citizen in any of these communities will depend on how he can and does participate in the momentous decisions that are made there. Participation in public and corporate affairs is not just a matter of voting at elections or the right to be heard through representatives at the tables of power. It is also a matter of freedom to inquire, to dissent, to communicate, to act creatively, so that one feels himself a part of a community, and not a passive outsider.

The passive employee, like the passive stockholder, loses this sense of participation, to the great detriment of a free society of free men. The old *virtù* in a free citizenry at the base of the structure is thereby lost, and power passes into the hands of a few, whose responsibilities become too heavy to be borne. The liberalizing arts and sciences then cannot be widely shared, nor can the responsibilities for governing society in all of its multifold aspects: in the private as well as the public sectors.

Conclusions

CORPORATE GOVERNANCE in its dynamic aspects and with respect to the internal affairs of a company involves the formulation of policies whose norms are only partly drawn from compromise. It is true that the conflict of diverse interests within the corporate community requires compromise, and that the balancing of these interests is a major way of setting up the norms of policy. But there are other formative influences. Justice in the governance of corporations is not solely a matter of bargaining and "deals." In every issue there are external forces that condition settlements. Earlier we considered these forces in terms of corporate ecology, or the adjustment to environmental requirements. Here we have seen how in two major types of policy issue there is another conditioning factor of great importance, though it is often overlooked.

With respect to stockholder and employee relations, as illustrated, we have seen that the institutional demands of a free society operate on corporate policy-makers who take the long view. The institution of private property, in the case of stockholders, is of such basic importance to a free society as we have known it that a new order of problems arises in the field of corporate financial policy. Beneficial ownership of an extremely passive kind, as contrasted with migrant managerial power passing into few hands in certain financial institutions, means that both corporate and public policy-makers must now grapple with the issue if private property as a social institution is to be preserved.

As to employee relations, the substance of corporate justice in policy making has to be found beyond bargains and compromises among stockholder, managerial, and other interests. This appears especially in the growing issue of employee freedoms, and not least in the problem of freedom to inquire, to write, to publish, and in general to communicate with the extracorporate world. This is a problem which has dimensions not inferior to those raised in Milton's *Areopagitica* and J. S. Mill's essay *On Liberty*.

John Milton had fallen under charges of contempt of Parliament for having issued a pamphlet without first having obtained a license for the publication. The "Printing Ordinance" issued by Parliament in 1644 required all publications to be licensed by an official censor. "Why," he pleaded, "should ye suppress all this flowery crop of knowledge and new light sprung up and yet springing daily in this city? . . . Give me the liberty to know, to utter, and to argue freely according to conscience, above all liberties."

CHAPTER *16*

The Future of Corporate Governance

A NEW AND BETTER WORKING MODEL of the corporation is sought today. Business leaders and public policy-makers need such a model for reasons that are perhaps less obvious to them than they are to those who struggle through the vast literature on corporations in an attempt to understand it as a major social institution of our time. The old models of juristic and economic theory do not suffice as keys to the role of corporations in the social fabric of our free nation and, indeed, in the rapidly evolving new structure of international economics and politics. The large industrial corporation is here to stay; but its real potential contributions to that new structure are little understood.

In the present book an attempt has been made to complement the received doctrines about the corporation with another approach—in terms of the corporation of today and the future as a private governmental system. The older conceptual frameworks have by no means outlived their usefulness. But the thesis here is that additional ways of looking at our corporate system can not only be useful but are vitally necessary because we now live in a transitional period when all free institutions are being put to the test of survival. It is conceivable, and probable, that among the important building blocks of the emergent free society, now locked in struggle with autocratic and totalitarian systems of government, will be the great national and transnational corporate enterprises which harden the sinews of peoples dedicated to human liberty.

To make this contribution, however, it is not enough for the great corporations to be marvels of efficient production. They must also stand for principles of freedom and justice as these principles are embedded in the noblest of our constitutional traditions. The traditions of Western constitutionalism, on the other hand, are not limited to rhetorical exhortation; in practice, they appear in the form of practical and workable restraints on the power to govern. And free men everywhere are becoming keenly aware of the fact that the power to govern is not, and must not be, a monopoly of the state. It is distributed pluralistically among both the public and the private sectors of society, in a society that cherishes human liberty.

The great corporations are therefore necessarily among the wielders of power in our society, and it is right that they should be. If they are reduced to powerlessness, they cannot perform the tasks demanded of them. Yet disturbing questions arise: how much power, and power to what ends? And, conceding the necessity of corporate power to govern, in whose hands will that power lie, and how will those who use it be held accountable, and to whom? These are not economic issues, but issues that run to the heart of the political philosophy of our age. They demand answers which are better than casual references to older doctrines of political justice.

To many observers of corporate governance it seems anomalous that our corporate polities are in effect self-perpetuating oligarchies by reason of their internal authority structures. The anomaly is that these allegedly autocratic enclaves persist in the midst of a society dedicated to constitutionalist principles with respect to public government, thus perpetuating a system of private governmental enclaves at odds with our public philosophy of government. This disparity in governmental forms and processes is increasingly being commented on, and has led to demands that the corporation be "constitutionalized," just as critics demand the introduction of responsible government in labor unions.

The problem is not an easy one to solve, partly because of the failure to see that the governing of men is a universal phenomenon not limited to the apparatus of nation-states, and partly because of the extraordinary success of the business system as seen in corporate growth—attributable to some extent, so it is said, to the very fact that the modern corporation is *not* governed in democratic fashion. Let us not be misguided, so the argument goes, into the baneful analogy of business administration with public government, nor into the false hope that the principles of politics can help us to find the true bases of business statesmanship.

The caveat is tardy and useless. It fails to take into account the fact that the concept of private government is no imaginary construct of academic minds, but is now widely accepted wherever men come to grips with the facts of political life. The corporation of the future is certain to be assessed not only as an element in the economy but also as a contributor—or as a deterrent—to freedom and order. As an integral part of social order in free societies it must accept the responsibilities as well as the advantages of its rule-making powers.

Yet, when this becomes the accepted mode of thought, it still leaves open the question of ways and means by which corporate governments can make their greatest contribution to a free society. Shall this be done by imposing upon corporate polities a form of constitutional government prescribed by law? Or shall it be done mainly within the corporate community itself, with minimal public regulation? Clear alternatives of this kind rarely turn out to be realistic. Undoubtedly, both methods will be tried. But one may hope, at least, that respect for corporate autonomy, like respect for the autonomy of all other private associations, will survive, and that its survival will be nourished by active efforts within the leading business corporations to bring their internal governmental systems into line with prevailing norms of equitable procedure.

The case for self-improvement in corporate self-government is a strong one. Nor does it rest entirely on the pluralistic arguments so often made today in defense of a free-enterprise system and the preservation of balance between the public and private sectors of our mixed economy. Public government, as it has evolved under contemporary ideals of constitutionalism, is not itself free from doubt. State and national governmental systems do not present a uniform picture of the pursuit of Public Interest and Justice to the exclusion of deals and compromises. We have not yet found all of the answers to the question of public accountability for public agencies; and within them are to be found not a few "irresponsible oligarchies"—a term often used in condemnation of corporate governments. Is it not conceivable that, left largely to their own devices though stimulated by public concern, the corporations may find novel forms of polity which are suited to their needs and are yet consonant with the best traditions of constitutionalism?

These traditions are fairly clear. They require any group of men who claim the right to control the lives and property of others to exercise their power with due respect for these rights. The necessity of power is not denied; its uses, however, must be harnessed to the legitimate ends for which it was originally created. The harnessing of power is effected not by preachment but by practices discovered—mainly in modern times—through experiment with constitutional devices such as representative government, the distribution of powers, and the rule of law—especially through the enforceability of fundamental law by courts on rule-makers and executives.

Corporations of the future could be left relatively free to design their own polities, provided that they adhere to these basic principles. They cannot, however, expect to be immune from the general rule of free societies that these principles be respected. Their problem of self-constitutionalization becomes the more acute, moreover, as the process of "cybernation" intensifies. The computerized public and private sectors will both face this problem to a high degree within the next decade because of the concentration of controls within relatively small groups of professionals. But no computer can be programed to dispense justice. The demand for fair dealing will not subside even though machines take over much of the work of thinking through knotty problems of organization and policy. It remains to be seen whether—in corporation or state—the appropriate constitutional devices can be found for holding the machines and their tenders to accountability by the governed.

As we have pointed out in this book, the search for reliable constitutional restraints has a much longer history in public and ecclesiastical polities than it has in business polities. The inventive genius of corporate constitution-makers need not be constricted by blind adherence to the traditional devices; but neither can the traditional designs be dismissed as quite irrelevant. Perhaps we shall stay on the right track, in our future experimentations with corporate governmental systems, if we keep in mind the watchword of the late distinguished jurist Learned Hand: "Liberty lies in the hearts of men and women; when it dies there, no constitution, no law, no court can save it."

Yet liberty is a word of many meanings. For the businessman it may mean freedom of enterprise and a high degree of corporate autonomy. But for the corporate constitutionalist liberty must mean more than that. It must mean human libery, the freedom of real persons from unjustifiable uses of power, and not merely freedom of corporate persons—as fictitious entities—from state power. Corporate autonomy, coupled with substantial efforts within the corporate community itself to modify corporate governance in accordance with prevailing norms of justice and fair dealings, can indeed be a means to the end of human liberty and the protection of the rights of persons and their property. But neither corporate autonomy nor public regulation of business can be relied upon alone to nourish the flowering of human personality. The modern corporation is not the only formative influence that contributes to the making of Organization Men.

The free man in a free society faces today a struggle that is different from the eternal struggle of past ages only as it has an organizational setting. His liberties are threatened today, as they always have been, by those who raise the banner of freedom for dubious purposes. One is reminded of the struggle for liberty of conscience and toleration in England four centuries ago. There, as J. W. Allen observes, in his study of *Political Thought in the Sixteenth Century*, Puritans and Catholics both attacked Tudor supremacy over ecclesiastical polity—but not for liberty of conscience. "They were contending for the liberty of their own consciences, not for those of other people. Both were, most of them, ready and eager to see the civil sword used for the establishment of the 'true religion,' which was simply their own, and the destruction of all other. So far as they were concerned it was merely an accident in the vast process of things, that their efforts to free themselves helped to enlarge human freedom. . . . The establishment in law of intellectual freedom and of freedom for the religious consciousness, was the triumph not of Peter or Paul, but of Gallio."

Zealots of the "true religion" obviously have their dangerous counterparts in the twentieth century, too. But in the interim we have surely learned something about the art and science of constitutional government; and it may be hoped that we have learned enough so that they can be applied to private as well as to public governments. The "judicious Hooker," writing in defense of the Establishment and attacking the critics of Tudor supremacy in religious matters, argued that "in polity, as well ecclesiastical as civil, there are and always will be evils which no art of man can cure, breaches and leaks more than man's wit hath hands to stop." Quietism of this sort, however, did not stop the advance of constitutional reform in both ecclesiastical and civil polity, in England and later in the colonies across the seas; and that advance was due in no small degree to the influence of Hooker's own dictum that "laws therefore human, of what kind soever, are available by consent." There are, in other words, evils in polity which the art of man can cure, given the will to do so and freedom on the part of the governed, using their right to exercise the consent of the governed, to explore the possibilities of improvement.

In corporate polity today the range of possibilities may be far wider than is ordinarily assumed. Concession theory notwithstanding, we are not bound in this respect by the rules of an Establishment; there is room for the exercise of ingenuity here as well as in the narrower range of administrative management, where modern businessmen have shown their inventiveness. The way is open to the younger generation of business leaders to institute constitutional reform in our great enterprises. It remains to be seen whether they will grasp that opportunity or leave the matter to public governments.

Notes

CHAPTER 1 The Study of Corporate Governance

1. Thus Professor Frederick M. Watkins pointed out in a paper, "The English Pluralists Reconsidered," prepared for the 1961 annual meeting of The American Political Science Association, that the early pluralists' doctrines have fallen into some disrepute because they emphasized the dangers of excessive authority in the state, whereas today the real danger is "the unprecedentedly rapid and widespread disintegration of political authority." "We can no longer afford, if we ever could," he said, "to rely on a decision-making process that asks the [public] government to stand idly by while pressure groups fight it out between themselves, expecting the spontaneous generation of public goods through the balancing of private interests."

2. ". . . we are seeing the gradual transition (in historical time of course not gradual at all) of our vast country from a system of individual possessory property (the norm a century ago) to a system of non-individual, non-statist, non-possessory economic and social power (a system of corporations, corporate insurance companies, and pension trusts, of labor unions, professional guilds, and voluntary associations) which has concentrated economic power to a degree unknown in recorded history." Adolf A. Berle, Jr., "Coherency and the Social Sciences," in Lyman Jay Gould and E. William Steele (eds.), *People, Power, and Politics* (New York: Random House, 1961), p. 10. The leaders of these "new institutions of [a] non-statist power system," said Berle, were now seeking new conceptions of stewardship

since their institutions had become detached from their original fields of responsibility.

3. John R. Commons, *The Economics of Collective Action* (New York: The Macmillan Co., 1950), Chapter 3, and *Legal Foundations of Capitalism* (New York: The Macmillan Co., 1924), Chapter 4.

4. Compare Peter B. Clark, "The Business Corporation as a Political Order," a paper prepared for delivery at the American Political Science Association's annual meeting in 1961, in which he distinguishes between unilateral and hierarchical decision-making procedures as to organization and personnel matters in a corporation, and the very different procedures in the same corporation which involve substantive decisions on business operations. The latter type of procedure is, he says, one that requires rather widespread consent by "concurrent majorities." These disparate types of decision process in the business corporation produce characteristic tensions in what he calls "the concurrent hierarchy."

5. J. L. Schaver, *The Polity of the Churches*, 4th ed. revised (Chicago: Church Polity Press, 1956); E. F. Jacob, "Nicolas of Cusa," in F. J. C. Hearnshaw (ed.), *The Social and Political Ideas of Some Great Thinkers of the Renaissance and the Reformation* (London: George G. Harrap & Co., 1925), Chapter 2.

CHAPTER 2 Constitutional Crisis in the Corporation

1. Some of these are noted in *The Meaning of Modern Business* (New York: Columbia University Press, 1960), pp. 308–309, and pp. 319 *f.*, where I discuss briefly the problem of corporate polity. See also Edward S. Mason (ed.), *The Corporation in Modern Society* (Cambridge: Harvard University Press, 1959), Chapters 2, 3, 4, 5, and 11. Part II, below, goes into the nature of corporate constitutions in detail.

2. The contributors to a corporate enterprise are (1) direct and (2) indirect, and their claims on its fruits are correspondingly different. Suppliers of capital and of managerial and other skills are direct contributors, for example, and are ordinarily regarded as "members" of the firm if they are security-holders or regular employees or officers in it. Their claims on its fruits are met in a different way than the claims of indirect contributors such as suppliers of goods under contract and the plant communities and public governments which provide a general framework for the enterprise.

3. See "The New Look in Corporation Law," *Law and Contemporary Problems*, Vol. 23, No. 2 (Spring, 1958).

4. Cf. Charles E. Merriam, *Systematic Politics* (Chicago: University of Chicago Press, 1945), Chapter 1.

5. Take, for example, three functionally similar corporations, each operating in a different "environment." Concretely, look at the cases of a major radio network in England, Radio Luxembourg, and an "unauthorized" radio station operating aboard ship in international waters off the coast of the European continent. Each of these organizations is designed to create audiences and to serve audiences by providing information, entertainment, enlightenment, or cultural identification. The English network, controlled by the government, observes—in practice—the code of British law. This spirit pervades its organization of talent, the quality of programing, and, eventually, the character of the audiences which it constructs. Radio Luxembourg, similarly, discharges its responsibilities in terms of its importance to the Luxembourg economy and the dignity of the state. But, at the same time, the authority of its broadcasts depends to a real degree upon the character of the sponsoring advertisers whom it serves throughout Western Europe. These advertisers may have plant and marketing facilities in any one, in several, or in all of the European countries reached by Radio Luxembourg's signal. And the diversity of audience response which reaches Radio Luxembourg disciplines the quality of the station's programing. The constitutional atmosphere guiding the work of the station's professional talent must be expected to differ from that found in the English station. The particularity of custom, code, and mode of British behavior is replaced by a "Continental" spirit which is expressed by wide tolerance for deviance of behavior in personal life. Finance, engineering, marketing, and legal decisions within the corporation reflect the complexity of the European economy as regulated by a variety of nation-states. In the end, the commonality of constitutional order at Radio Luxembourg is importantly similar to the basic elements which have tied Western Europe into the framework of the Coal and Steel Community and, finally, into the Common Market.

The characteristics of those two different problems in corporate management of authority relationships are highlighted by the case of the radio station which operates in international waters. Apparently this station has no national home. Operating outside the bounds of international control over communications facilities, it is a "pirate" corporation, at first glance. Its law is that of its managers. Its relations with its employees are presumably achieved in free bargaining situations. Its link with its audiences seems to be uncontrolled. But, in fact, if its governing principles should become a stench in the nostrils of its audiences; if it should impose upon the legal rights of established transmission channels of other stations; if it should not earn the respect of advertisers of products and services in the markets reached by its broadcasts—if any one of these statements were true, the station would be forced off the air. The responses of employees, audiences, advertisers, and the controllers of international communications systems discipline the operation of the "pirate." In fact, that nation which taxes the income of the share-owners in the outlaw station undoubtedly holds a benevolent view toward the operation. And this final relationship certainly modifies the display of naked power of the corporation. It may be an outlaw, but the corporation simply does not exist in anarchy. The fact that the managers chose to operate as outlaws suggests that they are not aware of the massive controls which discipline their business.

6. Carl Kaysen, "The Corporation: How Much Power? What Scope?" in Edward S. Mason (ed.), *The Corporation in Modern Society* (Cambridge: Harvard University Press, 1959), p. 105.

CHAPTER 3 Constitutional Foundations of Corporate Governments

1. James Bryce, *Constitutions* (New York: Oxford University Press, 1901), pp. 93–94.

2. *Ibid.*, p. vii.

3. C. H. McIlwain, *Constitutionalism, Ancient and Modern* (Ithaca: Cornell University Press, 1940).

4. *Ibid.*, p. 24.

5. Thomas M. Cooley, *A Treatise on Constitutional Limitations*, 7th ed. (Boston: Little, Brown & Co., 1903), Vol. 1, p. 4. Cooley's treatise was first published in 1868 and was for several decades the leading commentary on the United States Constitution.

6. This apt phrase comes from the title of Herbert J. Spiro's book *Government by Constitution: The Political Systems of Democracy* (New York: Random House, 1959), in which he systematically compares eight constitutional democracies: the United States of America, Canada, Great Britain, France, Germany, Italy, Switzerland, and Sweden.

7. Sir George Cornewall Lewis, *Remarks on the Use and Abuse of Some Political Terms* (London: Printed for B. Fellowes, 1832), p. 4.

8. Aristotle, *Politics*, Book VI (IV in the old order), Chapter xi. C. H. McIlwain, *The Growth of Political Thought in the West* (New York: The Macmillan Co., 1932), pp. 76 *f.*, presents a clear analysis of these passages in the context of Greek experience.

9. Quoted by Edward S. Corwin, in *The Constitution and What It Means Today*, 12th ed. (Princeton: Princeton University Press, 1958), p. xv. The observation was made when Hughes was governor of New York.

10. *Ibid.*, pp. 132, 140, 145, 174–175, 284.

11. Herman Finer, *The Theory and Practice of Modern Govern-*

ment, revised ed. (New York: Holt, Rinehart & Winston, 1949), pp. 116–117.

12. *Ibid.*, p. 117.

13. Scott Buchanan, *The Corporation and the Republic* (New York: The Fund for the Republic, 1958), pp. 4–5.

14. *Ibid.*, p. 14.

15. *Ibid.*, p. 15.

16. *Ibid.*, p. 15.

17. *Ibid.*, p. 19.

18. *Ibid.*, p. 22.

19. *Ibid.*, p. 22.

20. *Ibid.*, p. 22.

21. *Ibid.*, p. 23.

22. *Loc. cit.*

23. *The Corporation and the Economy: Notes by W. H. Ferry, Followed by a Discussion.* (Santa Barbara, Calif.: Center for the Study of Democratic Institutions, 1959). The participants were A. A. Berle, Jr., Scott Buchanan, Eric Goldman, Clark Kerr, John Courtney Murray, S.J., Reinhold Niebuhr, and I. I. Rabi. Remarks of the following consultants were included: Robert M. Hutchins, chairman of the meetings, John Cogley, W. H. Ferry, Hallock Hoffman, Paul Jacobs, Frank K. Kelly, Walter Millis, James Real, and Edward Reed.

24. *Ibid.*, p. 82.

25. *Ibid.*, p. 87.

26. *Ibid.*, p. 87.

27. *Ibid.*, p. 88.

28. A. A. Berle, Jr., *Economic Power and the Free Society: A Preliminary Discussion of the Corporation* (New York: The Fund for the Republic, 1957), p. 9. He said that in at least one case a New Jersey court had held that a self-perpetuating oligarchy was illegal. A life-insurance company had gained control of a trust company by buying a majority of the shares and had thereafter caused the trust company to purchase a majority of its own shares.

29. *Ibid.*, p. 10.

30. *Ibid.*, p. 13.

31. *Ibid.*, p. 16.

32. *Ibid.*, p. 18. This thesis had been explored in detail by Berle in "Constitutional Limitations on Corporate Activity—Protection of Personal Rights from Invasion through Economic Power," *University*

of *Pennsylvania Law Review*, Vol. 100, No. 7 (May, 1952), pp. 993–955. "Though true corporation law," he wrote, "has abandoned the task of regulating relations between the corporation and the community, the large corporation, monopoly or concentrate (and in some cases highly competitive, multi-unit industries) is encountering a rapidly growing and extremely powerful field of law, quasi-law, and public expectations as to conduct hardening into law." The new law was "crystallizing in two distinct areas": one in which a system of industrial planning was gradually building up and the corporation as an entity was dealt with as a contributor to economic results acceptable to the community; the other, "a body of rules governing the rights and positions of individuals with whom the corporation deals as a supplier." *Ibid.*, p. 936. Berle noted "the tendency to give specific constitutional or legal protection to individuals in their dealings with private units wielding great economic power," and "a quiet translation of constitutional law from the field of political to the field of economic rights." *Ibid.*, p. 942. See also, by the same author, "Legal Problems of Economic Power," *Columbia Law Review*, Vol. 60, No. 1 (January, 1960), pp. 4–23. At p. 10: "Especially where a power organization, be it corporation or labor union, has statutory privileges from which the power derives, the due process and other constitutional restrictions may well apply."

33. Berle, *Economic Power and the Free Society*, p. 18. The question of judicial review of corporate action as "state action" is taken up again later in this chapter.

34. Earl Latham, "The Commonwealth of the Corporation," *Northwestern University Law Review*, Vol. 55, No. 1 (March–April, 1960), p. 33.

35. *Ibid.*

36. Latham, *op. cit.*, p. 35, citing by way of illustration the case of *Greene* v. *McElroy*, 360 U.S. 474 (1959), involving industrial security procedures in corporations governed by federal standards.

37. Earl Latham, *Political Theories of Monopoly Power* (College Park, Maryland: Bureau of Governmental Research, College of Business and Public Administration, University of Maryland, 1957); "Anthropomorphic Corporations, Elites, and Monopoly Power," *American Economic Review*, Vol. 47, No. 2 (May, 1957), pp. 303–310; "The Body Politic of the Corporation," in E. S. Mason (ed.), *The Corporation in Modern Society* (Cambridge: Harvard University Press, 1959), pp. 218–236.

38. Bayless Manning, "Corporate Power and Individual Freedom: Some General Analysis and Particular Reservations," *Northwestern University Law Review*, Vol. 55, No. 1 (March–April, 1960), pp. 38–53.

39. *Ibid.*, p. 53.

40. *Ibid.*, p. 51.

41. Thus, says Manning, in an informative statement about an infringement of "freedom of speech" in the realm of public law, there are five elements that can be identified with specificity: (1) the institution acting to encroach upon the freedom (e.g., Congress or a state legislature), (2) the action taken (e.g., a law forbidding some utterance), (3) the area affected (e.g., an utterance such as picketing with placards), (4) the persons affected (e.g., strikers), and (5) the normative consensus (many people are agreed in condemning the encroachment and they feel justified in rallying others to oppose it by established procedures). Manning, *op. cit.*, pp. 47–49.

42. To say that corporations threaten because they have "power," writes Manning, is no help in deciding "what it is we do not want an institution to do, or how to go about blocking it, or what it is we want the institution to do, or how to go about stimulating it." Manning, *op. cit.*, p. 50.

43. Thus he denounces the "common disease carried by the 'corporation bug,' " leading to what he regards as unhealthy preoccupation with the legal structure, legal theory, and legal history of the corporation as a *persona ficta*—a disease he calls Platonism—because it "tempts us to focus upon the peculiar internal aspects of the corporate form rather than upon the impact of the enterprise on society." Manning, *op. cit.*, pp. 39–40. Obviously, one can be interested in its impact, as a system of private government, on both internal and external groups. "Society" is also a term of ambiguous reference. Preoccupation with the corporate form, however, is properly the object of Manning's criticism on another ground: "it serves admirably to conceal the real actors in a given situation." *Op. cit.*, p. 42.

44. Manning, *op. cit.*, p. 42.

45."It is not 'Power' we fear, but the power to effectuate particular policies to which we object. The question is—what are they and who is in a position to carry them out. Until we find out, we cannot design defenses"—i.e., defenses of "Individual Freedom" against "Corporate Power." Manning, *op. cit.*, p. 46.

46. *Ibid.*, p. 53.

47. *Ibid.*

CHAPTER 4 Roots of Authority

1. Earl Latham, "The Body Politic of the Corporation," in Edward S. Mason (ed.), *The Corporation in Modern Society* (Cambridge: Harvard University Press, 1959), p. 220.

2. E. Merrick Dodd, Jr., "Company and Corporation Law," *Encyclopedia Britannica*, 1958 ed., Vol. 6, p. 149.

3. *Ibid.*

4. *Ibid.*

5. *Ibid.*

6. Carl J. Friedrich, *Constitutional Government and Democracy* (Boston: Little, Brown & Co., 1941), p. 136.

7. Edward S. Corwin, *The "Higher Law" Background of American Constitutional Law* (Ithaca: Great Seal Books, a Division of Cornell University Press, 1955), reprinted from the *Harvard Law Review*, Vol. 42 (1928–1929), pp. 149–185 and 365–409.

8. *Ibid.*, p. 89. Italics in the original.

9. On the more extended analysis of governance in nonstate associations see David B. Truman, *The Governmental Process* (New York: Alfred A. Knopf, 1951), Part II. Charles S. Hyneman makes a distinction between "legal governments" and "the near-equivalents of legal government" in *The Study of Politics* (Urbana: University of Illinois Press, 1959); he says that "the central point of attention in the scholarly effort of American political scientists is the government of the state" (p. 25). But power and influence are the center of attention in the works of many political scientists. The study of the "authoritative allocation of values for a society" is the political scientist's field, according to David Easton in *The Political System* (New York: Alfred A. Knopf, 1953). Compare T. I. Cook, "The Political System: The Stubborn Search for a Science of Politics," *Journal of Philosophy*, Vol. 51 (1954), p. 128. Compare Robert A. Dahl, "Business and Politics: A Critical Appraisal of Political Science," in Robert A. Dahl, Mason Haire, and Paul Lazarsfeld, *Social Science Research on Business: Product and Potential* (New York: Columbia University Press, 1959), pp. 3–44, and especially the section on "The Business Firm as a Political Order."

10. In historic Congregationalism the local church is autonomous and independent of all external control by other ecclesiastical bodies; the associations, conferences, and the general council are agencies of the local churches and, as such, possess only derived powers. "The ideals of Congregational Church government are the independence of the local congregation and the fellowship of the independent churches for mutual counsel and for the prosecution of those enterprises which no single church alone could compass." Oscar Stearns Davis and Matthew Spinka, "Congregationalism—United States," *Encyclopedia Britannica*, 1958 ed., Vol. 6, pp. 250–253 and sources there cited.

11. J. L. Schaver, *The Polity of the Churches*, Vol. 2, p. 73.

12. Latham, *op. cit.*, p. 223.

13. The "contract" between state and corporation can be interpreted as reserving to the state large areas of the police power that no state can bargain away, for example. Under most charters and statutes

drawn after the Dartmouth College case these "reserved powers" were specifically referred to. After 1868 the Fourteenth Amendment was increasingly invoked, rather than the contract clause, by corporations as a protection against the police power. Carl B. Swisher, *American Constitutional Development*, 2nd ed. (Boston: Houghton Mifflin Company, 1954), Chapters 8 and 11.

14. E. H. Warren, *Corporate Advantages Without Incorporation* (1929).

15. Adolf A. Berle, Jr., and Gardiner C. Means, "Corporation," in *Encyclopedia of the Social Sciences*, Vol. 4, pp. 420–421.

16. *Ibid.*

17. Abram Chayes, "The Modern Corporation and the Rule of Law," in E. S. Mason (ed.), *op. cit.*, p. 40.

18. *Ibid.*, p. 41.

19. *Ibid.*

20. Eugene V. Rostow, "To Whom and for What Ends Is Corporate Management Responsible?" in E. S. Mason (ed.), *op. cit.*, p. 51.

21. Arthur Stone Dewing, *The Financial Policy of Corporations*, 5th ed. (New York: The Ronald Press Co., 1953), Vol. 1, pp. 16–17.

CHAPTER 5 The Core and the Periphery of Corporate Constitutional Law

1. Wilber G. Katz, "The Philosophy of Midcentury Corporation Statutes," *Law and Contemporary Problems*, Vol. 23, No. 2 (Spring, 1958), pp. 177–192, where it is shown that the "enabling act" theory of recent state corporation statutes exhibits a "major concern . . . lest application of common law doctrines should be unduly restrictive of corporate management" (p. 185).

2. *Ibid.*

3. *Ibid.*

4. *Ibid.*

5. Frank D. Emerson, "The Roles of Management and Shareholders in Corporate Government," *Law and Contemporary Problems*, cited.

6. Elvin R. Latty, "Some Miscellaneous Novelties in the New Corporation Statutes," *Law and Contemporary Problems*, cited, p. 367.

7. *Ibid.*, p. 369.

8. On the distinction between "participants" and "members" of an organization, see Chapter 2 above, note 2. Also the distinction, in

analyzing world politics, between states as formal participants and the much wider variety of "minor members of the international cast" of characters who actually engage in the "factual process of coercion across state boundaries"; Myres S. McDougal and associates, *Studies in World Public Order* (New Haven: Yale University Press, 1960), pp. 247–249 and p. 27.

9. The rational and natural-system models are compared by Alvin W. Gouldner, "Organizational Analysis," in Robert K. Merton and others (eds.), *Sociology Today: Problems and Prospects* (New York: Basic Books, 1959), pp. 400–427.

10. *Ibid.*, p. 417.

11. This section follows the analysis of Gouldner, *op. cit.*

12. H. H. Gerth and C. Wright Mills (trs. and eds.), *From Max Weber: Essays in Sociology* (New York: Oxford University Press, 1946), p. 196.

13. Gouldner, *op. cit.*, p. 405.

14. *Ibid.* Gouldner describes such responses as "taking the form of crescively developed defense mechanisms" that are shaped importantly "by shared values which are deeply internalized in the members" of an organization.

15. Gouldner, *op. cit.*, p. 405. He mentions some of the ways in which organizational instabilities are generated, thus leading to disequilibrium in the view of natural-system organization analysts: the manipulative treatment of human beings as instruments in violation of cultural norms that insist upon human dignity; impairment, through ceaseless rationalization drives, of the spontaneous homeostatic controls that have contributed to the organization's equilibrium; and the self-generation, through such rationalization, of new administrative problems that have to be planfully resolved. *Ibid.*, p. 418.

16. The deep suspicion of mechanistic planning in large organizations is evident in the writings of Auguste Comte and Edmund Burke and their disciples. See the references to Comte in Gouldner, *op. cit.*, and Burke's *Reflections on the Revolution in France* (1790), in part a diatribe against constitutions drawn up *de novo*.

17. Selznick's discussion of two types of commitment in organizational behavior that identify the conditions under which a high frequency of unanticipated consequences may be expected to occur is relevant here: commitments enforced by the social and cultural environment, and commitments enforced by the centers of interest generated in the course of action. The "co-optative mechanism" he describes is also highly suggestive for the student of comparative corporate constitutional development. See Philip Selznick, *TVA and the Grass Roots* (Berkeley and Los Angeles: University of California Press, 1953), and particularly those portions reproduced in Albert H.

Rubenstein and Chadwick J. Haberstroh (eds.), *Some Theories of Organization* (Homewood, Ill.: The Dorsey Press and Richard D. Irwin, 1960), pp. 111–123.

18. Board and shareholder relationships with these groups are ordinarily channeled through the corporation officers, though there may be significant exceptions not analyzed here.

19. I have developed this point in some detail in *The Meaning of Modern Business* (New York: Columbia University Press, 1960), Chapter 14: "Public Relations and Corporate Interests." In an organization whose activities are very heavily centered in the external field, the failure of executive management to take a unified view of external relationships can have the most serious consequences. To illustrate, take the case of a governmental military-intelligence organization. In simplest outline, bureaus, departments, and branches of the government propose to the military-intelligence organization certain categories of knowledge in which they have interest—the so-called "essential elements of information." The fact-gathering organization consolidates the categories and organizes to collect critical bits of information which can be related to the several interests. It finds that evaluation and interpretation of bits and scraps of fact are necessary facets of its work. It notes that in the competition among bureaucratic elements of the government some interpretations influence the power positions of specific offices or departments, deteriorating some and raising the importance of others. Yet all offices are "clients" of the intelligence service. Again, with limited resources at its disposal, the intelligence organization must allocate its efforts so as to serve the "best interests" of the government as a whole. Thus the intelligence service calls upon its plans-and-policy section to review and formulate strategic objectives of the government in order that its own work will be critically guided in the most important directions. The foreign operations of the intelligence service may impinge upon the freedom of action of the government. Thus, when disclosure was made about the flights of the U-2 aircraft over the Soviet Union, our government was put into a position where it suffered some embarrassment. At the same time, the executive who is responsible for the work of the intelligence organization must arbitrate among the competing interests of governmental bureaus, among competing interests of his operating arms, among competing interests of other intelligence services representing other governments, and among competitive interpretations of his own nation's objectives, policies, and interests. And he must balance his decisions in such fashion as to maintain confidence in the reliability and validity of the output of his service. If he is guided solely by the latter interest, the charge may be made that he tailors his reporting according to what his clients find credible. If he is guided solely by his interpretation of national objectives, he is open to the charge that he is playing politics with the nation's policies. If he is guided by sensitivity to the power position of his clients, he is

open to the charge that he blocks necessary changes in the power structure of the government. In the end, where critical issues are involved, the weighing and balancing of competing claims become central to the executive's work. And in these central functions he must often liken his situation to that of the sailboat which is guided to its port by the compass of major objectives while jibbing and tacking along the way.

20. McDougal and associates, *op. cit.*, pp. 13–14, discuss the nature of authority in terms of expectations.

CHAPTER 6 Functional Bases: *Traditional Views*

1. "Purpose," as used here, includes more than "product" or the kind of purpose that L. H. Gulick and L. Urwick had in mind in *Papers on the Science of Administration* (New York: Institute of Public Administration, 1937) in the theory of departmentalization for formal organizations. Nor should purpose be confused with proclaimed but inoperative objectives.

2. The concession theory states, as has been indicated, that a corporation can be created only by or under legislative authority, and, as a mere creature of law, is established only for those special purposes indicated in the sovereign act by which it is created. The concession theory has long been orthodox in English and American law.

3. On participation in organizations see James G. March and Herbert A. Simon, *Organizations* (New York: John Wiley & Sons, 1958), Chapter 4, especially pp. 89–93, where the relevant participants include other than employees.

4. Thomas I. Cook, *History of Political Philosophy from Plato to Burke* (New York: Prentice-Hall, 1936), p. 687.

5. See Edward S. Mason, "The Apologetics of 'Managerialism,'" *The Journal of Business*, Vol. 31, No. 1 (January, 1958).

6. See Richard Eells, *The Meaning of Modern Business* (New York: Columbia University Press, 1960), pp. 77*f*.

7. Morris Janowitz, "Changing Patterns of Organizational Authority: The Military," *Administrative Science Quarterly*, Vol. 4, No. 4 (March, 1959), pp. 473–493; by the same author, *The Professional Soldier: A Social and Political Portrait* (New York: The Free Press of Glencoe, 1960).

8. Stephen A. Richardson, "Organizational Contrasts on British and American Ships," in James D. Thompson and others (eds.), *Comparative Studies in Administration* (Pittsburgh: University of Pittsburgh Press, 1959), pp. 39–54. On authoritarian systems related to organizational structure of authority, see also R. A. Cloward and

others, *Theoretical Studies in Social Organization of the Prison* (New York: Social Science Research Council, 1960).

9. The principle of congregational polity, in which authority derives from the whole congregation and arises in church officials only by delegation of its members, is rejected in some churches for doctrinal reasons:

> If the ruling office within the Church is one of human arrangement and if it is dependent for continued existence upon the will of the people, then this position of the independents can be maintained. If the Church is like a republic in which the chosen officers carry out the wishes of the voters, then congregational polity is correct. However, the Church is not a republic but a monarchy, even an absolute monarchy, wherein Jesus is King forever and His word the unalterable constitution. And it is the King of the Church who instituted the ruling office in His ecclesiastical realm. Though the office bearers are chosen by the people, this is but Christ's way of calling them to office, and their authority comes not from the people but from the King of the Church. . . . And the power to rule in the Christian Church is not as in a democracy an exercise of authority that reckons merely the will of the majority but one which reckons first of all with the will of Christ from whom that power proceeds. J. L. Schaver, *The Polity of the Churches* (Chicago: Church Polity Press, 1947), Vol. 1, pp. 73–74.

10. William J. Goode, "The Sociology of the Family: Horizons in Family Theory," in Robert K. Merton, Leonard Broom, and Leonard S. Cottrell, Jr. (eds.), *Sociology Today: Problems and Prospects* (New York: Basic Books, 1959), pp. 178–196; A. L. Kroeber, *Anthropology*, new ed. (New York: Harcourt, Brace & World, 1948); R. H. Lowie, "Relationships Terms," *Encyclopedia Britannica*, 1958 ed., Vol. 19, pp. 84–90; Leopold Pospisil, "Kapuku Papuan Political Structure," in Verne F. Day (ed.), *Systems of Political Control and Bureaucracy in Human Societies*, Proceedings of the 1958 Annual Spring Meeting of the American Ethnological Society (Seattle: American Ethnological Society, University of Washington, 1958), pp. 9–22; M. F. Nimkoff and R. Middleton, "Types of Family and Types of Economy," *American Journal of Sociology*, Vol. 66, No. 3 (November, 1960), pp. 215–225.

11. See *Psychiatry*, Vol. 20, No. 3 (August, 1957), "On Some Convergences of Sociology and Psychiatry," esp. the papers by Erving Goffman, "A Sociologist's View"; Maxwell Jones, "The Treatment of Personality Disorders in a Therapeutic Community"; Stewart E. Perry and Gertrude N. Shea, "Social Controls and Psychiatric Theory in a Ward Setting"; and Morris S. Schwartz, "Patient Demands in a Mental Hospital Complex." Also Oscar Grusky, "Organizational Goals and the Behavior of Informal Leaders," *American Journal of Sociology*, Vol. 65, No. 1 (July, 1959), pp. 59–67. Also

R. McCleery, *Policy Change in Prison Management* (East Lansing: Governmental Research Bureau, Michigan State University, 1957); and Erving Goffman, "The Nature of Deference and Demeanor," *American Anthropology*, Vol. 58, No. 3 (June, 1956), pp. 473–502.

12. See, e.g., John J. Corson, *Governance of Colleges and Universities* (New York: McGraw-Hill Book Co., 1960); Philip Taft, *The Structure and Government of Labor Unions* (Cambridge: Harvard University Press, 1954); J. A. C. Grant, "The Gild Returns to America," *Journal of Politics*, Vol. 4 (1942), pp. 303–336 and 458–477; Grant McConnell, "The Spirit of Private Government," *American Political Science Review*, Vol. 52, No. 3 (September, 1958), pp. 754–770; Alexander H. Leighton, *The Governing of Men* (Princeton: Princeton University Press, 1946); Charles E. Merriam, *Public and Private Government* (New Haven: Yale University Press, 1944); Oliver Garceau, *The Political Life of the American Medical Association* (Cambridge: Harvard University Press, 1941).

13. See Charles E. Merriam, *Public and Private Government* (1944), Chapter 1, and *Systematic Politics* (Chicago: University of Chicago Press, 1945), pp. 236–239; *The Professional Thief; by a Professional Thief*, annotated and interpreted by Edwin H. Sutherland (Chicago: University of Chicago Press, 1937), Chapter 9; and Frederic M. Thrasher, *The Gang*, rev. ed. (Chicago: University of Chicago Press, 1960).

14. Consider, for example, such problems as the government of the ill, the young, the aged, etc., regarded as groups that are subjected to various kinds of control system that are distributed among a number of organized institutions and therefore not ordinarily made the focus of scientific attention as integral control systems simply because of the absence of *single* institutionalized authority patterns. Compare J. S. Mills' study *The Subjection of Women* (1869) and Aristophanes' *Lysistrata*.

15. Peter F. Drucker, *Concept of the Corporation* (New York: The John Day Company, 1946), pp. 20–21.

16. See Mason, note 5 above. On the multiplicity of corporate goals today, see Eells, *op. cit.*, Chapter 6.

17. Adolf A. Berle, Jr., and Gardiner C. Means, *The Modern Corporation and Private Property* (New York: The Macmillan Co., 1932), a classic statement of the theory of separated ownership and control which was foreshadowed in the works of Veblen, Rathenau, and W. Z. Ripley, and has influenced many writers on corporation theory during the past quarter of a century. Note especially Berle and Means, *op. cit.*, pp. 352–357, on "the law of corporations . . . as a potential constitutional law for the new economic state" with "business practice . . . assuming the aspect of economic statesmanship."

18. Neither juristic nor political theory offers today a clear-cut and generally acceptable doctrine to explain the relationship of authority between stockholders and those who manage a corporate enterprise. Theories of agency and representation are inadequate. The "fiduciary relationship" has been suggested as the more appropriate one. Lloyd E. Dewey, "The Board of Directors," in J. I. Bogen (ed.), *Financial Handbook*, 3rd ed. (New York: The Ronald Press Co., 1956), p. 394; and E. M. Dodd, Jr., "Company and Corporation Law," *Encyclopedia Britannica*, 1958 ed., Vol. 6, p. 150, on the fiduciary obligations of directors and officers.

19. James Burnham, *The Managerial Revolution* (New Midland Books ed., Bloomington: Indiana University Press, 1960; original ed., New York: The John Day Company, 1941). He declared (pp. 82 *f.*) that the real managers are "the operating executives, production managers, plant superintendents and their associates [who] have charge of the actual technical process of producing" and not those more highly placed and paid company officials ("finance-executives") whose function is to guide it toward a profit, or the "finance-capitalists" among directors and bankers. The legal "owners" (stockholders) were dismissed as mere passive recipients of whatever dividends the directors decide to declare. ". . . with profit in the capitalistic sense eliminated, the technically necessary functions of the finance-executives . . . become part of the management functions" of the real managers "if management is extended over all or most of industry," which is, in turn, subordinated to some noncapitalist goal (p. 85). Compare the observation of Berle and Means, *op. cit.*, p. 356, that the "control" group in large corporations might well "develop into a *purely neutral technocracy* balancing a variety of claims by various groups in the community and assigning to each a portion of the income stream on the basis of public policy rather than private cupidity." (Italics not in original.)

20. "The position, role, and function of the most privileged of all groups, the finance-capitalists, are . . . *entirely* bound up with capitalist property and economic relations"; and, while "the preservation of the capitalist relations is not an absolutely decisive question for the managers [of the productive mechanism]," the preservation of "capitalist property and economic relations is decisive even for the continued existence of this [finance-capitalist] group." Burnham, *op. cit.*, p. 91; italics are Burnham's. It should be noted that in his recent edition Burnham says that his statement of the hypothesis of the managerial revolution in 1941 seems "too rigid and doctrinaire" to him in 1960, but that subsequent events have not weakened the validity of his general argument.

21. Burnham, *op. cit.*, p. 92.

22. Burnham, *op. cit.*, p. 92.

23. *Ibid.*, p. 154.

24. *Ibid.*, p. 94.

25. *Loc. cit.*

26. *Ibid.*, p. 95. Burnham's analysis was directed primarily at "the managerial world system of superstates" and not at the internal constitutional structure of corporations as we analyze it here.

27. As indicated, for example, in the monographs published by the Fund for the Republic and the Center for the Study of Democratic Institutions, and in E. S. Mason (ed.), *The Corporation in Modern Society* (Cambridge: Harvard University Press, 1959).

28. Drucker, *The Practice of Management* (New York: Harper & Brothers, 1954), p. 37. Joseph A. Schumpeter, *The Theory of Economic Development* (Cambridge: Harvard University Press, 1934) held that "enterprise" is "the carrying out of new combinations," and "enterprisers" include not only independent businessmen but also "'dependent' employees of a company, like managers, members of boards of directors, and so forth, or even if their actual power to perform the entrepreneurial function has any other foundations, such as the control of a majority of shares" (pp. 74–75). ". . . shareholders *per se* are never entrepreneurs, but merely Capitalists, who in consideration of their submitting to certain risks participate in profits" (p. 75, n. 1). "The entrepreneur is never a riskbearer" (p. 137).

29. See Robert A. Gordon, *Business Leadership in the Large Corporation* (Washington: The Brookings Institution, 1945), p. 145 and pp. 349–350; Sidney Weinberg, "A Corporate Director Looks at His Job," *Harvard Business Review*, Vol. 27, pp. 585–593; B. Ruml, "Corporate Management as a Locus of Power," in *Social Meaning of Legal Concepts* (New York: New York University School of Law, 1950), Vol. 3, *The Powers and Duties of Corporate Management*, pp. 235 *f.*; Courtney C. Brown and E. E. Smith (eds.), *The Director Looks at His Job* (New York: Columbia University Press, 1957).

30. Lewis D. Gilbert, *Dividends and Democracy* (Larchmont, N.Y.: American Research Council, 1956). The "shareholder democracy" urged in Gilbert's book would not be regarded by most traditionalists as the most effective way of assuring proper returns to holders of equity capital.

31. Thorstein Veblen, *The Theory of Business Enterprise* (New York: Mentor Books, The New Library of World Literature, 1958; first published by Charles Scribner's Sons, 1904), p. 16.

32. *Ibid.*, p. 89.

33. *Ibid.*, p. 114.

34. *Ibid.*, pp. 135–136.

35. Schumpeter, *op. cit.*, p. 128. See note 28 above.

CHAPTER 7 Functional Bases: *Recent Trends*

1. "Capitalism," *Encyclopedia Britannica,* 1958 ed., Vol. 4, p. 801.

2. "A so-called 'capitalist society' now ceases to be dominated by the normal, or, rather, the classically assumed motivations of property-holding 'capitalist' or entrepreneur investors. Large corporations increasingly become institutions in themselves not primarily identified with, and certainly not expressions of, their stockholders. They must make profits, but it is even more important that they satisfy consumer demand. They must detach profits by way of dividends, increasingly for distribution to satisfy pension and other claims; but equally they must maintain continuous employment (as far as possible) and accumulate part of their profits as additional capital to meet future needs. In general, their administrators have acquired the power and must assume their share of the burdens and responsibilities inherent in the service-of-supply system of a vast and democratic state." Adolph A. Berle, Jr., in the introduction and commentary, Paul P. Harbrecht, S.J., and Adolf A. Berle, Jr., *Toward the Paraproprietal Society* (New York: The Twentieth Century Fund, 1960), pp. 5–6.

3. Theodore O. Yntema, Vice President–Finance, Ford Motor Co., in a statement before the Subcommittee on Antitrust and Monopoly, Committee on the Judiciary, U.S. Senate, Feb. 4–5, 1958. He referred to stockholder profits and losses as "the rewards and penalties for superior, or inferior, service to the consumer rendered by their companies."

4. Chester I. Barnard, *The Functions of the Executive* (Cambridge: Harvard University Press, 1953), p. 154, note 7.

5. On this organizational equilibrium and the "balance of incentives" compare March and Simon, *op. cit.*

6. Barnard listed, besides material inducements, "personal nonmaterial opportunities, desirable physical conditions, ideal benefactions" as specific inducements, and as general incentives, "associational attractiveness, adaptation of conditions to habitual methods and attitudes, the opportunity of enlarged participation, the condition of communion" as a suggestive if not complete inventory. Barnard, *op. cit.*, p. 142.

7. The "method of persuasion" include "(a) the creation of coercive conditions ["homicide, ostracism, outlawing, incarceration, discharge" were "expressions of the power of organizations to persuade by force"]; (b) the rationalization of opportunity [propaganda]; (c) the inculcation of motives." Barnard, *op. cit.*, pp. 149–153.

8. *Ibid.*, pp. 158–159.

9. C. I. Barnard, "Elementary Conditions of Business Morals," *California Management Review,* Vol. 1, No. 1 (Fall, 1958), p. 2.

". . . to a large extent management decisions are concerned with moral issues [and] cooperation among men, through formal organizations of their activities, creates moralities. . . ."

10. See Barnard, *Organization and Management: Selected Papers* (Cambridge: Harvard University Press, 1948), p. 112.

11. *Ibid.*, pp. 112–113.

12. *Ibid.*, p. 118. In this paper Barnard applied to the customer relationship all of the principles he had earlier developed, in *The Functions of the Executive,* to the employer-employee relationship, since he thought that "the economy of incentives" applies equally to both.

13. *Loc. cit.*

14. See Edith Tilton Penrose, *The Theory of the Growth of the Firm* (New York: John Wiley & Sons, 1959), pp. 18 *f.*

15. Charles E. Lindblom, "Democracy and Economic Structure," in William N. Chambers and Robert H. Salisburg (eds.), *Democracy in the Mid-Twentieth Century: Problems and Prospects* (St. Louis: The Washington University Press, 1960), p. 62.

16. Analyzed at length in Robert A. Dahl and Charles E. Lindblom, *Politics, Economics and Welfare* (New York: Harper & Brothers, 1953).

17. Lindblom, *op. cit.*, p. 62, note. On the "investor electorate" it has been suggested that "perhaps the power of corporate governors would be more acceptable if they had to stand for re-election in the constituency of a free capital market" instead of financing capital expansion from withheld earnings. Kingman Brewster, Jr., "The Corporation and Economic Federalism," in Edward S. Mason (ed.), *The Corporation in Modern Society* (Cambridge: Harvard University Press, 1959), p. 83.

18. Cf. Nelson N. Foote (ed.), *Household Decision-Making* (New York: New York University Press, 1960); Lincoln Harold Clark (ed.), *Consumer Behavior* (New York: New York University Press, 1958); S. H. Britt, *The Spenders* (New York: McGraw-Hill Book Co., 1960).

19. Cited in Eells, *The Meaning of Modern Business,* (New York: Columbia University Press, 1960), Chapter 6, "Corporate Goals," and Chapter 15, "The Well-Tempered Corporation," especially pp. 316 *f.* on the coordinate economic functions of the corporation, pp. 319 *f.* on the coordinate political functions, and pp. 326 *f.* on the coordinate social and cultural functions.

20. Carl Kaysen, "The Corporation: How Much Power? What Scope?" in Mason (ed.), *The Corporation in Modern Society,* pp. 102–103.

21. Other ways of limiting "business power," suggested by Kaysen, are the promotion of competitive markets through a more vigorous

antitrust policy, and "broader control of business power by agencies external to business," *op. cit.*, p. 103. Kaysen sees little likelihood of much change in a third way: the internal organization of the corporation as a means of "institutionalizing within the firm the responsibility for the exercise of power"; but "some mixture" of the second and third of these did seem to him to be possible.

22. Louis O. Kelso and Mortimer J. Adler, *The Capitalist Manifesto* (New York: Random House, 1958), pp. 157–158 and p. 170. The authors propose a number of other concomitant reform measures to effect a "transition to Capitalism" from what they believe now to be a "laboristic economy."

23. See Neil Chamberlain, "The Corporation and the Trade Union," in Mason (ed.), *The Corporation in Modern Society*, pp. 121–140: ". . . union members enjoy little or no differential wage advantages over their unorganized brethren, . . . the unions' chief contribution to their members' welfare has been to free them from the tyranny of arbitrary decision or discriminatory action in the work place." Cf. Paul M. Herzog and Morris Stone, "Voluntary Labor Arbitration in the United States," *International Labour Review*, October, 1960, pp. 301–326.

24. Robert K. Merton, "Bureaucratic Structure and Personality," *Social Forces*, Vol. 18 (1940), pp. 560–568; and *Social Theory and Social Structure*, 2nd ed. (New York: The Free Press of Glencoe, 1957); P. Selznick, "Foundations of the Theory of Organization," *American Sociological Review*, Vol. 13 (1948), pp. 25–35, and *TVA and the Grass Roots* (Berkeley and Los Angeles: University of California Press, 1949); A. W. Gouldner, *Patterns of Industrial Bureaucracy* (New York: The Free Press of Glencoe, 1954); James G. March and H. A. Simon, *Organizations* (New York: John Wiley and Sons, 1958).

25. Max Weber, *The Theory of Social and Economic Organization*, tr. by A. M. Henderson and T. Parsons (New York: Oxford University Press, 1947). References here cited are in the second edition by The Free Press of Glencoe. Weber's study was originally published at Tübingen, Germany, in 1922 as a part of his *Wirtschaft und Gesellschaft.*

26. See R. K. Merton and others (eds.), *Reader in Bureaucracy* (New York: The Free Press of Glencoe, 1952), pp. 18–33; Weber, *op. cit.*, pp. 324–340.

27. March and Simon, *op. cit.*, p. 36.

28. See Albert Lepawsky, *Administration: The Art and Science of Organization and Management* (New York: Alfred A. Knopf, 1952); Harwood F. Merrill (ed.), *Classics in Management* (New York: American Management Association, 1960); Dwight Waldo (ed.),

Ideas and Issues in Public Administration: A Book of Readings (New York: McGraw-Hill Book Co., 1953).

29. See Merton and others (eds.), *Reader in Bureaucracy*, cited above.

30. Classic examples of dysfunction abound in American business and are referred to in the commonplace observation that the first generation works in shirt sleeves, the second generation in a stuffed shirt, and the third generation again in shirt sleeves. Observers of the retail trades see the continuing ebb and flow of such patterns in the rise of family-owned department stores, the merging of these (when in third-generation hands) into the giant chains, and the simultaneous rise of "new" first-generation stores, which today are more likely to follow discount-house formats. Throughout these life histories of business enterprises one could expect that a chart of the pattern of authority relationships among the owners and managers would reveal that nonrational pressures were bottling up authority in weak flasks and energizing abrasive elements simultaneously. Explosions within family businesses have been widely noted for their bitterness.

At the same time, some family businesses have escaped the crude outcomes at the first level of resolution. Seeking to distinguish between the roles of owners and managers, families have "found a place" for their new generations within the family enterprise while introducing professional managers into the life-stream of business operations. But unsystematic observation suggests that no corporation can become great and outstanding among its competitors when family-ordained policies and governing principles continue to prevail.

Within such corporations, large though they may become, the characteristic dysfunction takes the form of slowness in adaptation to changing market conditions, a failure to interpret correctly, and in time, the meaning of changes in customer needs, and an overelaboration of the process of decision-making when investment policies are under consideration. For example, one large company in the forest-products industry has always had (into the third generation) a member of "the family" as its chief executive officer. Although the corporation enjoys half-billion-dollar sales annually and will continue to earn very great capital gains from continuous-process logging on its extensive forest acreage, serious questions are being raised about the company's long-range objectives. Should it continue to prize wood and wood products as intrinsically superior forest products? Should it move toward breaking down the cellulose and lignin in the tree and become a chemical marketer? Should it focus upon providing systems of wood products adapted to residential-home construction—that is, to become a marketer of homes? There are other important alternatives, but in the range from lumber-producer to chemicals-marketer to marketer of homes greatly different orders of financial problems can be raised. To move forward dynamically will require the assumption of risks as great as those taken by the founders of the corporation generations ago. And the costs of the different decisions can be readily brought forward: costs of a change in specifications of manpower required, costs in establishing and managing market-intelligence systems, costs in the break-up of established relationships which have been maintained with lumber-dealers and trade associations and labor unions.

Faced with issues of such magnitude, it is questionable that the constitutional structure of the corporation—controlled by "a family"—will be able to cope with the decisions. Relative harmony is maintained as long as the present course of "active consideration of the issue" is maintained. But the essential dysfunction within the structure continues to spin off, as if by centrifugal force, professional managers who come to the company expecting to aid in resolution of the issue and to participate in the drama of a major corporate rebuilding activity. Disillusioned by years of inaction, they depart.

Such a corporation, as traditionally designed in structure, continues to serve an economic purpose and to provide economic value to the society. But the pattern of family-controlled authority relationships within the corporation appear to deter it from moving forward on a course of growth and expansion.

CHAPTER 8 The Powers of Constitutional Corporations

1. R. A. Dahl and E. C. Lindblom, *Politics, Economics and Welfare: Planning and Politico-Economic Systems Resolved into Basic Social Processes* (New York: Harper & Brothers, 1953), pp. 99–112.

2. *Ibid.*, pp. 112–117.

3. Jean Jacques Rousseau, *The Social Contract, or Principles of Political Right*, Book I, Chapter 3.

4. Thomas Hobbes, *Leviathan*, Part I, Chapter 10.

5. Arnold Brecht, *Political Theory: The Foundations of Twentieth Century Political Thought* (Princeton: Princeton University Press, 1959), pp. 346–347.

6. *Ibid.*

7. *Ibid.*

8. Selznick, in his interesting discussion of "coöptation . . . the process of absorbing new elements into the leadership or policy-determining structure of an organization as a means of averting threats to its stability or existence," points to the significance of co-action of internal power centers with certain power centers in the community environment. Such coöptation may be formal and legitimized by law, or operate quite informally. Philip Selznick, *TVA and the Grass Roots* (Berkeley and Los Angeles: University of California Press, 1953).

9. H. D. Lasswell and A. Kaplan, *Power and Society* (New Haven: Yale University Press, 1950), p. 133. They define authority as "formal power," thus presuming a "political formula" that is "the source and basis of legitimacy"; authority alone is "power of low weight," and the "weight of authority varies with the prestige of the authorities" (pp. 134–135). Similarly, authority has been defined as "institutionalized power" by Robert Bierstedt, "An Analysis of Social Power," *American Sociological Review*, Vol. 15 (1950), pp. 730–738; and by Max Weber as legitimized "imperative coordination," in *The Theory of Social and Economic Organization*, tr. by A. M. Henderson and T. Parsons (New York: The Free Press of Glencoe, 1947), p. 324. Cf. Robert K. Merton, "Bureaucratic Structure and Personality," in Alvin W. Gouldner (ed.), *Studies in Leadership* (New York: Harper & Brothers, 1950), pp. 47–68, where authority is regarded as "power of control which derives from an acknowledged status," and a power that inheres in the office and not in the particular person who performs the official role.

10. Myres S. McDougal and associates, *Studies in World Public Order* (New Haven: Yale University Press, 1960), pp. 13–14.

11. Henri Fayol, *General and Industrial Management*, tr. by Constance Storrs (London: Sir Isaac Pitman & Sons, 1949), Chapter 4, quoted in Harwood F. Merrill (ed.), *Classics in Management* (New York: American Management Association, 1960), p. 219.

12. Bertrand de Jouvenel, *Sovereignty: An Inquiry into the Political Good*, tr. by J. F. Huntington (Chicago: University of Chicago Press, 1957), pp. 29–33. He also speaks of "the faculty of inducing assent" and "the ability of a man to get his own proposals accepted." Power, he adds, is the capacity to make oneself obeyed, whereas authority "is exercised only over those who voluntarily accept it." "Authority ends where voluntary assent ends," he writes, and "police regimes come in when prestiges go out." Only the "margin of obedience" is won by force or the threat of force.

13. Dahl and Lindblom, *op. cit.*, pp. 114–115.

14. Hugo Krabbe, *The Modern Idea of the State*, tr. by George H. Sabine and Walter J. Shepard (New York: Appleton-Century-Crofts, 1922): ". . . the modern idea of the state no longer finds the basis of subjection in the authority of the sovereign, but in the law which is valid by its own force . . ." (Chapter 10, iii, G.).

15. Walter B. Miller, "Two Concepts of Authority," in James B. Thompson and others, *Comparative Studies in Administration* (Pittsburgh: University of Pittsburgh Press, 1959), pp. 93–115. "Just as the Fox related himself directly to supernatural power, and to the procedural rules governing collective action, so he deemed it his inviolable right to respond *directly* to the rules governing general behavior. The intensity of Fox resentment to *external* direction was matched by an

equally intense conformity to *internalized* cultural directives" (p. 111, italics not in original). "Manitu power," among the Fox was not admired or adored but feared: it was "both dangerous and immoral for one individual to exercise any substantial control over others."

16. Chester I. Barnard, *The Functions of the Executive* (Cambridge: Harvard University Press, 1938), p. 163.

17. *Ibid.*, p. 184.

18. *Ibid.*, p. 220.

19. Chester I. Barnard, "Elementary Conditions of Business Morals," *California Management Review*, Vol. I, No. 1 (Fall, 1958), p. 2. Italics not in the original. Note that Barnard speaks of "moralities," thus recognizing the possibility of conflicting codes of behavior that arise from the very nature of coordinated effort in any large organization. This fact is seldom appreciated by outsiders.

20. See Mary Parker Follett, "The Illusion of Final Authority," *Bulletin of the Taylor Society*, Vol. 11 (1926), pp. 243–246.

21. Barnard, *The Functions of the Executive*, p. 163.

22. Herbert A. Simon, *Administrative Behavior*, 2nd ed. (New York: The Macmillan Co., 1957), p. 125.

23. *Ibid.*, p. 135.

24. Alfred D. Chandler, Jr., "Henry Varnum Poor: Philosopher of Management, 1812–1905," in Wm. Miller (ed.), *Men in Business: Essays in the History of Entrepreneurship* (Cambridge: Harvard University Press, 1952), pp. 254–285, esp. at p. 272 and sources there cited.

25. *Ibid.*, p. 271.

26. Richard Eells, *The Meaning of Modern Business* (New York: Columbia University Press, 1960), Chapter 2, distinguishing between the corporation as traditionally conceived in corporation law and the revised concepts of the "metro-corporation" and the "well-tempered corporation" of contemporary literature.

CHAPTER 9 The Multinational Corporation

1. David Lilienthal, "Management of the Multinational Corporation," in Melvin Anschen and George Leland Bach (eds.), *Management and Corporations 1985* (New York: McGraw-Hill Book Co., 1960), p. 220. See also Barbara Ward, "The Western Corporation and the Underdeveloped Economies," *ibid.*, pp. 159–182; and Raymond Vernon, "The American Corporation in Underdeveloped Areas," in E. S. Mason (ed.), *The Corporation in Modern Society* (Cambridge: Harvard University Press, 1959).

2. Ward, *op. cit.*, pp. 158–182.

3. Lilienthal, *op. cit.*, p. 219.

4. C. I. Barnard, "Concepts of Organization," in his *Organization and Management* (Cambridge: Harvard University Press, 1956), Chapter 5, p. 112.

5. *Ibid.* "In the sense of ultimate analysis an organization is a composition of cooperative *acts*" (p. 118).

6. Dahl and Lindblom, *op. cit.*, Part IV.

7. *Ibid.*, pp. 227–271. "Hierarchy" is a process of economizing characterized by a high degree of unilateral control by leaders over non leaders, encountered not only in bureaucratic organizations but also in national economies where there is a deliberate, conscious, and presumably rational adaptation of economic means to national purpose.

8. *Ibid.*, pp. 272–323. "Polyarchy" is characterized by a relatively high degree of control by nonleaders over leaders and thus a means of controlling hierarchy, not only by democratic voting but also through social pluralism in which competing voluntary associations play an important part in leader control. The preconditions of polyarchy are detailed by Dahl and Lindblom, *op. cit.*, pp. 287–323.

9. *Ibid.*, p. 371, presents a convenient diagrammatic synopsis of the interrelationships between rational calculation and control—the two basic kinds of social process—and the four central sociopolitical processes (price system, hierarchy, polyarchy, bargaining), as these affect economizing in all of its aspects. "Rational calculation," for Dahl and Lindblom, is aided by discussion, codification, quantification, sampling, delegation, etc., and the mechanisms used for goal scheduling include voting, the market, delegation, and autonomy. The four basic methods of "control," referred to earlier, are spontaneous field control, manipulated field control, command, and reciprocity.

10. Harbison and Myers, *Management in the Industrial World: An International Analysis* (New York: McGraw-Hill Book Co., 1959), p. 8.

11. *Ibid.*, p. 47.

12. *Ibid.*, pp. 60–61. Cf. Rensis Likert, *New Patterns of Management* (New York: McGraw-Hill Book Co., 1961).

13. *Ibid.*, p. 363.

14. Clark Kerr, *Industrial Relations and the Liberal Pluralist.* (Reprint No. 80, Institute of Industrial Relations, Berkeley: 201 California Hall, University of California, 1955); also Clark Kerr, John T. Dunlop, Frederick H. Harbison, and Charles A. Myers, *Industrialism and Industrial Man: The Problems of Labor and Management in Economic Growth* (Cambridge: Harvard University Press, 1960), especially Chapter 10, "Pluralistic Industrialism."

15. *Ibid.*, pp. 367 and 376.

16. Richard Eells, *The Meaning of Modern Business*, pp. 313 *f*. This refers to those economic functions for society as a whole with respect to which private corporations unavoidably must exercise some authority and assume some responsibility over and above the economizing processes within their own administrative orbits.

17. W. W. Rostow, *The Stages of Economic Growth: A Non-Communist Manifesto* (Cambridge, Eng.: Cambridge University Press, 1960), Chapter 6, "The Age of High Mass-Consumption," and p. 156. "Man's ultimate economic problem," writes Rostow of "a problem that we of this generation can set aside," may be one of "babies and boredom, the development of new inner human frontiers, outer space and trivial pleasures—or, may be, destruction, if the devil makes work for idle hands." The powers required for governing business corporations at the stage "beyond mass consumption," as Rostow describes it, would certainly be very different from what they are, and must be, at the earlier stages of economic growth where the job to be done requires extraordinary skill and power for managers of productive organizations.

18. Sir William P. Hildreth in *The Washington Post and Times-Herald*, May 22, 1960, Section K, page 8.

19. Paul P. Harbrecht, S.J., *Pension Funds and Economic Power* (New York: The Twentieth Century Fund, 1959), p. 277.

CHAPTER 10 American Patterns of Constitutional Restraint

1. Arthur W. Macmahon (ed.), *Federalism, Mature and Emergent* (Garden City, New York: Doubleday & Co., Inc., 1955), p. 4. In the Canadian federation, provincial powers are delegated while those of the central government are residual.

2. *Ibid.*, pp. 10–11.

3. For a critical analysis of the separation-of-powers doctrine, see Albert Lepawsky, *Administration* (New York: Alfred A. Knopf, 1952), Chapter 3; Herman Finer, *The Theory and Practice of Modern Government*, revised ed. (New York: Holt, Rinehart & Winston, 1949), Chapters 6 and 7; Robert G. Neumann, *European and Comparative Government*, 3rd ed. (New York: McGraw-Hill Book Co., 1960), Part V, Chapter 4; Carl J. Friedrich, *Constitutional Government and Democracy*, rev. ed. (Boston: Ginn & Co., 1950), Chap. 10.

4. "The trouble with the old (tripartite) classification is twofold: Legislature, executive, and judiciary are alike in that they all make policies, and the making of policies is their main function. But what distinguishes the types of policies they make is not the same as what distinguishes legislation from the execution of laws, nor is it the same as what distinguishes either of these from adjudication." Herbert J.

Spiro, *Government by Constitution: The Political Systems of Democracy* (New York: Random House, 1959), p. 13.

5. "What is colloquially, if erroneously, spoken of as the separation of *powers* is operationally only the distribution of specific state *functions* among different state organs." Karl Loewenstein, *Political Power and the Governmental Process* (Chicago: University of Chicago Press, 1957), p. 36. He prefers to speak of the "separation of functions" since the term "powers" must be understood to be "merely figurative," and proposes a "new tripartism of state functions based on the distinction between policy determination, policy execution, and policy control." *Ibid.*, p. 42.

6. "Constitutionalism is a political system in which several independent power holders co-exist and co-operate." Loewenstein, *op. cit.*, p. 53. It "includes several patterns of government, all characterized by the existence of several independent power holders among whom the exercise of power is constitutionally distributed and who are required to co-operate, by pre-established constitutional procedures, in the formation of the will of the state." *Ibid.*, p. 70.

7. Loewenstein, *op. cit.*, p. 184.

8. *Ibid.*, p. 185.

9. As contrasted with the purge in the Soviet state. The purge is not an isolated phenomenon arising from emergency, but a necessary and continuous part of the Soviet system. See Zbigniew K. Brzezinski, *The Permanent Purge: Politics in Soviet Totalitarianism* (Cambridge: Harvard University Press, 1956).

10. See Alexander Heard, *The Costs of Democracy; Financing American Political Campaigns* (New York: Doubleday & Co., Inc., 1962).

11. Spiro, *Government by Constitution*, pp. 34 *f*.

12. *Ibid.*, pp. 34–35. Emphasis supplied.

13. Loewenstein, *op. cit.*, p. 52: "Autocratic government, by contrast, is characterized by the absence of any techniques by which the political responsibility of the single power holder could be effectively invoked, short of revolution."

14. It is sometimes forgotten that the Declaration of Independence preceded the Declaration of the Rights of Man and of Citizen in France by thirteen years. From France the idea spread throughout Europe and ultimately to other continents. The American idea had antecedents in the English Bill of Rights (1 Wm. & Mary, Sess. 2, Ch. 2) in 1689, the Petition of Right (1628), and Magna Carta (1215). The first bill of rights in an American state constitution was that of Virginia (1776), followed soon thereafter by those of Pennsylvania, Maryland, North Carolina, Vermont, Massachusetts, and New Hampshire.

15. In the discussion following Hutchins' paper on *Two Faces of Federalism*, cited above, Mr. Justice William O. Douglas said that "we have in Washington, D.C. now, in the city itself, between 60,000 and 65,000 arrests every year that they call 'arrests for interrogation.' There is no charge. There is sheer suspicion. They are not the kind of people who sit around this table. They are not from the churches and the banks and the medical professions. They are the second- and third-class citizens. Last year there were 65,000 of them, which is rather appalling to me in a democratic society. . . . No charges were ever made. They were held for a day or a week and then turned loose." *Op. cit.*, pp. 94–95. He pointed out that there had been no positive standard as to how long a prisoner could be held incommunicado; in a California case the prisoner had been held incommunicado five days and a confession had been obtained. "The court held that it didn't make them puke. It didn't make five of them puke. I will be glad to send you my dissenting opinion." *Ibid.* This referred to what Justice Douglas called the "visceral application of law": the determination of what violated natural law and due process by asking —in a phrase attributed to Justice Holmes— "Is the thing that happened to this man something that makes you puke?" If not, then no violation. See, generally, William O. Douglas, *The Right of the People* (New York: Doubleday & Co., 1958) and Osmond K. Fraenkel, *The Supreme Court and Civil Liberties* (New York: Oceana Publications, 1960). Mr. Justice William J. Brennan says that "far too many cases come from the states to the Supreme Court presenting dismal pictures of official lawlessness, illegal search and seizure, illegal detention, attended by prolonged interrogation and coerced admission of guilt, denial of counsel and downright brutality." Second annual James Madison Lecture on the Constitution and the Bill of Rights at New York University Law School, as reported in *The New York Times*, February 16, 1961.

16. Loewenstein, *op. cit.*, p. 331.

17. Eighteen years after the adoption of the Fourteenth Amendment the Supreme Court held unanimously in *Santa Clara County* v. *Southern Pacific Railroad Co.*, 118 U.S. 394 (1886) that corporations were "persons" under the terms of the Amendment, and the rule has stood against occasional dissenting opinions (Justice Black in *Connecticut General Life Insurance Co.* v. *Johnson*, 303 U.S. 77 (1938), and Justice Douglas and Black in *Wheeling Steel Corporation* v. *Glander*, 337 U.S. 562 (1949) 572, 668. The theory that the word "person," instead of "citizen," was deliberately inserted in the draft of the Amendment so as to cover corporations as well as natural persons is discussed in Howard J. Graham, "The 'Conspiracy Theory' of the Fourteenth Amendment," *Yale Law Journal*, Vol. 47 (1938), pp. 371–403, and Vol. 48 (1938), pp. 171–194.

18. Corporations do not, of course, become private governments by virtue alone of their "personality" as conferred by law and protected

by the Fourteenth Amendment. Unincorporated groups also exercise the powers of private government over their members and even outsiders. But the special protection of the Fourteenth Amendment is not open to them as it is to fictitious persons in corporate form.

CHAPTER 11 Restraints by Public Government

1. 4 Wheaton 518.

2. 9 Cranch 42. Cf. James J. Robbins, "The Private Corporation –Its Constitutional Genesis," *Georgetown Law Journal*, Vol. 28, No. 2 (November, 1939), pp. 165–183.

3. 9 Cranch 42, p. 52.

4. 4 Wheaton 518, at pp. 688–689. The English precedents on which Justice Story relied made no such public-private classification of corporations. They did, however, make it quite clear that the King's courts were extremely hesitant to review intracorporate disputes (the cases involved colleges, hospitals, foundations, and other eleemosynary institutions) and that the visitatorial power enjoyed by the attorney-general in the case of corporations, such as boroughs, created for public purposes did not extend to charitable institutions founded on property granted by private persons. In such instances the visitatorial power was reserved to the grantors and their successors. Thus, in *Green* v. *Rutherforth*, 1 Ves. Sr. 462, 472, 27 Eng. Re. 1144, 1149 (Ch. 1750), Hardwicke, L. C., declared that "the original and nature of visitatorial power . . . is the property of the donor, and the power everyone has to dispose, direct and regulate his own property" since "the nature of this power is *forum domesticum*, the jurisdiction of the founder." On this and other English precedents see Robbins, *op. cit.*, pp. 177–178. None of these precedents involved as did the Dartmouth College case, any alleged legislative encroachment on the government of eleemosynary institutions. They all went to the question of judicial review of the acts of corporate governments. It is interesting to observe that the English courts often referred to these as private governments.

5. Albert J. Beveridge, *The Life of John Marshall* (Boston: Little, Brown & Co., 1919), Vol. 4, p. 276.

6. *Trustees of Dartmouth College* v. *Woodward*, 4 Wheaton 518.

7. It has become fashionable again to trace the origins of the modern business corporation to "bodies corporate and politic" erected by royal authority in colonial times for essentially public purposes. But the historical record hardly supports this view. See Shaw Livermore, *Early American Land Companies: Their Influence on Corporate Development* (New York: The Commonwealth Fund, 1939), esp. the "Editor's Introduction" by Julius Goebel, Jr.

8. A. A. Berle, Jr., "The Theory of Enterprise Entity," *Columbia Law Review*, Vol. 47, No. 3 (April, 1947), pp. 343–358.

9. *Ibid.*, p. 352.

10. *Ibid.*, p. 344.

11. *Swift & Co.* v. *U.S.*, 196 U.S. 375 at p. 398 (1905).

12. John R. Commons, *Legal Foundations of Capitalism* (New York: The Macmillan Co., 1924), Chapter 5, "Going Concerns," and *The Economics of Collective Action* (New York: The Macmillan Co., 1950), pp. 34, 118, 355.

13. Stated succinctly by Arthur S. Miller, *Private Governments and the Constitution* (An Occasional Paper published by the Center for the Study of Democratic Institutions, Santa Barbara, California, 1959). The legal citations immediately following have been provided by the kind permission of Professor Miller.

14. *Interstate Commerce Act* (1887), Sec. 3(1). See *Mitchell* v. *U.S.*, 313 U.S. 80 (1941); *Henderson* v. *U.S.*, 339 U.S. 816 (1950); *Bob-Lo Excursion Co.* v. *Michigan*, 333 U.S. 28 (1948).

15. *Home Telephone and Telegraph Co.* v. *Los Angeles*, 227 U.S. 278 (1913). See also *Grovey* v. *Townsend*, 295 U.S. 45 (1935); *United States* v. *Classic*, 313 U.S. 299 (1941); *Smith* v. *Allwright*, 321 U.S. 649 (1944); and *Terry* v. *Adams*, 345 U.S. 461 (1953), which applied the rule to political parties and other associations that excluded Negroes from primary elections.

16. *Marsh* v. *Alabama*, 326 U.S. 501 (1946).

17. *Steele* v. *L. & N. R.R. Co.*, 323 U.S. 192 (1944).

18. *Ibid.*

19. *NAACP* v. *Alabama*, 357 U.S. 449 (1958).

20. See Arthur W. Macmahon (ed.), *Federalism, Mature and Emergent* (New York: Doubleday & Co., 1955), Part III: "Functional Channels of Relationship," and the essay (Chapter 26) by Carl J. Friedrich on "Federal Constitutional Theory and Emergent Proposals." Also A. Maas (ed.), *Area and Power: A Theory of Local Government* (New York: The Free Press of Glencoe, 1959); Robert M. Hutchins, *The Two Faces of Federalism: An Outline of an Argument about Pluralism, Unity, and Law* (Santa Barbara, California: Center for the Study of Democratic Institutions, 1961); and Arthur S. Miller, *Private Governments and the Constitution* (Santa Barbara, California: Center for the Study of Democratic Institutions, 1959). "Our generation of constitutional lawyers is discovering a new dimension in our federal structure—the dimension of private governments. . . . Our society is in fact a federation not merely of forty-eight states, but of a considerably greater number of private sovereignties, governments, and communities as well. . . . Is constitutionalism *plus*

freedom of associations the latest and most refined trick of the age-old enemies of justice and liberty who went underground and persuaded mankind that they cannot possibly be tyrants for the simple and conclusive reason that they are not governments?" Alexander H. Pekelis, *Law and Social Action* (Ithaca: Cornell University Press, 1950), pp. 97–98 and p. 103. Pekelis, like other students of Robert L. Hale at Columbia Law School, had become much interested in the problem. See Robert L. Hale, *Freedom Through Law: Public Control of Private Governing Power* (New York: Columbia University Press, 1953).

21. But without undue emphasis on the distributive functions of power balancing as distinguished from the necessary mobilization of power resources to get things done collectively; see Talcott Parsons, *Structure and Process in Modern Societies* (New York: The Free Press of Glencoe, 1960), Chapter 6, "The Distribution of Power in American Society"–a critique of C. Wright Mills's *The Power Elite*. *Cf*. Frank Tannenbaum, "The Balance of Power in Society," *Political Science Quarterly*, Vol. 61, No. 4 (December, 1946), pp. 481–504.

22. See Macmahon (ed.), *op. cit*., and Robert R. Bowie and Carl J. Friedrich (eds.), *Studies in Federalism* (Boston: Little, Brown & Co., 1954).

23. See Jack Stieber, Walter E. Oberer, and Michael Harrington, *Democracy and Public Review: An Analysis of the UAW Public Review Board* (Santa Barbara, California: Center for the Study of Democratic Institutions, 1960).

24. Wolfgang G. Friedmann, "Corporate Power, Government by Private Groups, and the Law," *Columbia Law Review*, Vol. 57, No. 2 (February, 1957), pp. 155–186, at p. 176.

25. Arthur S. Miller, *Private Governments and the Constitution* (Santa Barbara, California: Center for the Study of Democratic Institutions, 1959).

26. *Ibid*., p. 12.

27. *Ibid*., p. 4.

28. *Ibid*., p. 12.

29. See W. Brooke Graves (ed.), *Major Problems in State Constitutional Revision* (Chicago: Public Administration Service, 1961), especially Part I, "Myth and Reality in State Constitutional Development" by Harvey Walker, and Part III, "The Content of State Constitutions," particularly Chapter 17, "New Constitutions for a New Era in State Government," by Charlton F. Chute.

30. A somewhat different classification of the control devices of constitutionalism is that of Karl Loewenstein in his *Political Power and the Governmental Process* (Chicago: University of Chicago Press, 1957). In addition to the constitution, he designates as "horizontal controls" (a) those which operate *within* a specific power-holder (gov-

ernment or "the administration," assembly or parliament, electorate and political-party cadres), or "intraorgan controls," and (b) those which operate *among* the several power-holders, or "interorgan controls." "Vertical controls," on the other hand, operate among the different levels of the state society in the form of (a) federalism as territorial pluralism, (b) "fundamental liberties of the individual as areas held inaccessible to all power holders," and (c) "the plural groups interposing themselves as shock absorbers between the power holders and the power addressees." Loewenstein, *op. cit.*, p. 18.

31. Walton H. Hamilton, "Constitutionalism," in *Encyclopedia of the Social Sciences* (1931), Vol. 4. "The writing down of the fundamental law, beyond peradventure and against misunderstanding," he says, "is an important political invention. It offers exact and durable language as a test for official conduct at the risk of imposing outworn standards upon current activities." But, he adds, "a shrewd jurist has written, 'Its unchanging provisions'—that is a popular gesture—'are adapted to the infinite variety of the changing conditions of our national life'—that is judicial sense. Where adaptability is, the eternal does not matter."

32. Edward S. Corwin, "The Constitution as Instrument and as Symbol," *American Political Science Review*, Vol. 30, No. 6 (December, 1936), pp. 1071–1085, at p. 1076. "While . . . the constitutional instrument exists to energize and canalize *public power*, it is the function of the constitutional symbol to protect and tranquilize *private interest or advantage as against public power*, which is envisaged as inherently suspect, however necessary it may be." The symbolic aspect of American constitutionalism has been evident in our heavy reliance on judicial review of legislation to check the use of governmental powers, mainly by invoking the Tenth Amendment against Congress. Historically, the Constitution had passed through three phases: from "(1) an instrument of national government, a source of powers" under Chief Justice Marshall's long tenure, to "(2) an object of popular worship, finally valued chiefly for the obstacles it interposed to the national power, to (3) a protection of certain minority interests seeking escape from national power." *Ibid.*, pp. 1072 and 1082. Corwin, in this essay, was a strong exponent of the Constitution as an "instrument." The pendulum swings, in our constitutional history, from emphasis on instrumental to symbolic aspects of constitutionalism. For a recent example of the former see Robert M. Hutchins, *The Two Faces of Federalism*, cited above.

CHAPTER 12 Restraints in the Corporate Constitution

1. See Chapter 5 above.

2. Karl Loewenstein, *Political Power and the Governmental Process* (Chicago: University of Chicago Press, 1957), p. 124.

3. *Ibid.*, p. 145.

4. The terminology adopted here is from Loewenstein, *op. cit.*, pp. 147–153, who prefers this "ontological" classification of constitutions to the "stock-in-trade classifications of the textbooks" distinguishing, for example, between written and unwritten or flexible and rigid constitutions, between monarchical and republican patterns of government, or between federal or unitary state organizations. "The *normative* constitution is the rule in western states with an established tradition of constitutional government and a relatively high degree of socioeconomic homogeneity," while "the *nominal* constitution has its habitat in states where western democratic constitutionalism has been implanted into a colonial or feudal-agrarian social order, without antecedent intellectual incubation or political maturation"; the *semantic* constitution, though without any specific breeding ground, "has become the common practice in the Soviet orbit." *Loc cit.*; italics supplied.

5. As, for example, in Richard Bendix, *Work and Authority in Industry* (New York: John Wiley & Sons; London: Chapman & Hall, 1956); Arthur Kornhauser, Robert Rubin, and Arthur M. Ross (eds.), *Industrial Conflict* (New York: McGraw-Hill Book Co., 1954); Frederick Harbison and Charles A. Myers, *Management in the Industrial World: An International Analysis* (New York: McGraw-Hill Book Co., 1959); and Alvin W. Gouldner, *Patterns of Industrial Bureaucracy* (New York: The Free Press of Glencoe, 1954).

6. The English Companies Clauses Act of 1845 and the acts of 1855 and 1856 left it to companies to adopt their own form of government, although the acts did propose model sets of bylaws which companies might elect to use. A member of Parliament observed that, "having given them a pattern, the State leaves them to manage their own affairs and has no desire to force on any of these little republics any particular constitution." Robert Lowe in *Hansard*, CXL, 134, as quoted by Bishop C. Hunt, *The Development of the Business Corporation in England 1800–1867* (Cambridge: Harvard University Press, 1936), p. 135.

7. Herbert Spencer, for example, wrote that the modeling of corporation government "so as to become a miniature of our national constitution" succeeded also in reproducing its "characteristic vices": "The direction, ceasing to fulfill its theory as a deliberative body whose members possess like powers, falls under the control of some one member of superior cunning, will, or wealth, to whom the majority become so subordinate, that the decision on every question depends on the course he takes. Proprietors (the stockholders), instead of exercising their franchise, allow it to become on ordinary occasions a dead letter; retiring directors are so habitually re-elected without opposition, and have so great a power of insuring their own re-election when opposed, that the board becomes practically a close

body; and it is only when the misgovernment grows extreme enough to produce a revolutionary agitation among the shareholders that any change can be affected." Lowe, *op. cit.*, pp. 135–136, quoting an article on "Railway Morals and Railway Policy" by Herbert Spencer in the *Edinburgh Review* (1854).

8. As Earl Latham argues in "The Body Politic of the Corporation," in Edward S. Mason (ed.), *The Corporation in Modern Society* (Cambridge: Harvard University Press, 1959), pp. 218–236, at p. 223. "Directors," he writes, "were given the authority to reshape the capital structure of the corporation at will" in the nineteenth-century trend toward freedom of incorporation, and the incorporators could "fix the allocation of fundamental functions in the corporation. The corporation thus acquired the constituent power from the state, and came to share the sovereignty. . . . The corporations have acquired the power to make their own constitutions." *Ibid.*, pp. 222–223.

9. Latham, *op. cit.*, p. 224, goes on to say that "the legal constituency of the corporation is the multitude of owners; it is they who are citizens of the corporate state. They are the lawful electorate. This electorate, like that of the public at large, holds the franchise which chooses the corporate legislature—the board of directors—and gives it legal authority to legislate." Latham's distinction between "constituent power" and the "legal constituency" which elects the "corporate legislature" is apparently drawn from Carl J. Friedrich's *Constitutional Government and Democracy* (Boston: Little, Brown & Co., 1941), which he cites in stating that "constituent power is the power to make the constitution which fixes the basic distribution of powers, rights, and functions in the society." Latham, *op. cit.*, p. 222.

10. See the section below on responsible government in corporations.

11. See Eugene V. Rostow, "To Whom and for What Ends Is Corporate Management Responsible?" in Mason (ed.), *The Corporation in Modern Society*, pp. 46–71, esp. at pp. 46–49: "This is the essence of the raider's offense: to attack the established management and to treat the fictional legal structure of the publicly-held endocratic corporation as if it represented reality. . . . the implicit power of managerial self-perpetuation is accepted the more readily when the challenge comes from men who buy stock in a corporation in order to participate in its control."

12. Three of the "most severe cases holding mergers illegal under the antitrust laws . . . concern attempted raids," writes Rostow, *op. cit.*, p. 47, n. 3, citing the Northern Securities case, 193 U.S. 197 (1904), *Hamilton Watch Co.* v. *Benrus Watch Co.*, 114 F. Supp. 307 (1953), and *American Crystal Sugar Co.* v. *Cuban American Sugar Co.*, 152 F. Supp. 387 (1957). "Statutes and judicial decisions frown on the purchase of stock for the purpose of exercising what the textbooks treat as one of the most fundamental privileges—that of

voting," and "courts and legislatures are unfriendly to stockholders' suits." Rostow, *loc. cit.*

13. With certain qualifications "the endocratic corporation is an autonomous body politic in a legal order of decentralized power," and "in such companies the stockholders obey the management, not the management the stockholders"; Rostow, *op. cit.*, pp. 51 and 53. The qualifications he mentions include the necessity of compliance with statutory regulation and the rules of securities exchanges that require disclosure of financial affairs of the corporation; antitrust laws, labor legislation, and other laws that impose certain patterns of conduct and define boundaries of power; and consciousness of fiduciary duty, fear of stockholders' suits and the "occasional appearance of the dread figure of the raider" (p. 51).

14. See Edward S. Corwin, *Court over Constitution: A Study of Judicial Review as an Instrument of Popular Government* (Princeton: Princeton University Press, 1938); and Charles Grove Haines, *The American Doctrine of Judicial Supremacy*, 2nd ed. (Berkeley and Los Angeles: University of California Press, 1932).

15. Bayless Manning, review of Livingston's *The American Stockholder* in *Yale Law Journal*, Vol. 67, No. 8 (July, 1958), pp. 1477–1496.

16. ". . . centers of significant nongovernmental [in our usage, private governmental] power within society . . . must be subjected to the rule of law. . . . The rule of law . . . is concerned with regularizing the use of power. But it is concerned with power in both its faces–not only as an evil, to be restrained, but as a resource to be harnessed in the service of society." Abram Chayes, "The Modern Corporation and the Rule of Law," in Mason (ed.), *The Corporation in Modern Society*, pp. 25–45, at pp. 31–32. Cf. the current corporation studies of the Fund for the Republic and the Center for the Study of Democratic Institutions.

17. For exceptions see Chayes, *op. cit.*, and Kingman Brewster, Jr., "The Corporation and Economic Federalism" in the same volume. Cf. W. H. Ferry, *The Economy under Law* (Santa Barbara, California: Center for the Study of Democratic Institutions, 1960), who proposes that "the economic order be brought under the political order," though not "the absorption of the economic order into the political order" (p. 44).

18. This has been challenged by Franz L. Neumann, "Federalism and Freedom: A Critique," in Arthur W. Macmahon (ed.), *Federalism Mature and Emergent* (New York: Columbia University Press, 1955), pp. 44–57. Neumann concluded that "there are no values (such as individual freedom) that inhere in federalism as such" and that "federalism cannot be defended successfully on the grounds that the inevitable tendency of a unitary state is toward political repression";

nor did he believe that "a division of constitutional power is the best guarantee of political freedom" (pp. 54–55). Federalism in the theory of Johannes Althusius—a towering figure in the history of federal theory—was a vehicle for providing some medium of active citizenship for the too numerous members of the nation-state, as distinguished from devices for the deconcentration of power; see Norton E. Long, "Institutional Framework for the Development of Responsible Citizenship," in Carl J. Friedrich (ed.), *Responsibility* (New York: The Liberal Arts Press, 1960), pp. 225–243, at p. 227.

19. Ernest Dale, "Some Foundations of Organization Theory," *California Management Review*, Vol. 2, No. 1 (Fall, 1959), pp. 71–84, at p. 83. He adds that when a company changes over from a centralized to a decentralized organization, the long- and short-run results may differ, as at Westinghouse; increase in profitability is the immediate impact, though with concomitant increase in administrative expense that more than offsets the gains. In the long run, however, increased costs are outrun by increased profits.

20. Harold F. Smiddy, "Management as a Profession," a paper prepared for ASME Report on *Ten Years Progress in Management —1950 to 1960* (New York, June, 1960, mimeographed). "The determinant level for responsibility, and authority, to make a particular decision should be the lowest organizational level where both the needed skills and *competence*, on the one hand, and the needed *information* —embracing understanding of both direct and environmental *impacts* of the decision—on the other hand, *can reasonably be* brought to exist; so such understanding and information can be brought to bear in choosing wisely from possible alternatives, or risks, as responsibility and need for decision arise."

21. Loewenstein, *op. cit.*, pp. 285–286. "The existence of interfederal barriers restricts the power of the central state toward the member states and vice versa." *Loc. cit.* He distinguishes between quasi-confederal associations of states in ancient Greece, in the early alliances of the Swiss cantons, and in the Union of Utrecht (1579), on the one hand, and real federations, on the other, as in the case of the U.S. federal Constitution of 1787, where there are "common organs with direct jurisdiction over the citizens of the associated states" and no preponderance of any hegemonial state.

22. As in the theories of the French syndicalists such as Georges Sorel, Paul Louis Hubert Lagardelle, and Edouard Berthe. Cf. G. D. H. Cole, *Self-Government in Industry*, 3rd ed. (London: G. Bell & Sons, 1918), and *Guild Socialism Restated* (London: Leonard Parsons, 1920). Also C. E. M. Joad, *Modern Political Theory* (Oxford: At the Clarendon Press, 1924), Chapter 4, and Wm. Y. Elliott, *The Pragmatic Revolt in Politics* (New York: The Macmillan Co., 1928), Chapters 4 and 6.

23. See "How to Let Go of Authority," *Nation's Business*, March, 1958, pp. 86–88, where it was pointed out that effective decentralization exists only where top management is really convinced of its value for the achievement of business objectives; also Perrin Stryker, "The Decentralizing of Blaw-Knox," *Fortune*, February, 1956, pp. 114 *f.*, where divisional autonomy without centralized controls is condemned. On the "discredited pyramided holding companies" of the 1930's, see Thomas C. Cochran, *The American Business System: A Historical Perspective, 1900–1925* (Cambridge: Harvard University Press, 1957), pp. 64 *f.* "The objective of decentralization," wrote Fayol, "is the optimum utilization of all faculties of the personnel . . . everything that goes to increase the importance of the subordinate's role is decentralization, everything which goes to reduce it is centralization"; Henry Fayol, "General Principles of Management," in Harwood F. Merrill (ed.), *Classics in Management* (New York: American Management Association, 1960), p. 232. The realignment of top men at General Electric gave rise to speculation that the company was pulling back its decentralization program in favor of tighter central control; "GE Reshuffles Its Roster," *Business Week*, October 5, 1957, p. 48. Cf. "Decentralization–How Much and When?", a panel discussion by Dause L. Bibby, V. H. Viot, and Ernest Dale, *Advanced Management*, January, 1959, pp. 14–20. On the role of profit-center decentralization, see Joel Dean, "Profit Performance Measurement of Division Managers," *The Controller*, September, 1957.

24. Douglas M. McGregor, "The Human Side of Enterprise," in Albert H. Rubenstein and Chadwick J. Haberstroh (eds.), *Some Theories of Organization* (Homewood, Ill.: The Dorsey Press and Richard D. Irwin, 1960), pp. 177–187, citing Drucker's concepts. "Delegation is not an effective way of exercising management by control," writes McGregor. "Participation becomes a farce when it is applied as a sales gimmick or a device for kidding people into thinking they are important. Only the management that has confidence in human capacities and is itself directed toward organizational objectives rather than toward the preservation of personal power can grasp the implications of this emerging theory" of participative and consultative management. *Op. cit.*, p. 186.

25. See C. J. Haberstroh, "Control as an Organizational Process," in Rubenstein and Haberstroh, *op. cit.*, pp. 331–336.

26. See especially Herbert A. Simon, *Administrative Behavior*, 2nd ed. (New York: The Macmillan Co., 1957), pp. 234–247; Ernest Dale, *Planning and Developing the Company Organization Structure* (New York: American Management Association, 1952), pp. 137–167 ("Delegation of Decision-Making: Decentralization"); and Robert A. Gordon, *Business Leadership in the Large Corporation* (Washington: The Brookings Institution, 1945), Chapter 4 ("The Chief Executive and the Diffusion of Decision-Making").

27. See, for example, Arthur T. Vanderbilt, *The Doctrine of the Separation of Powers and Its Present Day Significance* (Lincoln: University of Nebraska Press, 1953). Chief Justice Vanderbilt was one of the leaders in the revision of the constitution of New Jersey. Cf. Carl J. Friedrich, *Constitutional Government and Democracy*, revised ed. (Boston: Ginn & Co., 1950).

28. In the French doctrine of separation of powers, the ordinary judiciary may not interfere with acts of the legislature or the executive. Checks against abuse of power by the latter are provided in the specialized administrative courts, which are within the executive branch, but administrative justice is dispensed in the final instance by a court of great independence and prestige, the Conseil d'Etat, and, more specifically, its Litigation Section. In addition, the Tribunal des Conflits decides jurisdictional disputes between the realms of ordinary and administrative justice. The triadic separation-of-powers system as understood in the United States does not apply. See Robert G. Neumann, *European and Comparative Government*, 3rd ed. (New York: McGraw-Hill Book Co., 1960), pp. 300–306.

29. Loewenstein, *op. cit.*

30. "... the doctrine that the making of rules and their application and the adjudication of controversies regarding the applicability of such rules in the main should be entrusted to different bodies is still valid. ... it rests upon a broad logical and psychological foundation. At any rate, governmental powers in a constitutional system should be divided between several relatively independent bodies or persons. ... against the advocates of a dictatorial concentration of power in one leader, the case for a separation of powers may be allowed to rest upon much broader grounds than are suggested by the limited doctrines of Locke and Montesquieu. ... The difficulties resulting from divided powers are great. But the consequences of concentrating power are disastrous." Friedrich, *op. cit.*, p. 188. Friedrich's comments were made with reference to public governments.

31. Delegation of authority, both in public government and in large corporations, has gone so far that "executives and administrators have taken over part of the legislative function ... [a tendency] much more marked in the large corporation, in which the board of directors has yielded a large part of its function or formulating policies to the executive group. ... In both, many 'policies' evolve without deliberate planning out of the acts and decisions of 'administrators.' And in both, the character and background of the 'administrators' are important independent variables operating within the not inconsiderable range of discretion permitted by formal grants of power and the pressures of affected interest groups." Gordon, *Business Leadership in the Large Corporation*, pp. 223–224.

32. The contrast between theory and practice in the functions of the board was examined in detail by Gordon, *op. cit.*, Chapter 6.

Gordon found that the situation varied greatly from company to company: "some boards do wield an independent control over at least a limited range of management decisions . . . [but] for the most part, the board of directors has surrendered its function of active decision-making in the large corporation" and "'outside' directors function, if at all, primarily as financial and business advisers." Gordon regarded "the withering away of the active leadership function of the board [as] unavoidable" since large-scale business leadership can be performed efficiently only by a single group of working officials willing and able to devote the necessary time to the business" (p. 146).

33. See "Reputations and Dividends," *Fortune*, August, 1959, pp. 80 *ff*. A dividend cut at Bethlehem Steel, it was pointed out, would affect directors' income since "the executive compensation program is tied in directly to the company's dividend policy: the executive bonus is calculated at 4½ per cent (cut last September [1958] from 6⅔ per cent) of the total cash payout to stockholders. . . . Directors who are officers of a company will also be concerned about the effect of their dividend decisions on any stock options they happen to have. Dividends are a most important factor in setting the price of stock, and officers who have exercised their options certainly are anxious to see the market price hold above the option price for at least the six-month period required to ensure a capital gain." *Ibid.*, p. 184.

34. Sidney Weinberg, "A Corporation Director Looks at His Job," *Harvard Business Review*, Vol. 27, No. 5 (September, 1949), pp. 585–593, at 586. He regarded outside directors as interpreters of the outside world to the executive managers, and as independent reporters to the stockholders. He thought that inside directors should not vote on their own compensation or assume any responsibility at a stockholders' meeting of justifying any salary levels or increases for themselves. For similar reasons, he thought that outsiders should be in the majority on the executive committee of the board.

35. The most extensive of these studies, based on case studies and statistical work, are: Solomon Ethe and Roger M. Pegram, *Corporate Directorship Practices* (National Industrial Conference Board Studies in Business Policy No. 90, January, 1949), a survey of 976 companies, chiefly in tabular form without identification of the companies; also NICB Studies in Business Policy No. 24, August, 1947, "Keeping Corporate Directors Informed," and No. 63, 1953, "The Corporate Directorship"—a survey of 254 companies; John C. Baker, *Directors and Their Functions* (Boston: Graduate School of Business Administration, Harvard University, 1945), in narrative form and without identification of companies, but both informative and critical; Robert A. Gordon, *Business Leadership in the Large Corporation* (Washington: The Brookings Institution, 1945), Chapter 6 and pp. 343–351; Melvin T. Copeland and Andrew R. Towl, *The Board of Directors and Business Management* (Boston: Graduate School of Business

Administration, Harvard University, 1947); and Courtney C. Brown and Everett E. Smith (eds.), *The Director Looks at His Job* (New York: Columbia University Press, 1957), valuable as a source of directors' own views as recorded from panel discussions, though without identification of the companies. See also American Institute of Management, *The Management Audit Series* (New York: 1953–1957), esp. Vol. 2, *Corporate Structure;* H. H. Spellman, *Treatise on the Principles of Law Governing Corporate Directors* (New York: Prentice-Hall, 1931); Robert C. Hardy and Robert D. Youle, "The Powers and Responsibilities of Corporate Directors," *Journal of Accountancy*, Vol. 82, No. 4 (October, 1946), pp. 280–296; Percival E. Jackson, *What Every Corporate Director Should Know* (New York: The William-Frederick Press, 1957); Myles L. Mace, *The Board of Directors in Small Corporations* (Boston: Graduate School of Business Administration, Harvard University, 1948); and Clarence G. McDavitt, *If You're a Bank Director* (Boston: Bankers Publishing Co., 1950).

36. Gordon, *Business Leadership in the Large Corporations*, p. 347.

37. *Ibid.*, p. 350.

38. Not, however, informal controls exercised by the press, radio, TV, and pressure groups having access to decision centers in the ministries. The same agencies of informal control operate, of course, in a presidential-congressional system.

39. Bayless Manning, *Yale Law Journal*, Vol. 67, No. 8 (July, 1958), pp. 1477–1496. For another suggested control mechanism, ingenious in its attempted solution of the vexations problem of minority stockholders' suits, see G. T. Washington, "Stockholders Derivative Suits: The Company's Role and a Suggestion," *Cornell Law Quarterly*, Vol. 25 (1940), p. 361.

40. *Ibid.*, p. 1490.

41. *Ibid.*, p. 1491. Manning assumed that the certificate-holder would have access to securities markets for quick and cheap disposal of his investment; also "free exit and transfer," in additional to full disclosure, would be the certificate-holder's principal protection, but with anticipated additional developments along three lines: "extension and variation of existing appraisal remedies for dissenters and radical streamlining of present clumsy procedures for appraisal; maintenance of a free and unmanipulated stock market; revision of the tax laws to permit limited shifts of investment from one stock to another without incurring tax liability." *Ibid.*, note 31, p. 1493. He also observed that a complete scrapping of existing shareholders voting machinery was not to be implied from de-emphasis of shareholder voting.

42. *Ibid.*, p. 1491.

43. *Loc. cit.* See also Manning's more recent article, "Corporate Power and Individual Freedom: Some General Analysis and Indi-

vidual Reservations," *Northwestern University Law Review*, Vol. 55, No. 1 (March–April, 1960), pp. 38–53.

44. See Miguel A. de Capriles, "Fifteen-Year Survey of Corporate Developments, 1944–1959," *Vanderbilt Law Review*, Vol. 13, No. 1 (December, 1959), pp. 1–19, at pp. 10–12 ("Corporate Management").

45. A. A. Berle, Jr., in W. H. Ferry and others, *The Corporation and the Economy* (Santa Barbara, California: Center for the Study of Democratic Institutions, 1959), p. 87. See also A. A. Berle, Jr., *Economic Power and the Free Society* (New York: Fund for the Republic, 1957), p. 18, in which he specifies four obligations in relation to which "great corporate power" is exercised: to supply the want in a corporation's area of production, to supply this at an acceptable and not an extortionate price, to provide at least some continuity of employment, and to give continuing attention to the technical progress of the art.

46. See comments by A. A. Berle in W. H. Ferry and others, *The Economy under Law* (Santa Barbara, California: Center for the Study of Democratic Institutions, 1960), pp. 47 *ff*. The institutions of "social accounting" he refers to are not intracorporate.

47. U.S. 64th Congress, 1st Session, Senate, *Senate Documents*, Vol. 26 (1916).

48. See, e.g., Geneva Seybold, "When Employee Turns Author," *Management Record*, Vol. 20, No. 2 (February, 1958).

CHAPTER 13 The Span of Corporate Policy

1. In *The Meaning of Modern Business* (New York: Columbia University Press, 1960), at pp. 364–368, I have brought together a variety of definitions of "policy" as the term is used in contemporary discourse.

2. *Ibid.*, Chapter 14, and "The Corporate Image in Public Relations," *California Management Review*, Vol. I, No. 4 (Summer, 1959), pp. 15–23.

CHAPTER 14 Corporation and Community

1. The term is used here as Kenneth Boulding uses it in his analysis of "social ecosystems" in *The Organizational Revolution* (New York: Harper & Brothers, 1953). He defines an ecosystem as "a self-contained and self-perpetuating system of interacting populations of various kinds." Corporations, of course, are *organizations*, not organisms that are precisely analogous with plants and animals as the latter are treated in the sciences of plant and animal ecology. A corporate ecology might therefore be dismissed as a discipline not closely analogous with these branches of biology. But the systematic emphases

in biological ecology upon environment (major and minor communities, the principles of succession and convergence, etc.), antecology and synecology, as major aspects of the science are all highly suggestive to the student of corporate growth and survival. In an eventual unification of sciences the apparent analogies may become identities at a higher level of abstraction that will be acceptable. Here we go no further than to suggest these possibilities. On the intimate interrelation between organization theory and the theory of organisms, see James G. March and Herbert A. Simon, *Organizations* (New York: John Wiley & Sons, 1958).

2. Abram Bergson, *The Real National Income of Soviet Russia since 1928* (Cambridge: Harvard University Press, 1961).

3. Simon Kuznets, *Capital in the American Economy: Its Formation and Financing* (Princeton: Princeton University Press, 1961), a study made for the National Bureau of Economic Research on a grant by the Life Insurance Association of America.

CHAPTER 15 Corporate Justice

1. James Finney Lincoln, *A New Approach to Industrial Economics* (New York: Devin-Adair Co., 1961). Mr. Lincoln argues that the consumer gets short-changed because "we let hired 'experts' concoct our relations with him and try to delude him about our products. We charge him all we can get out of him," and that industrialists try to eliminate competition by patents, tariffs, and so-called fair-trade laws. Management, he says, treats the worker as an enemy who gets advancement in income and status only from the labor union that compels management to grant these gains. At Lincoln Electric Co. an advisory board of elected representatives from each department has met twice monthly since 1914. Paid life insurance for all employees was begun in 1915, pay geared to cost-of-living index in 1923, and a stock-purchase plan in 1925. Since 1934 a profit-sharing plan has paid out more than $100 million.

2. Louis O. Kelso and Mortimer J. Adler, *The Capitalist Manifesto* (New York: Random House, 1958), especially at p. 157 and pp. 204–207. See the discussion of this and similar positions in Richard Eells, *The Meaning of Modern Business* (New York: Columbia University Press, 1960), Ch. 4 and pp. 218 *ff*.

3. Paul P. Harbrecht, S.J., and Adolf A. Berle, Jr., *Toward the Paraproprietal Society* (New York: Twentieth Century Fund, 1959–1960), pp. 37–38.

4. Richard Eells and Clarence Walton, *Conceptual Foundations of Business* (Homewood, Illinois: Richard D. Irwin, 1961), p. 177.

5. *Ibid.*

6. *Ibid.*, p. 191.

7. Harbrecht and Berle, *op. cit.*, especially at pp. 27 *ff*.

8. *Ibid.*, p. 33. After control of productive property was severed from ownership in the first instance by the corporate device, control was then "free to migrate since it was attached to shares of stock and, to some extent, to bonds, which could be bought and sold."

9. *Ibid.*, p. 37.

10. *Ibid.*, p. 40.

11. Robert Tilove, *Pension Funds and Economic Freedom* (New York: The Fund for the Republic, 1959).

12. The point is well made in *The Public Interest in National Labor Policy*, a report by an independent Labor Study Group for the Committee on Economic Development and published by CED in New York in 1961.

13. Oscar and Mary Handlin, *The Dimensions of Liberty* (Cambridge: Harvard Univeristy Press, 1961).

14. *Ibid.*, pp. 12–13.

Index